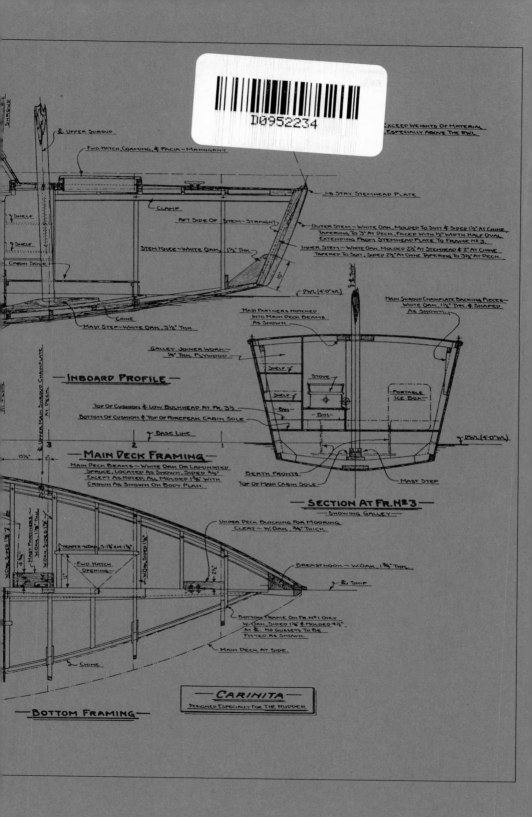

℄ UPPER SHROUD

FWD. HATCH COAMING, & FACIA ~ MAHOGANY

CLAMP

AFT SIDE OF STEM ~ STRAIGHT

STEM KNEE ~ WHITE OAK    1½" THK.

CLAMP

SHELF

SHELF

CABIN SOLE

CHINE

MAST STEP ~ WHITE OAK, 3½" THK.

EXCEED WEIGHTS OF MATERIAL ESPECIALLY ABOVE THE PWL

JIB STAY STEMHEAD PLATE

OUTER STEM ~ WHITE OAK, MOLDED TO SUIT & SIDED 1½" AT CHINE TAPERING TO 3" AT DECK, FACED WITH ½" WIDTH HALF OVAL EXTENDING FROM STEMHEAD PLATE TO FRAME № 3.

INNER STEM ~ WHITE OAK, MOLDED 2½" AT STEMHEAD & 2" AT CHINE TAPERED TO SUIT; SIDED 2½" AT CHINE TAPERING TO 3½" AT DECK.

PWL (4'-0" WL)

MAIN SHROUD CHAINPLATE BACKING PIECES ~ WHITE OAK, 1½" THK. & SHAPED AS SHOWN.

MAST PARTNERS NOTCHED INTO MAIN DECK BEAMS AS SHOWN

GALLEY JOINER WORK ~ ¼" THK. PLYWOOD

## — INBOARD PROFILE —

TOP OF CUSHION & LOW BULKHEAD AT FR. 3½

BOTTOM OF CUSHION & TOP OF FOREPEAK CABIN SOLE

℄ BASE LINE

3      2      1

## — MAIN DECK FRAMING —

MAIN DECK BEAMS ~ WHITE OAK OR LAMINATED SPRUCE, LOCATED AS SHOWN, SIDED ¾" EXCEPT AS NOTED, ALL MOLDED 1⅝" WITH CROWN AS SHOWN ON BODY PLAN.

℄ UPPER MAIN SHROUD CHAINPLATE AT DECK

15½"

SHELF

STOVE

SHELF

PORTABLE ICE BOX

DR.

DR.

BERTH FRONTS

TOP OF MAIN CABIN SOLE

MAST STEP

## — SECTION AT FR. № 3 —
— SHOWING GALLEY —

UNDER DECK BLOCKING FOR MOORING CLEAT ~ W. OAK, ¾" THICK

MAST PARTNERS W. OAK, 1⅜" THK

W. OAK SIDED 1⅝"

W. OAK SIDED ¾"

W. OAK SIDED 1⅜"

DEADWOOD ~ W. OAK, 1⅜" THK.

HEADER ~ W. OAK, 3-1⅛ EA 1⅜"

FWD. HATCH OPENING

W. OAK SIDED 1½" ?

2½"

℄ SHIP

BOTTOM FRAME ON FR. № 1 ONLY W/ OAK, SIDED 1⅝ & MOLDED 4½" AT ℄. NO GUSSETS TO BE FITTED AS SHOWN.

MAIN DECK AT SIDE.

CHINE

## — BOTTOM FRAMING —

## — CARINITA —
DESIGNED ESPECIALLY FOR THE RUDDER

# Cruising at last

## SAILING THE EAST COAST

### ELLIOTT MERRICK

## THE LYONS PRESS

Guilford, Connecticut

An imprint of The Globe Pequot Press

*A boat is not just a boat, you know.*
*It is a winged Pegasus, or a Magic Carpet, taking you to new*
*places, new friends, and new thoughts.*

*Millions of people would like to go cruising in their own*
*sailboats. If my wife and I at sixty and seventy could do it, so*
*can they. This book is for them.*

—Elliott Merrick

The Lyons Press is an imprint of the Globe Pequot Press.

10 9 8 7 6 5 4 3 2 1

ISBN 1-58574-767-X

Printed in the United States of America

Designed by Paul L Schiff

Library of Congress Cataloging-in-Publication data is available on file.

Design drawings of Carinita are reproduced with permission from A. Mason Design:

CARINITA, Design Number S-023 ©1952 by A. Mason. These represent details and design features as elements of a design prepared by A. Mason and are to be used only for work authorized in writing by the designer. These drawings shall not be copied, reproduced directly or indirectly, in whole or in part, nor shall they be used for any other manufacturing purposes and any unauthorized use will be considered an infringement of these rights. All rights of invention and design are reserved by the designer.

The designs, and accompanying copyrights, of A. Mason, N.A., are currently owned, in their entirety, by A. Mason Design. Anyone interested in purchasing a set of construction plans, specifications, and construction information for CARINITA may contact:

A. Mason Design
ATTN: Anita C. Mason
20281 Anza Drive
Salinas, CA 93908-1202
Telephone: 1-831-455-2554
Fax: 1-831-455-2415
E-mail: amason@a-mason-na.com

# Table of Contents

| | | |
|---|---|---|
| Editor's Note | .................................................................. | v |
| Preface | Port Royal Sound and Inland Passages ............... | vii |
| CHAPTER I | *Prelude to Cruising:* A Boat Is Born ..................... | 1 |
| CHAPTER II | St. Helena Sound to Savannah River;<br>Charleston Harbor and Approaches ................... | 19 |
| CHAPTER III | Approaches to Cape Fear; Cape Fear to<br>Wilmington; New River to Cape Fear;<br>Cape Lookout to New River Inlet ....................... | 29 |
| CHAPTER IV | Pamlico Sound—Western Part;<br>Cape Hatteras—Wimble Shoals to<br>Ocracoke Island ................................................... | 41 |
| CHAPTER V | Mobjack Bay and York River Entrance ............... | 45 |
| CHAPTER VI | Cove Point to Sandy Point .................................. | 51 |
| CHAPTER VII | Annapolis Harbor; Sandy Point to<br>Susquehanna River; Chesapeake &<br>Delaware Canal, Salem River Extension;<br>Delaware River—Smyrna River to Wilmington .... | 61 |
| CHAPTER VIII | Delaware Bay; Little Egg Inlet to<br>Hereford Inlet; Absecon Inlet ............................. | 77 |
| CHAPTER IX | *Interlude:* About the Jib ....................................... | 87 |
| CHAPTER X | Greenwich Point to New Rochelle; Long<br>Island Sound's South Shore—Oyster and<br>Huntington Bays; Stratford to Sherwood<br>Point; Long Island Sound—Eastern Part;<br>Block Island Sound and Approaches ................. | 91 |

Chapter XI     *Interlude:* About Our Compass ............... 109

Chapter XII     Narragansett Bay; Cape Cod Canal
and Approaches ..................... 113

Chapter XIII     Portsmouth to Cape Elizabeth; Casco Bay ......... 123

Chapter XIV     Casco Bay ............... 145

Chapter XV     Damariscotta, Sheepscot, and Kennebec
Rivers; South Bristol Harbor, Christmas
Cove; Muscongous Bay; Penobscot Bay
and Approaches ..................... 153

Chapter XVI     *Interlude:* Coastal Cruising .................. 179

Chapter XVII     Frenchman and Blue Hill Bays
and Approaches ..................... 183

Chapter XVIII     Cape Elizabeth to Cape Cod Bay;
Cape Cod Canal and Approaches ........... 189

Chapter XIX     Martha's Vineyard to Block Island; Block
Island Sound—Point Judith to Montauk Point;
Block Island Sound and Gardiners Bay,
Long Island .......................... 197

Chapter XX     Fishers Island Sound; North Shore of Long
Island Sound—Niantic Bay and Vicinity;
Connecticut River—Long Island Sound to
Deep River; Long Island Sound—Eastern Part;
Long Island Sound—Western Part ......... 209

Chapter XXI     Hudson River—New York to
Wappinger Creek .................. 219

Chapter XXII     Sandy Hook to Little Egg Harbor; Little Egg
Inlet to Cape May.................. 227

Chapter XXIII     Cape May to Cape Hatteras; Cape Hatteras
to Charleston; Port Royal Sound and Inland
Passages .......................... 245

Author biography ........................249

# Editor's Note

This book is compiled from several short pieces Elliott Merrick wrote about cruising the East Coast of the United States. Though they recorded adventures that occurred on several different cruises in various years, he intended to unify them into a single narrative so that they would seem to be the log of a single summer's cruise, a job he never finished.

His daughter, Sue Merrick Hoover, asked me if I could see a book here—and, if so, could I edit it into shape? I was so taken with these splendid stories that I said I would give it a try. Rather than attempting to squeeze them into the form that Merrick intended, which might require some distortions of the text, and perhaps even some rewriting or interpolation of our own words (which would inevitably appear to limp alongside Merrick's own lucid prose), we have simply arranged them in the order that follows him down to Maine in the summer, and back to Hilton Head in the fall. There are obvious gaps in this progression, but we trust the reader will be as grateful as we are for what is in this record, and not worry about what is missing.

Of his crew, Merrick wrote: "The reader of these stories should know that MM, my mate, is two different women. The first, my wife Kay Austen, an extremely courageous and capable trained nurse, was the mother of my three children. She died at age ninety-four. After some years, I married Patricia Herring Stratton, an accomplished portrait painter and widely known equestrienne whose early life was involved with horses rather than sailboats.

"Looking back through that window of memory Wordsworth characterized as 'emotions recollected in tranquillity,' it has seemed impossible for me to sharply differentiate. Suffice it to say that without these two greathearted women I could never have made the cruises described in this book. I hope the unutterable joy of our good days, when the bow wave sparkled white, and the sky was so blue you lost yourself in it, and our bird's-wing mains'l leaned toward the horizon, has offset the cold, wet hours at the tiller and repaid them in part for the loving care of me."

Upton Birnie Brady
Hartland Four Corners, Vermont
December 2002

# Preface

## PORT ROYAL SOUND AND INLAND PASSAGES

When we could get away from work, my wife and I towed our little Penguin sailing dinghy down to the coast at Hilton Head, South Carolina, on a homemade trailer made from the front wheels of an old Dodge. In those days, 1965, Hilton Head had not been developed yet, and was a wonderland of beaches, coves, and creeks for small-boat exploration.

An eleven-and-a-half-foot Penguin as a daysailer is ridiculous, of course. But if it's all you have, and if your crew-wife can shift her weight in lively fashion, it's surprising how far you can travel. You have to keep an eye out for squalls, be alert, and change your plans according to the weather. But it's full of adventurous uncertainties, and wasn't the object to get away from the old humdrum?

Every day the wind blew strong and steady. Every morning we tumbled into the little boat, hoisted sail, and leaned away upchannel or downchannel, whichever way the tide was running; we didn't care. We had our lunch and slickers, water, a half-sized sail to put up in a blow, and a pair of seven-foot spruce oars in case of calm. We had a little box compass if it should get foggy, but it never did. And in the bow was stuffed a rubber bag containing a pup tent, mosquito bar, and some iron rations if we should get stranded for the night.

Hilton Head Island, three miles wide and eleven miles long, is a lovely spot on the coast of South Carolina not far below Beaufort and not far above Savannah, Georgia. It was October, and nobody much was around, for people don't go to the Carolina beaches in the spring and fall when those shores are blue and silver; they only go when it's blazing hot. The Intracoastal Waterway runs inside the whole length of the island, and the marina-with-motel where we were staying catered to passing craft.

As we tacked northward, the channel wound between bright green marshes with shores of oyster shell or mud, past islands and a little bay where shrimp boats were tied up to a fish wharf, past a beached shrimper cast up by a recent hurricane. When we landed on a spit for lunch and a swim, we chose the oyster shell, putting on old sneakers first and anchoring the boat in knee-deep water so it wouldn't get cut on the sharp edges. "Hey, give me your knife," said Kay first thing, and started prying oysters out of the clusters and eating them then and there.

Piling aboard again and tacking past a grass point, we suddenly opened up the vast expanse of Port Royal Sound, wide as the sky, blue and sparkling, with white shoals breaking to seaward. In that low, flat country, where nothing much limits your view but the curve of the earth, we could even see the faint black matchstick of Hunting Island Lighthouse some twenty miles away. At this magic gateway was a stretch of broad white sand, not a house, not a soul, just the windy sea and the sunlight winking. It is wonderful how the hurricanes keep this sea-island region free, flooding the marshes and sand spits, periodically sweeping them clean, so that the entrance to Port Royal Sound looked the same as it probably did in 1562, when the Frenchman Jean Ribault sailed in here to make the first Protestant settlement in the New World. The spot he picked was Parris Island, where the U.S. Marine base now is, several miles up the bay. We didn't care about all that. We tacked a long way out the great blue bay toward the ocean. It was so wide we could scarcely see across, and rough enough to flip in a dollop of water now and then. But we kept within half a mile of the beach and figured we could haul up there if things got too bad. It was wonderful to see how the little boat could take it, both of us sitting up to windward feeling happy and free.

By and by we doused the sail, rowed ashore through the small surf, and ran along the sand to a stranded tree beneath whose root was a pool filled with Caribbean shells, many of them new to us. Among them were two Panamas, shiny, new-minted, and alive, each poking himself about on his single foot like a man on a pogo stick. Back of the beach was a high sandbank and a forest of longleaf pine, where we sat and watched the yachts go by. This is the season when they are streaming south along the waterway for Florida or somewhere. Mostly motor cruisers they were, rolling heavily down the choppy sound from Beaufort, across and into "our" channel, exhausts smoking, ports shut, only a solitary figure at the wheel. Why were they hurrying so, we wondered. Would it be any better in Miami or the Bahamas or even Antigua? Did they never think of this island sleeping in the sun, with its ancient Spanish wells and ruined forts and lonely beaches?

Karl Woodring, the marina man who soon became our friend, told us, "Most of them are paid captains taking the boat to Miami or Bimini or somewhere for the owner, who will fly down later."

While we were watching, two tall ketches came dipping across the sound. Neither showed an inch of sail, both motoring busily like oil barges, though they had a fair wind and could have been running all the way across the sound to Hilton Head and through the Skull Creek channel, down Calibogue Sound to Savannah and on, running outside for twenty-mile stretches and ducking in again with nothing to do but jibe the stays'l and main occasionally. The wind was so strong they could have run all day under stays'l and jib if they were too lazy to hoist the main. Standing on the windy beach, we hated to see them miss such a sail.

So we got aboard the peanut shell and poked into the huge sound, where the tide was ebbing like a millrace and the wind was pushing in with great power from the sea. Out there we stood on end and splashed and spattered and dipped the gunwale, even luffing. As the squalls swept over, we could have gone bottom-up a dozen times if I hadn't let the sheet run. This maneuver consists merely of straightening one's bent arm. Every other wave bounced in a pint or so over the undecked bow, and our old motto of "One to sail and one to bail" became no joke. It was lonely and dark as the sun went under. We didn't feel very confident out there in the huge rough sound, balancing like tightrope walkers, the sail thundering, the water coming in. We were both sitting on the gunwale, hiking out to windward as the squalls beat us down. Kay gave me that smile reserved for occasions when the going gets impossible.

We looked longingly down Port Royal Sound, wishing we could go farther, as we had planned from the chart. But that required a deck this day. None too soon we turned tail and beat it out of the welter for the sheltering arms of the waterway and "home." We flew south down the channel, reaching most beautifully between the red buoys and beacons to starboard and the black ones to port that make this one of the best-marked channels in the world. A drizzle began to fall, and a grayness made all the country dim. But soaring past the marshes, the boat's white bow wave looked bright and saucy, as though it had color.

Our marina quarters contained a nice big bed and a gas stove and plenty of books and a heater for coolish nights when we came in wet, and some whiskey and grub, so what else does anybody need? The channel was so close that even through the rain, we could see a red nun nodding on the tide in a particularly knowing way. As darkness fell, the mysterious throb of diesels came over the water to us and the wash of passing craft lapped the shore. A bonus we hadn't counted on was the swing bridge downchannel half a mile or so. In the night a tug-with-barges bound down the waterway blew for the bridge, three wild, impressive blasts like some plumed knight before the castle. Waking from sleep, we hopped out of bed and watched the red and green eyes go by, wondering what sort of man the skipper must be to keep from running aground in that crooked channel. "Perhaps we'd better drink a very small toast to save his soul from the perils of the sea?" And so we gulped a slug and pulled up the blanket shivering with delight to know that we could sail again first thing as soon as the sun came up.

There are quiet days, too, reaching down side channels where the marsh grass shields the water, and we slide softly over winding sheets of pale green glass. You wouldn't think there was a breath, until you turn and see the track rippling in a long V between the marshes. There are birds and a strange semitropical sky. On former trips north of here we have sailed down channels divided from the ocean only by a narrow sandspit. You see the ocean's rim, and the surf pounding white on the beach, and you skirt it for miles in the calm. It can't get at you, though it seems to try. It is like sailing in a South Seas lagoon where the combers roar just outside the reef. Often we have landed and walked through the low dunes to swim in the breakers. Then we climb aboard and wing away again. There are advantages to a little boat.

It has taken us several visits to get some feel for the sea-island country, "the low country," the hurricane land half drowned at every high tide. It was not always so quiet as now. For instance, at the time of the Revolutionary War Hilton Head Island alone had some twenty-two prosperous plantations. The slave population was immense, as many as four hundred slaves on one plantation near Beaufort. This was the land of large labor forces, very black African tribesmen from Angola.

It was along this coast that all the moonlight-and-magnolia myths of plantation days began; only they weren't myths during that fabulous hundred years when the planters were so wealthy and aristocratic they took a fancy to classical Greek customs and the hopped-up chivalry of romance as fictionalized by Sir Walter Scott and satirized by Mark Twain. From way below Savannah to a little above Charleston the sea-island plantations flourished. Bricks, silverware, furniture, books, and the latest fashions were being briskly imported from England and France as early as 1750. In the heyday of this land, Christmas dances lasted two weeks. Rice and indigo made fortunes. Sea-island cotton, the longest-stapled fiber then known, brought a dollar a pound, and in Paris they had to have it for the weaving of the sheerest cloth. Nobody else in the world was successful with sea-island cotton—only these low-lying kingdoms.

The bustling port of Charleston was the hub of this universe, considered itself the seat of culture in the New World—still does, in fact.

Everything went by boat among the watery mazes of this coast, where even now the main roads are twenty miles back from the sea. Even now you cannot really see it except from a boat. Every plantation had its wharf or wharves, and the ruins of many still stand drunkenly in the tide. Owners went to Charleston on business by boat, and the same held for all local freight, inter-island sociability, and trading. Many plantation approaches and flowered allées led down to a dock. My lady went to church in a plantation barge, sitting on an upholstered cushion, rowed by slaves, with a pretty little parasol to shield her from the sun. There is such a plantation barge in the Charleston museum now. During most of the 1800s, a weekly steamboat plied among the sounds and estuaries between Savannah and Charleston.

We drift on the tide around the corner of a wooded, grown-up island inhabited only by the descendants of a few slaves who fish and crab and oyster silently, almost invisibly among these sea reaches—and there inside the point are the black sticks of the old wharf for which the steamer used to blow. One stands up in the boat and imagines cotton bales rolling down the gangplank, the black smoke rolling, the red bandannas, the swarm of people. It is ghostly, and even I, a damn Yankee, know why the Charlestonians cannot forget their long-gone dream that was ended by the boll weevil and the freeing of the slaves. I have to blink and do a double take to remember that this is only woods and marshes, and the distant sound of surf on the outer beach, and seabirds calling. So we sail on by, silently, seeing nobody all afternoon except a black man far away in a black, flat-bottomed skiff, tonging oysters at a bed known only to himself. We used to try to talk to such people, but no more. They do not understand us, and we seldom comprehend a single word of the singsong Gullah dialect.

Hilton Head is the essence of all this. Far down its Port Royal beach we had hauled up one day and were walking the sand, when we came on a black woman crabbing in a low-tide pool. She had on a blue dress and a straw hat with a red ribbon around it. I suppose she came from one of the little six-acre clearings back in the piney-woods, given to a slave ancestor after The War. Hilton Head Island was a big Federal base; there were close to fifty thousand Yankees on the island during Civil War days. Anyway, I asked her politely, "Where is the point, please, the Hilton Head they speak of. Is it far?" She seemed to reply as though sweetly singing, "Ee do be gone li. Hi lo do be, will you?" To my unaccustomed ear it sounded pleasantly insane but not very instructive. I can only hope she remembers me with the same kindly wonder. At any rate, we kept on, past a rusty steel tower and the old steam gun emplacement. Then suddenly we came out onto the sea beach and met the whole Atlantic Ocean face to face. It is a magnificent beach, eleven miles long and nearly two hundred feet wide at low tide. There was nobody on it but us. We swam immediately in the cool and creamy waves, the temperature about seventy. We felt like Robinson Crusoe, or a couple of Spanish conquistadores ranging north from St. Augustine. As we wandered down the frills of foam with the sandpipers, Kay tucked her arm in mine and said, "Do you suppose Columbus ever had half as much fun as we do?"

Sitting in a hollow of a dune facing the surf, a conviction comes to me that it is important to be here listening to the jumbled cadence of waves, trying to understand what the sea is saying. It takes time; it does not come all at once; perhaps it never comes. Only by being childlike, asking nothing . . . The sea in its great strength is not for us; we are for it. This lonely beach is full of whispering and wonders, and a black flock of geese stringing down the sky. We cannot know, we cannot understand, but that is no matter. We can be here watching the bent dune grass trace lines in the sand. We can examine a sand dollar, fragile, perfect, and see it shrink the affairs of men to pinpoints.

How is it, I wonder, that absolute essentials such as this interlude by the sea have become luxuries? Perhaps it is that we have gone and must go full circle. From primitive hunger needs, bark shacks, and skin clothes we "advance" to our present civilization. Whereupon we long for the wilderness, the wild ocean shore. Perhaps it is only by losing the primitive sense of oneness with nature that we can value it and learn to win back to perceptiveness again. Sometimes the hardworking things of my life seem valueless compared to this selfless, savage moment of being that can never be sought or bought, only listened for, opened to, humbly, rarely.

Ooom whoOOM! goes the surf, and the white manes blowing backward.

I haven't any answers. Burrowed into a sand dune, watching the waves roll in from so far away, I only know that existence is stronger than any of us and will do for us all one day. And here are we, middle-aged, adventuring again as we used to. Now we've raised our young and can go once more to the wild places where nature rules and man hasn't changed everything. Maybe these travels will be even better than the youthful ones. Captain Slocum was not young when he sailed around the world in a home-built boat, with a battered alarm clock for a chronometer.

Next morning we set sail down channel the other way for Calibogue Sound, determined to get to its seaward end. The breeze was ahead, but the tide was fair. The swing-bridge tender waved gaily to us from his pinnacle cab, pleased perhaps that he needn't open for our nineteen-foot mast as we tacked under. A tug with two barges was coming up—worst hazard of the waterway. We had a fine whitecap breeze, and gave him a wide berth, throwing spray already. Strapped down tight, we beat and beat from side to side of the widening bay. We beat all morning until past noon, by which time the bay was two miles wide. The last of the ebb bucking the fresh sea wind kicked up a chop that stood as high as our heads, but it wasn't breaking, so we thrashed on, shouldering up over them, lost in the trough. An oysterman went by, an old shrimper by the looks of her, towing a cluster of skiffs that skittered like leaves. The wind's whistle in the rigging went up a note or two. We had to luff as the gunwale dipped flush with a wave and a cupful ran along it and into the boat.

So we slogged on, with the tide shoving us seaward, till at last we came to the beautiful beach, Braddock Point, at the south end of the island. The water is deep to the shore, scoured by the tide, and we could just about sail her up onto the sand. Porpoises are nearly always fishing there in the channel, diving and blowing, revolving like the rim of a wet wheel. Leaning against a wind that was making sand whisper among the low dune grass, we pushed out toward the long point and the ocean till we could see the harbor markers of Savannah, and a freighter coming in. The breadth of the seascape and the wind and distance made us feel as though we had traveled a thousand miles.

Black clouds were advancing from the west, and we heard

thunder rattling out of them. The day was getting on; it was time to fly home before the wind got up any more.

I hadn't known a Penguin could plane, but the breaking chop (you could plainly hear its seething) sprang her loose and we rushed up the bay in a white gash, shroud like a fiddle string, sail hard as ivory. It seemed incredible that nothing was popping. The seas threw the stern around and the wind picked up and hurled us. The green bow wave hardened and heightened. The whole boat trembled, close to ultimate hull speed and beginning to drive under. Gingerly we inched ourselves aft an inch or two, balancing fore and aft as well as side to side. We were tacking downwind to avoid a jibe, for, steer as I would, she yawed. Sometimes as she flew, overtaking wave after wave and tobogganing down their backs, I thought for sure she'd broach, but with help she never quite managed it. That was a run! Once we rounded up and bore off on the other slant. I wouldn't have thought such a little boat could stand it.

Kay was shifting weight to perfection whenever the boom lifted or we made a swoop-and-roll. "Are you scared?" I asked.

"No," she said, "I'll go anywhere you will."

Fair winds never bother her, it's the windward slogs when we're filling up, and they bother us both. I was about to tell her if she wasn't scared she ought to be. But that seemed inappropriate return for such faith.

It was a shame to end that sleigh ride, but the keyed-up tension without room for the slightest eye wink was getting grim. We were sure to swamp soon at this rate, so I steered into a channel known as Town Creek, were we found ourselves purling over smooth water in the lee of a high shell bank. There we anchored and breathed a sigh and ate lunch. It was three o'clock and high time. Then we put up the half-sized storm sail (which I made and roped, sitting by the fire winter evenings years ago) and romped home under perfect control, doing about five knots. The bridge tender waved again as we roared under. The bay was darkening, the storm clouds almost upon us. Just as we tied up at our dock mooring, down came the rain in curtains and sheets. But we were pretty wet already.

Karl was there to greet us. "You ought to have a little outboard motor," he said, "so you could be sure of getting back when you go way down the bay."

He was right, of course. I didn't reply, for I didn't like to admit that the boat is so small we almost sink it with our minimum necessary gear even without a motor. And then, too, I didn't like to remind him how blessed were past generations, waiting for the tide, digging clams or making love meanwhile, utterly unable to get back to the office.

The gas heater fire felt cozy that night and when the tugboats blew for the bridge in the wild windy darkness, for once I didn't hanker to be out there at all.

Everything good soon ends. We had to get back to work. As we hauled our trailer away, I was thinking that what I love about boats is the look of them slicing through a head sea or running like great birds. And the places they take you to and the thoughts they make you think. And letting yourself be cradled in the wind's arms. And the strength and danger and eternal verities they allow you to share. We wished we had a bigger boat with bunks for sleeping aboard, and a stove. But still, a little boat is exciting for poking into tiny creeks where oysters grow, or hauling up on a beach to picnic and swim and run on the sand.

We changed the Penguin's species and called her *Duckling* because of the saucy way she tipped up her stern. Kay and I trailed the Penguin to Cape Cod, to Maine, where we ventured two miles out in the ocean one mild day, but were unable on another rougher occasion to sail even on Castine Harbor. We trailed to the Chesapeake, to Edisto, to Captiva and Sanibel, time and again to Hilton Head, and to a number of TVA lakes.

Meanwhile time was passing and we still had no cruiser we could sleep in. Having owned so many precarious boats, we knew what we must have: a craft that could take it in storms, a boat with self-bailing cockpit and a cabin we could shut up tight when waves were coming over, a boat for the ocean.

Because we could spend only thirty-five hundred dollars, and even in those days that wasn't much, all the boats we looked at had something wrong with them. They leaked, the cockpit drains were too small, the rudder fastenings were flimsy, the cabin windows too big and breakable, the chocks like toys. A common fault was a toothpick mast with only two shrouds, both attached to a single, common chainplate. Some had only one shroud each side. I knew enough about boats to realize that these wire guys hold up the mast and take such strains they sometimes pull a whole boat out of shape; hence there must be, as on all good old boats, three on each side, namely the topmast shroud, the lower forward shroud, and the lower aft shroud, each with its very strong chainplate designed never to pull out of the hull.

Our search was hopeless. It sometimes seems silly in this fiber-glass age to build a wooden boat, and often it is. But in our case the best course appeared to be spending our money for the finest materials money could buy and putting them together in my spare time. I already had a little experience in building the Penguin and knew how strong modern plywood and glues can be. I could see that a good little boat is infinitely more desirable than a big one in need of endless repairs.

I didn't 'specially crave to sail around the Horn or across the Atlantic, or even race to Bermuda (though I sure would have tried Bermuda if I had known anyone faintly disposed to ask me). I was tired of reading around-the-world cruise books by the Hiscocks, the Smeetons, Robinson, Slocum, et al., or studying how to jibe a spinnaker, while not possessing a spinnaker. Rather than reading glorious descriptions of the new and speedier seventy-footer some millionaire had just commissioned for the Southern Racing Circuit, I myself must do something.

I looked and looked for designs that were rugged but not tubby, something seagoing though small, a hull that was good to windward, relatively fast, made for amateur building. Performance seemed to us more important than luxurious accommodation.

I went to the New York Boat Show, something I'd vowed to see for years. It was a sort of study. It helped me to learn, to see and compare prices, materials, quality, and to be aware of new methods of rigging and other matters of vital import. The thing is held in the huge Coliseum on Columbus Circle, four floors, each acres in extent, attended by a total of over three hundred thousand people in the ten days of its run. There were forty-foot sail cruisers there, with their great masts and sails towering to the mezzanine. Each person paid admission, so it is easy to see why it was run. But another great reason was that suppliers were trying to interest the large-scale retailers, too. There were many couples from Brooklyn whose yearly yachting obviously consists of a visit to this show. And very savvy boat technicians, and old-hand Bermuda racers, and every gradation you can imagine. A chap about twenty-three intrigued me; he kept badgering various experts on the best and cheapest place to get a cast-iron keel made—the best foundry. He had under his arm the most battered roll of blueprints ever seen, tied up in a frayed piece of twine, and yes, you guessed it, he was building a boat. His is a twenty-nine-footer, very ambitious. I felt like saying, "Hail, brother." But managed to restrain myself. I met a very knowing aluminum mast expert and got some advice and supplies I needed. There were whole floors of outboards, outboard runabouts, little outboard cabin cruisers, but of course I didn't go aboard any of those. What interested me was the great number of twenty-two-, twenty-three-, twenty-four-foot sail craft with cabin and keel, really seagoing, all in fiberglass. They are called Midget Ocean Racers—the M.O.R.C. The C is for "Class." Boats are so expensive, people buy these now instead of the big ones they'd like. They have three or four bunks, a little stove, head, and immense amount of stuff crammed into every last available inch. Many are spoiled by cramming in too much. Each is a little different; each has advantages and disadvantages in seaworthiness, speed, room below, room in the cockpit, rig, etc. I learned an immense lot.

Four years before retiring, I found what I was looking for, and began building my cruising sloop.

# CHAPTER I

# *Prelude to Cruising*

## A BOAT IS BORN

SHE WAS TWENTY FEET OVERALL, a design by naval architect Al Mason. Details of the Carinita appeared in *Rudder Magazine* and *How to Build 20 Boats,* from which many have been built. Forty of them were sailing on rough, windy San Francisco Bay, and a few were said to carry spinnakers in forty-knot blows. She has a thousand-pound fin keel like a Star, and a Lightning rig. Mason laid her out with a self-bailing cockpit, two bunks, and a stove. She can really carry her sail in a big breeze, and a little ship much like her has crossed the Atlantic. Boats reflect your personality, pocketbook, and desires—whether you'll be sailing mostly in shoal water, whether you prefer speed or stability, strength or light weight. Some boats even have as their principal feature twin keels so they can sit upright in the mud. Every boat is a compromise, with the owner trying for as much of everything

1

as possible. We needed a strong deck and tight hatches, among other things.

Building the Carinita took place against a background of a nine-to-five job, a small farm with six head of beef cattle, and the writing of more books and magazine stories. This is why it took four years to put together such a simple craft.

It didn't seem possible I could do it. But you just begin, one step at a time. First you draw the plan full scale on old plywood sheets. Then you start making the curved tiller or the frames and knees. Pretty soon you've got such a stack of frames and parts, and ordered so much hardware, you can't possibly quit. Drawing lines, making frames, building the boat becomes an absorbing, gladsome, instructive, satisfying aspect of your life. After a hard day at the office, trying to learn about forestry at the same time as teaching foresters to write, I'd go out a few hours. The work in my old shed full of shavings and wood bits made me feel that the day hadn't been entirely wasted.

I bought always the best regardless of cost, bronze screws and bolts that glittered like gold, straight-grain white oak with no sapwood, and any crooked piece thrown away, so that I used only about half the wood I bought. Chainplates were to be of rugged bronze.

I sent away to England for the half-inch, five-ply, all-mahogany plywood to plank my boat. This plywood was put together with waterproof glue so strong that I boiled a sample for seventy-two hours, then charred it in the oven, and still couldn't knock the plies apart with an ax.

While I was testing my plywood hull planking, one of my friends remarked, "I didn't know you were going to sail on boiling water." This was typical of many inspired witticisms to come. I was

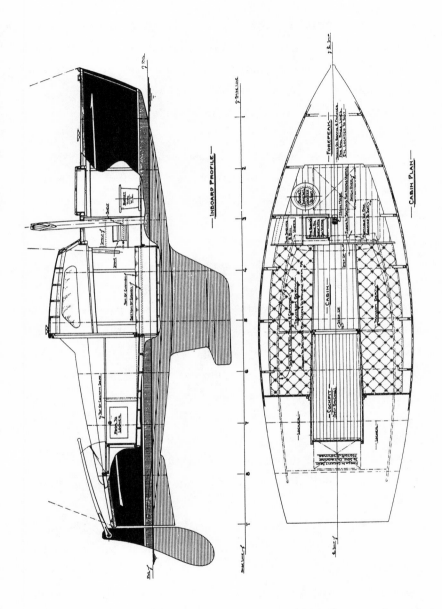

*I added a bridge deck, which had a window with my compass under it. A table slid in and out, and there was room for a waste basket and a 5-gallon jerrycan of water with a flexible hose to a pump.*

a little more surprised than pleased to discover how many clever comments were elicited by my trial-and-error boatbuilding methods. But I provided so much amusement for so many people that—as often happens—a change took place and I wound up feeling like a public benefactor. I was like a miser with my boxes of bronze screws. It's fun to have an excuse for working with such stuff. Epoxy glue is so good that if you make a mistake, if a joint is a little slack or a piece is an eighth of an inch too short, you just glue in a wood shim or a patch, which makes the assembly stronger than it would have been otherwise.

Saturdays and Sundays, working on my boat became quite a lot of fun as she took shape. The boatworks was an old shed not far from the house. My little grandson, Marty, whose parents, Kim and Hazel Merrick, lived nearby, liked to join me in the shop and get nice and grubby, the same as Grandpa. He would climb among the bare frames and stand in the half-finished bow shouting, "I see land, pull in the sails, throw out the anchor!" He heard so much about epoxy that it became one of his favorite words. Sometimes, after things went askew with my amateur building, we'd be walking up to the house for lunch. I'd be grumbling about joints that didn't fit, and he'd put his little hand in mine and look up saying, "Never mind, Poppa, fix it up with epoxy."

In our vacation, to keep us going during the years of building the Carinita, we chartered a twenty-six-foot sloop out of Camden, Maine, for a week. It was all very unsatisfactory. The absentee owner had already chartered the boat for two weeks previous to our arrival. We were appalled to find gasoline leaking into the bilge. The baggy nylon mains'l, which had been made in Denmark, was sufficiently

*I decided that considering her thousand-pound keel, she was under rigged. So I added a masthead forestay and masthead genoa, but retained the 7/8 stay also.*

5

torn to be useless. The compass didn't work, and neither did the stove, which we dared not light anyway. By the time we had taken the main to a sail maker and found a mechanic to repair the gasoline line, our week was nearly over.

Then, in our precious days off another year, we chartered a thirty-footer out of Georgetown, Maryland, on the Chesapeake, and that was scarcely any better. It was May, and happened to be an extremely frigid May. Almost all our sailing was done in long johns, flannel shirts, sweaters, parkas, and mittens. I didn't know how to reef the mains'l, so our only method of shortening down was to sail with nothing but the working jib, and that didn't get us to windward. I hadn't learned how to back the boat with the engine in tight quarters, and as a result, in St. Michael's overcrowded basin I seesawed back and forth, reverse and ahead, in the same old crescent till we drifted up against some pilings and warped ourselves around by hand, while a group of sidewalk superintendents immediately materialized, of course, and commented on the proceedings. Although I had taken the Power Squadron course in piloting, in fact even the advanced course, I wasn't expert with charts, and was always apprehensive that I'd wreck somebody else's valuable boat. This craft had automatic running fresh water, provided by a silly little electric pump under the starboard bunk. This meant that every time you wanted a drink of water and turned on the faucet—in the night, for instance, when my all-girl crew was asleep—the pump shook everybody awake with loud grumbling noises.

I must confess I learned a lot, to wit: the sidewise thrust of a propeller is important; hand pumps are better for fresh water than electric ones; mains'l reefing is a primary consideration; and when trying to claw to windward on an ice-cold blowy day with working jib only, squalls will flatten you because you can't luff up. I also learned, once again, that somebody else's boat for a week is an expensive pain in the neck, since all the glorious independence and zest you went for is totally absent. If we had signed up with an established charter company instead of an owner, perhaps we'd have done better. Perhaps not.

In any case, the spare-time boatbuilding went with renewed vigor after we returned from these expeditions.

For so many years we had been wishing to cruise the coast of Maine in our own boat. At this period in my existence I was reading so many scores of cruising yarns and accounts of boatbuilding by naval architects, in addition to a huge batch of jolly, salty articles by yacht designers specializing in esoteric terminology, that I began to get indigestion of the cranium. My mind reeled under an avalanche of incomprehensible verbiage known only to the experts to such an extent that in a mental lapse I composed a tale combining as many garbled technicalities as possible. It was called "Nightmares of a Backyard Boat-builder," and it was printed in a nice little magazine. It went like this:

So one day while leaving Falmouth for orders I rowed out from Wapping Oldstairs to be aboard at the turn of the tide and had a not inconsiderable adventure. I was at this time master of a not inconsiderable hermaphrodite brigantine carrying ostrich feathers out to the Ambiguous Islands.

Now it just so happened that the chine strip of the taffrail log had got fouled in the turnbuckle connecting the deadeyes with the foremast gallows cringle, where we flew the old Blue Ensign upside down at the leach of the mizzen. Since my sextant had been askew ever since falling under the lazarette, I was put into a quandary.

Nevertheless, we dropped down the estuary after having stowed the cargo booms under the mast step. All being 2-block and the yards frapped with rotten stuff, I ordered the hook graveled and the main courses set. This put a strain on the forward bitts that made the old hulk strain and groan. However, Wilcox Crittenden has invented a bronze fitting just for this, and since our plywood planking was well set in resorcinol phenolic resin, we rode easily enough despite the mutterings of the crew. Taking my adz in my hand, I went below, where I was busy putting gussets on both sides of the futtock shrouds. . . .

And so on.

After printing my fantasy, the nice little magazine soon folded and was no more. Meanwhile, I pressed on with my white oak and my plywood and my glue that was stiffening and ruining all my work clothes. Marty's dad, our thirty-five-year-old son, Kim, was a wonderful help, especially with the great twelve-foot slabs of plywood. I thought it was awful he was not working on his own boat, but he seemed to enjoy it. Kay helped with painting on glue, bolting things, mopping up the glue that squeezed out. We began to get quite good at it and make marvelous progress at last.

When the three-hundred-dollar supply of bronze screws began to run short, I backed out a few and used them elsewhere; once the glue had set, screws were unnecessary. My boat became all one piece, every part strengthening every other part. I'm no great shakes as a carpenter, but I learned how to do things easier and quicker— for instance, using scissors to make a paper pattern and employing that to fashion an awkwardly shaped wood piece. By the time I was finished, I really knew how to do the job.

The really great advantage to having built my own boat is that

I learned so much—so much that helps me to maintain her, repair, improve, and be independent of the busy and uninterested boatyard repair men. All this work enables you to cruise with greater confidence, prepared to fix almost anything that goes haywire in the all-corrosive grind of the sea.

I was very proud of my boat, all through the period of working on it, sometimes an hour a day, sometimes all day, sometimes not at all. My boat was twenty feet, four inches overall; waterline length eighteen feet; beam six feet, nine inches; draft three and a half feet. The secretary of the Carinita Association in San Francisco became a cherished pen pal and gave me many helpful pointers. He sold and shipped to me an iron keel from their molds. He advised me that early boats pulled too hard on the tiller, and so current builders were shifting the fin keel four inches farther aft to avoid too much weather helm. I was hesitant to make such a radical change in plan, but did so and it worked out well; only in the lightest air did we subsequently have any lee helm.

I put the thousand-pound fin keel on with ten bolts of half-inch-diameter stainless steel through six inches of white oak in various glued-together pieces, so that it ought to stay for a hundred years. I put bronze rods edgewise into the rudder so it couldn't split. The long tiller is of heavy locust wood. The mast is tubular aluminum, slightly oversized. The standing rigging is of stainless-steel wire rope also one size larger than specified, as are turnbuckles, chainplates, halyards, sheets, cleats, genoa slides, and all other points of strain. In fact, I can't think of anything that isn't a point of strain in a hard-driven sailcraft. It mustn't be too heavy; but, on the other hand, it must be able to take a beating in storms.

ELLIOTT MERRICK

When I got discouraged by all the work, I reminded myself how lucky a man is to have a boat to work on and how I had longed to have a seagoing boat for thirty years. In the bending and gluing and clamping when I needed five hands Kay often helped me, getting so involved we sometimes went without meals. One of my worst troubles was with a motorboat company that sold me epoxy that wouldn't stick. It was old and its shelf life long past. I learned to buy fresh resin and hardener.

While I was in a mess and covered with dust, I fiberglassed the hull so that teredos couldn't bore into it no matter how worn the copper paint became. And, having learned a little about handling resin, I covered the decks and cabin with Dynel or Vectra cloth laid in resin. The whole tough structure of white oak framing and plywood skin was fastened twice—bolted or screwed with bronze, and glued with epoxy or resorcinol.

I was so proud of my creation that I made a list of her features:

- Construction: Cabin and coaming sides are half-inch plywood plus quarter-inch plywood (total three-quarters of an inch) glued together in place with a curve built in. Cabin sides are fastened to the deck and deck stringers with bronze screws, bolts, and glue, also tape fiberglassed, in a joint much stronger than in average boats. Cabintop is made of two thicknesses of quarter-inch plywood (total half an inch) glued together over a curved mold, very rigid. Two men can jump on it. Fixed cabin ports (two on each side and one amidships forward) are of bronze and three-eighth-inch Plexiglas, with rims on both sides bolted together, set in Thiokol, very strong, no leaks.

10

Forward and lazarette hatches are of varnished half-inch plywood with white oak sills. Both hatches bolt down on rubber gaskets by means of eight bronze toggle bolts. Sliding companion hatch of oak and mahogany rails, with three-eighth-inch Plexiglas to let light into the cabin.

In the stern deck is a shallow, watertight well (draining overboard) to accommodate the outboard motor clamp screws. The lazarette, where gasoline is stored, is ventilated by two bronze screwplates four inches in diameter, on the port and starboard stern deck. These are covered in turn by six-inch chrome clamshells, one pointing forward, one aft; these ventilators can be closed in stormy weather.

Cockpit seats are six feet long and watertight, no opening lids. Cockpit drains (two) are an inch and a half with Wilcox Crittenden highest-quality bronze seacocks. In the cockpit sides are three four-inch plastic screwplates (Holt-Allen) for ventilation in harbor. A five-inch gimbal compass is positioned amidships under a half-inch plate glass watertight window in the eleven-inch bridge deck. Adding a bridge deck was one of my alterations to the plan.

- Deck Hardware is Merrimon, bolted through oak backing pads below deck. Genoa sheet-block slides are three and a half feet long. Extra strong bow and stern chocks. Foredeck mooring cleats (two) are oversized bronze, each through-bolted with four five-sixteenths-inch Everdur bolts to a one-inch white oak pad that extends under the deck to the stem. Grab rail of quarter-inch stainless wire through bronze eye-bolts that in turn are through triangle-shaped oak blocks, deck, and under-deck pads. The grab rail is four and a half inches high. Toe rail amidships. Chainplates are Merrimon bronze with three-eighth-inch Everdur bolts through foot-long white oak boards glued inside hull. Turnbuckles are oversized Merrimon bronze, with toggles.

- Cabin Interior: Mahogany varnished. Bunks are four feet "sit up" and two and a half feet of foot well extending under the cockpit seats. Bunks have three hinged lids and three foam cushions corresponding. Cushions are blue with white piping. Under each bunk are two plastic dishpans and four plastic baby's bathtubs for clothes, tools, food, spares, books, etc. Also, at the foot end of each bunk is an additional two-foot "crawl-in" space for bedding, charts, or infrequently used supplies. Above the port foot well is a shallow chart drawer; to starboard, a mahogany plywood pullout table. Against the port after cabin bulkhead is a gimbal kerosene lamp; starboard, a Wilcox Crittenden Galley Gal freshwater pump with a rubber hose to a five-gallon jerrycan stowed abaft the mahogany companion ladder (and under the bridge deck); the hinged plywood dishpan shelf folds down Pullman-style so that water pumps into it. Room under the bridge deck for wastebasket. Two flat jerrycans of water stow under the cockpit sole (which is also extra strong, with glued oak "floors"); also a bilge pump. Pullman-type hammocks on brass coat hooks beside each bunk.

The cooking cupboard is made of African mahogany plywood, screwed and glued to form a strong, rigid bulkhead beside the mast. A one-burner kerosene Primus pressure stove in the cooking compartment is lined with a removable aluminum box to whose exterior sheet asbestos is cemented. A one-inch air space all around, except at the top, where a two-inch space contains a sliding plywood shelf as a heat baffle; this shelf slides all the way out to be used also as a cutting board. The door to the cooking box is hinged down, with bracket chains to form a horizontal shelf in front of the stove when open. In case of fire, flames could probably be suffocated by closing the door. In rough weather, pots cannot tip over in the box, except via the front door, which could be closed and small ventilator hole opened at bottom of the door for cooking. All hinges are of solid brass (no plated, which rusts), with walnut turn buttons to close the doors. Underneath the stove box is a deep cupboard with room for cutlery, china, cups, pots and pans, canned goods, utensils, a bin for alcohol and gallon cans of kerosene, a compartment for liquor.

- Forepeak has room for two spinnaker poles to the starboard close under deck. A dress clothes bag hangs on hooks on the forward side of the cooking cupboard. Toilet bucket to port under the hatch. Space for sails, small camping icebox, and Avon inflatable dinghy in its bag. I also carried a small battery to power the running lights. We planned to get the battery charged at marinas. We had an oil lantern, but would not travel at night if we could help it.

It was going to be a wonderfully sound, strong boat. People had come from miles around to look at it. And always asked, of course,

"How are you going to get it out?" Finally Kim and I knocked down the chimney of the old shed, cut away most of that wall, and, using the car, hauled the boat out onto the lawn. It was a job of several days to jack the boat up and attach the keel. There were times when I was discouraged. I had no idea that the final stages would be such a bottomless Grand Canyon of work, work, work.

So there at last was my boat, in the water, and we walking back and forth on the dock, looking at her from every angle. She wasn't leaking, she wasn't listing. She rocked a little at the float in Hilton Head Harbor Marina, South Carolina, wanting to be off.

There being no proper hoist, we had to walk the mast up. It was thirty feet long, but we had seven people to help us, with four long guy ropes so that our beautiful new spar couldn't fall. The marina owners and management men were there, gay as crickets and pulling twice too hard. Boats are like that—everybody helps. A young merchant marine first mate who was a powerhouse was going to lift the thing into its deck hole. He and his French wife had bought an old mahogany-planked ketch and were living aboard at the dock while he repaired it between freighter voyages.

About all I had to do was to stand on the heel of the mast and encourage the hauler-uppers to pull in unison and a little less vigorously. Shrouds and stays for the mast are a problem in a new boat, since you have to know the lengths from upper mast to deck fittings, and you only have an inch or two of come-and-go on the turnbuckles. You can hardly know the lengths till you put the mast up. So I had attached cheap wire to the upper mast, and as soon as we got the spar up I pulled these wires tight and crimped them to give me my lengths. Some people like to do everything by math, but I like simple ways. Then we took the mast down again, and I spent a day tap-tapping at my Nicopress gadget making strong end loops around thimbles in the stiff wire rope. I had to remind myself, I'm retired now and don't have to work at educating the kids or paying off the mortgage. If I work all day at rigging a sailboat and take joy in it, fine, why not?

Marty, Kim, and Hazel came down to help out. Marty brought along some wonderful crayon pictures of the boat that he had been making, but none showed any mast, because he had never seen the mast up. He had portholes, cabin, keel, outboard, winches, fittings, rudder, and just about everything else. Two people were looking out the single porthole. "That's Mom and Dad. Gran, you're down below making sandwiches."

One day Marty, Hazel, and Kay went off to the beach to swim. Kim and I sailed out Port Royal Sound about four miles into the ocean, with a good whitecap breeze. Then we had a six- or seven-mile run back before the wind, with the beautiful blue-and-white spinnaker drawing like horses. We were surfing a bit, we were going that fast. It was terrific. As we got way into the sound it became even better and we were both in heaven till I cut a buoy too close and we ran aground, bong! on a shoal about two feet deep, brought up all standing with main out one side and spinnaker the other. We got the sails down—something of a flapping tangle. We jumped overboard and soon got her off, no damage, except some slight blemish to my reputation for growing nautical competence. Ah well, must do, to learn.

We worked a month fitting out and completing endless final jobs. As we put in floorboards, finished varnishing, painted the deck, made a mast coat, sewed a canvas cockpit cover, bolted down deck hardware, we got to know boat owners and waterside people, just like family. A lot of casuals are always wandering around the boatyards, looking, learning, yearning, talking, some quite genuine and appealing, some quite fake. One supercilious soul said to me, "Messing about in boats is such fun, a lot of people would rather mess around permanently than sail them." He was deliberately baiting and insulting me, and it hurt because I felt we had been at the dock fitting out too long. There is always something more you could do to prepare for storm or breakdown. I managed to mumble merely, "How true, friend. Have you made many voyages?"

Speaking of voyages, I didn't want to do any special gung ho thing like racing around the world backward without touching anywhere, or trying to beat the clock like Chichester, which seems to me a stunt spoiling the simple joy you went for. I just wanted to sail my own boat from South Carolina to Maine and back, to experience the gladness and see whether I could improve my piloting and gain confidence. We wanted adventure, and we wanted to be in Maine as many weeks as possible, where the islands are remote and satisfying.

We had beautiful new sails from a sail maker: main and working jib, a red-and-white genoa, a blue-and-white spinnaker, and a storm jib. Sail area was 187.5 square feet. Our cruising anchor was a twenty-pound Danforth, with a twenty-five-pound CQR plow for emergencies. We bought an English five-horse Seagull outboard motor with a long shaft.

Stowage limits finally settled our problem. When we couldn't stash another sea anchor or foghorn, when every item we needed or were likely to need was packed under about seven other items, we decided we must be "in all respects ready for sea." So many charts on the bunks lifted the cushions up a good two inches. There was nothing left to do but leave or sink ourselves.

It was a lovely breezy morning when we sailed away northeastward, up the Intracoastal Waterway, bound for the coast of Maine more than a thousand miles away. The golden-green marsh grass was undulating in the fresh wind like some hula hip-wiggle on a geographic scale. We couldn't believe it was really us, pushing straight across the wide blueness of Port Royal Sound like genuine seagoers. Now we had a strong deck and a self-bailing cockpit, two bunks, a splendid compass, anchors, reefing arrangements.

The boat has a wide stripe of royal blue at the sheer, set off by varnished cabin, white topsides, and red bottom paint. We call our ship *Sunrise* because she is a dream like "The sanguine sunrise, with his meteor eyes" that flames over the ocean on summer mornings. When we got to Maine we would be sailing out a wooded channel from a cove in a blueberry-and-balsam island where nobody lives, out toward the brightening sea, only the music of ripples at the bow, only seagulls and the lap of waves on ledges.

# CHAPTER II

# St. Helena Sound to Savannah River

# Charleston Harbor and Approaches

IT IS VERY HARD FOR AN OUTSIDER not brought up among boats and yacht clubs to learn to cruise. It's sort of like learning to be a lion tamer—you don't have room for very many mistakes.

The first night out, in a place called Old House Creek, I ran aground by going farther in than necessary, being too careful—but soon got off again. Since we drew only three and a half feet, I found I could jump overboard and push off while Kay stood on one side hanging to the shrouds to list us and lift our keel a little.

Next day in the Coosaw River, on long broad stretches between markers I got a chance to try the compass courses I'd been learning about in Power Squadron piloting classes at home. My compass was a first-class instrument. In that small cockpit, with a long tiller, sitting practically over the bridge deck, I could look down and quite readily see its dial under the glass window. At the end of the

19

Coosaw River's long open expanse we encountered one of the many tricky features of the waterway. As we left the broad expanse for a narrow cut, the second channel marker was higher and more prominent than the first. Only just in time did we see the first and avoid grounding again.

We found that when running all day from one numbered marker to the next, a major difficulty was to remember whether we had passed, say, No. 12, or were coming to it. It was important to follow the magenta line on the waterway strip chart, as the good water wasn't always a straight shot between markers. Some people tape their charts on a board and move a pushpin from the marker just passed to the one ahead. That's a pretty good system except that I hate to be making holes in the chart.

We sailed as much as we could, motorsailing where the channel bent to windward. In such cases we could haul the main in flat and motor along with the kicker, but we had to pull down the genny because it flapped and chafed badly against the mast. The channels were so crooked we could seldom use the spinnaker.

The books I had read came in very handy. Two things: While I was pulling the jib down in a narrow channel tossing us hither and yon, Kay got into a wild jibe that wrapped the main around the spreader. "What'll I do now?" she asked calmly. With equal poise I remembered what I'd read in the book by Eric and Susan Hiscock, who have sailed around the world twice in their thirty-foot sloop, and their account of a similar jam and calmly replied, "Just jibe her back where she came from." It worked like a charm, and we blessed our slightly oversized mast and marvelously designed rigging, too. Also, when hauling down sails in a squall the ever-present danger of losing the halyard's bitter end up the mast limits one's clawing and wrestling. So they have a snap hook, and so have we, on the end of each and clip it to a rope loop at the base of the mast, thus freeing hands, teeth, arms, and legs for more important pursuits.

We encountered few boats, as this was not the season. Those that passed us were usually "boat jockey" professionals taking a motor cruiser north from Florida for absentee owners. Between Hilton Head and Charleston, gluey black mud predominates—good holding ground, but very dirty when the anchor comes aboard in the morning. After leaving Beaufort, South Carolina, we encountered mostly marshes, marshes, heat, and bugs at night. But we were well screened for the latter, and had heard about spraying the screens with kerosene to keep out no-see-ums. It was necessary to find an anchor spot before dark, out of the channel, because the tugs and broad barges that travel at night are a menace in narrow places. Generally we made about thirty-five miles a day with our little outboard motor humming away at four and a half knots. The British Seagull outboard was a dream for starting easily and having relatively powerful thrust from its large propeller. At docks I could turn it completely around and thus go astern. It was screwed to our well in the port afterdeck. We couldn't have it centered because of the outboard rudder. The arrangement worked well, except when *Sunrise* was heeled to starboard, thus lifting the long-stemmed prop so that it sometimes raced. Perhaps I should have made a well on each side. But the Seagull had a serious fault, in that its one-quart gas tank had to be filled by hand, and this, of course, fairly often when we were running all day along what I came to call the Motorway. I'd be kneeling on the small afterdeck with can and tube, and a tough job holding on with no hands when we were rolling and pitching. I could get my shoulder against the backstay, which helped some. Already I was noticing that American outboards are self-feed, with a hose from tank to engine. We carried two six-gallon portable outboard gas tanks in the lazarette, which was bulkheaded off from the boat's interior. I carried a little hand pump for pumping gas into my filler can. We were very scared of having fumes accumulate in the bilge because of many boat explosions so caused. Therefore, when pouring gas into our little motor, I closed the ventilators and put in the companionway hatch boards. It was all quite primitive in comparison with the great diesels that roared past. But we felt independent and happy just the same.

It was great fun to come out of the marshes into the Ashley River and be sailing in Charleston Harbor itself. Our little cruiser hurried down the harbor to give us a look at the rows of antebellum houses along the Battery. Cynics used to say, "Too poor to paint, too proud to whitewash," but the houses all seemed to be painted up in stylish fashion. A freighter was going out past Fort Sumter, and a destroyer coming up the Cooper River fork where the navy base lies. Another famous expression—ghost of the city's long-ago style and prominence—is, "Charleston—where the Ashley and the Cooper Rivers come together to form the Atlantic Ocean." It occurred to me that the Battery is a descriptive and historical term, in that it dates from the day when shore guns were able to be bigger and have longer range than any guns that ships could carry, and so the Battery was good defense against enemy invaders. Charleston had three other forts at the harbor entrance.

We returned up the Ashley River to the Charleston Municipal Marina, a great, concrete-walled square along the riverbank. The friendly dock master, appropriately named Mr. Keel, told us he was filled up. "But we never turn anybody away." And so he found us a berth rafted beside a thirty-five-foot sloop that was itself tied to the wall. Every time we went along the walkways to the shore or to the "facility" we had to climb over our neighbor's decks, which I thought would be embarrassing, but they didn't seem to mind or to pay any attention. We learned later that Mr. Keel tells everybody on arrival and assignment that they may have neighbors, even three deep. The ebbing and flowing tide ran through the marina with great speed. In an embrasure of the wall was a large dead fish. It had been there so long that after a day for stocking ice, water, and groceries, we didn't miss the fish any when we departed.

The church spires stuck up from the city as we were beating out the harbor against a fresh breeze, those warning fingers pointing skyward. Threading behind Isle of Palms and Bull Bay, we motor-sailed into the marshes and birdlands of Cape Romaine National Refuge. The sun rose out of the marshes and went down in them again. Birds were everywhere, red-winged blackbirds, gulls, oyster-catchers, rails, terns, herons.

Here were an almost endless variety of winding tidal channels curling among the marshes exposing mud and oyster bars among the coarse grass. Many of these channels ran out to the shallow sea-coast, miles away, and it would have been fun to follow them in a dinghy, out to the uninhabited beaches of the lonely ocean shore. But Maine was calling, the bugs were pests, and no matter how you try not to succumb, the Intracoastal Waterway seems to instill in everybody that demon urge to get on, get on, make miles. The sun went down in red and gold swirls across the western sky. We dropped the anchor in a gurgling creek where the rising tide made frying-pan sounds as it lapped the banks. We put up the nets. It was too hot to cook. But about nine-thirty Kay warmed up a can of hash. Then we turned in and lay sweating on our bunks, listening to the hum of the millions of mosquitoes.

We anchored out most nights, disliking marinas except for necessary fuel, water, and sometimes ice. Largely because of this we ran aground quite often, looking for a niche somewhere outside the dredged channel and the tugboat traffic. We sailed as much as we could, frequently combining motor and sail in the long, straight canal cuts that link rivers and bays and tidal creeks. Piloting and chart work are endlessly exacting, and someone must steer all the time. We stayed happy and healthy despite the heat, and the boat proved strong and rugged.

Weston Martyr (who by the way wrote the best cruising story ever published, namely "Smith versus Lichtensteiger," in the little book called The £200 Millionaire) has a delightful bit in one of his tales in which he tootles on his foghorn to galvanize bridge tenders into action as he and his jolly crew sail and motor along the canals of Holland. Loud or soft, sweet or harsh, he claims he had to guess, at a distance of fifty yards, whether the Dutch keeper needed rousing or soothing. He says it takes great skill to play on the foghorn with subtle tones, as the instrument wasn't designed for such performances. Nevertheless, delays were lengthy if he made the wrong guess.

I thought of this when we came to waterway bridges. Will the bridge tender open promptly? Shall I pull the sail down? Will we have to circle? Is there water enough for circling? Is anybody else coming the other way? What about all that road traffic? Shall I speed up or slow down? You never know what His Majesty the bridge tender is going to do. Some open when you're far away; some won't budge till you're right on top of them. If you have wind and current behind you, it's tricky, so tricky that some boatmen carry a stern anchor in case the engine should fail at a crucial moment. Sometimes a tug-and-barge or a fast motor cruiser are coming through from the other direction and there's no room for passing in the narrow span, so you say to yourself *Watch out!* The bells ring, the lights flash, the roadway gates go down, and the long rows of trailer trucks glare at us as we sail through the water lane. We are prepared to circle at every drawbridge, and if we have the genny poled out or the spinnaker up, we douse it a mile above the bridge.

When I am sailing through a bridge with a fair wind, main broad off, I find nearly always the wind flaws and we jibe in the middle of the bridge opening where there's no room to steer off for avoiding a jibe, and no room to swoop off course either. So what to do? In such case I've learned to sheet the main amidships so it can jibe however it wants to without harm. Once when we were soaring thus with fair wind through a narrow bridge opening, a very fast motor cruiser with huge wake came roaring up on our tail with the evident intention of passing us in the bridge opening, where an unavoidable jibe on our part would surely result in collision. I wasn't about to have that happen, so I gave him four vigorous blasts on the air horn to signify *Emergency! Don't pass!* Seeing his bow sink, I knew he'd gotten the message. He must have been one of those aggressive ones who will ask, "How long did it take you to get to Norfolk?" And when I answer, "Three weeks," he'll smirk and let us know, "It took me three days." Anyway, when we got through the bridge he followed close behind, and as he came alongside to pass he switched on his power with a great thrust and shouted, "Why

25

don't you get rid of that antique relic!" His great white wake followed after him like a tail, while I was inventing devastating squelchers that never had a chance to get used. Unlike this fellow, most people were very considerate with their wakes.

All this horn-blowing business went through my head when, motoring along the waterway one day in North Carolina, we came upon a bridge where nobody was blowing at all. Instead seven yachts were anchored quiet as mice in a basin before the bridge. "What's the trouble?" we asked.

"Bridge machinery is broken," we were told. "Sent for mechanics but they can't fix it till tomorrow afternoon." It was one of those turning affairs, pivoting on a little center island, thus opening two channels, one on each side.

It seemed like a long time to sit there. We wondered whether to go down the Edisto River to a breaking inlet full of shifting sandbars, then around by sea, entering through another wreck-making channel, but discretion seemed the better part, so we anchored also. By and by we looked up from our books to see a large green shrimp boat named *Miss Julie* swishing along the channel. Her skipper hollered to the nearest yacht, "Hey! What's the matter?"

"Bridge machinery busted. Can't turn to open. They can't fix it till tomorrow."

"The hell you say!" intoned *Miss Julie's* happy-looking captain. He steamed up close to the bridge, went into reverse, and floated there within feet of the bridge tender while engaging in earnest conversation. His loud voice came over the water: "Here, take my line. Make fast to that girder there, and I'll pull 'er open."

The bridge tender did as directed, and while we all watched goggle-eyed, *Miss Julie* slowly backed, tightening the heavy towrope.

The man had marvelous control, reminding me of the skillful way shrimp boats slide into a berth at a crowded dock, and they do it all the time.

When Shrimper applied the power to his taut line, the bridge began to turn. Bit by bit as he backed, water channels appeared on both sides of the bridge tender's island. Among the fleet, anchors started coming in, motors began to bark. Pretty soon we all went through except the shrimper, who stood by looking pleased. *Sunrise* lingered to see what would happen about the automobiles and trucks now waiting on the road.

"I'll pull 'er shut for you," we heard him shout. The towrope was made fast to the opposite end of the bridge, he pulled a little sidewise at first, then straightened out as the span half closed and gradually shut. It seemed an inspired performance.

"Cast me off," he yelled as the autos moved across the closed bridge, which the bridge tender proceeded to do with alacrity, as though he feared our friend would tear the bridge from its foundations just for a lark. As he steamed on up the waterway, he shouted, "Can't open till tomorrow! Too bad. Too damn bad!" Then he gave seven toots on his horn. Why seven I'll never know. They resembled derisive laughter.

"What a man!" Kay murmured.

I couldn't help commenting, "He ought to be chairman of somebody's board of directors."

# CHAPTER III

# APPROACHES TO CAPE FEAR

# CAPE FEAR TO WILMINGTON

# NEW RIVER TO CAPE FEAR

# CAPE LOOKOUT TO NEW RIVER INLET

AT THE SOUTHPORT MUNICIPAL MARINA on a windy evening we made a mess, as usual, of tying up to four pilings in a slip. As you enter the slip it is necessary to get a line immediately onto the windward post that will hold your stern. This has to be done as your bow passes by this outer, windward post, and the line taken smartly aft as the boat slides past. We missed this and banged around between the pilings, unable to reach out fifteen feet to the windward ones or lasso them against the breeze. But finally we got tied up, with only a few more scars to our rail, and went ashore for a shower.

At Southport one comes out of the marshes to a seagoing place where the ships pass by going up the Cape Fear River to

Wilmington, North Carolina, or coming down. Many fishing boats berth there, too.

That black windy night a big motor yacht came in and put on a real exhibition of seamanship. She was about eighty feet long, of graceful design with a clipper bow. She had a crew of three, who were probably captain, deckhand-mate, and steward-cook. The owner was aboard also, but he didn't assist in the docking—just looked on. The vessel came into a narrow basin where there was no room for her to turn. The restricted space between boats and wharves prevented her from getting closer to the tie-up dock than thirty feet. As soon as she lost way, a brisk broadside wind began blowing her down onto a cluster of nearby yachts. Disaster was imminent, and everybody knew it. But like lightning two heaving lines shot out one from her bow and one from her stern. Shore workers quickly hauled them in, and their attached cables. The captain shouted, "Stern line forward, bow line aft!" The big spliced eyes were in this fashion looped over bollards, giving him a bow spring and a stern spring, the two crossed in an X. All this had to be done in a twinkling.

Then he went slowly ahead on his engines, which pulled his bow toward the dock as the bow spring tightened. His deckhand was meanwhile winching in the sagging aft spring. Next, the skipper went slowly astern, which tightened his stern spring, pulling the ship's stern in and allowing some take-up on the bow spring. All this in the gusty blackness, with very few shouts. Ahead and reverse he steamed, hauling himself a little closer each time, until in a few minutes he was within about three feet and could put out breast lines that enabled him to winch himself alongside. His crew was well trained, and he was a master hand himself. The accommodation ladder quickly came down to accommodate the owner, who stepped ashore to telephone, as calm as could be.

In view of our bumbling tie-up performance, I felt great admiration for the skipper who had so neatly averted disaster. That evening I learned something about docking maneuvers that has stood me in good stead ever since.

Here at Southport, a time of big wind and rain overtook us, so *Sunrise* stayed tied up while the crew rested and reveled in a "harbor day." I was feeling condescending toward the mere motorboats berthed around us. When one of their owners who had just docked his sportfisherman came walking by on the pier, I said to him, "Blowy today."

"Yes," he replied, "I've just come in from the Gulf Stream sixty-five miles out, and it's really dirty out there."

So much for condescension.

Sailing up the supposedly flooding Cape Fear River next day, the skipper of *Sunrise* picked up a little more sea lore. The tidal currents in the Cape Fear River are formidable. To find when the favoring flood current would begin at Southport, I had, therefore, looked up the time of low water in my tidal levels book.

There are two tidal information books issued by the U.S. government. One tells you at what time high and low tide will occur for each day at specific coastal points, and also the range between high and low tides—whether a few inches or nineteen feet as in parts of Maine. The other is called Tidal Current Tables, and I never paid much attention to that one, although I carried it along. In a little boat that can motor at only five knots, the tide is extremely important. If we have a two-knot current with us, we are making seven knots; if we have a two-knot current against us, we make only three, which is less than half and means a huge difference in the day's run. Cruisers on the waterway are constantly mindful of high and low water, which occur about one hour later each day. If you should touch or go aground in those endless shallows on a rising tide, you can probably get off quite soon; but on a falling tide the reverse holds true. The marshes seem drowned at high tide, and they stick out surprisingly at the bottom of the ebb, changing all the appearance of the coast. It had seemed to me that the tidal levels tables were the ones that concerned us, but the Cape Fear River taught me otherwise.

This river has tidal currents running as much as five knots on the ebb and flow. The great ships creaming in from the sea, bound up for Wilmington, North Carolina's greatest port, seem to pay no attention to the current, having lots of power.

At low tide, eleven A.M., we said good-bye to our new friends at the Southport State Marina and cast off. A big wonderful wind was boosting in from the sea, fair for us, fair for up the river. Hoisting main and jib, away we went, expecting wind and current both to favor us. But the current in the river was still running out fast, and wind-against-current made it very rough. We pitched and tossed in blue-black waves with breaking crests, making a few miles upriver, but it was slow despite the fair wind. "What do you suppose is the matter?" I said to Kay. "Maybe you didn't figure the times right," she answered. "Did you allow for Daylight Saving?"

I got out my tide tables and pencil again, but couldn't see anything wrong with my figuring. Then I looked into my book of tidal current tables and found what the trouble was. It's a strange paradox, but when the current is running out from a huge inland area and the volume of water is enormous, the ebb current will some-times continue to run seaward for as much as three hours after the tide begins to flood. So we bucked the tide all the way up, and was it rough!

Time and again the great wind from the sea would grab the mains'l and knock us rail-down, slewing us off at right angles to our course no matter how we bent the tiller. It was a real broach, and we didn't like it. For Bermuda or Transpac racers with a crew of four to eight powerful men, to broach carrying too much sail is bad enough, but at least they're in the open ocean and have room to round up and lie battered on their sides. We had breaking sandbars beside us, and each broach forced us closer, a truly out-of-control situation, with the hard-over rudder unable to hold us on our course before the wind.

Everything was quite desperate in the fast head current and breaking chop, when up from astern came a powerful yawl. She must have been fifty feet overall, and her people were having a relaxed and splendid time, as cruisers are supposed to do. Lolling in the cockpit were two bronzed and capable-looking sailors with their women, under complete control, no sweat, no broaches, and why? Well, of course! Their main and mizzen were furled in this lashing fair wind and narrow channel; they were running with genoa only. Having all sail well forward (and nothing aft to push the bow up into the wind), their great jib was pulling the bow as though they were being towed; they ran straight and could follow the channel easily.

"Hey, hey, look at that," I hollered, and jumped for our main halyard. I had often read of cruisers in gales pulling the main down with the wind in it, not rounding up into the wind as we generally did. We had no room to round up in this instance, so I loosed the halyard and began pulling down the Dacron. I got it down, but in the process broke two of the ash sail battens where they had been beating against the shrouds and spreaders on the way down. I should have sheeted in the sail to keep it off the shroud. Later I bought some plastic battens that are much tougher than wood. In the rushing river and wind, the situation had seemed pretty desperate to us at the time, but months later we smiled to think of ourselves on the Cape Fear River, inept cruisers who had half panicked because they had to do something and hadn't known just what to do. Good sailors in blows in narrow waters have to do something and do it right and do it fast, till it becomes second nature and they don't think about it twice.

Under a jib alone it was a cinch. We began to enjoy the scenery, a huge expanse of sand and distance to starboard, a wooded shore and the extensive military loading port of Sunny Point to port. That upper part of the river is peppered with so many ranges and channel markers that the superfluity becomes confusing to a stranger and undoes the very purpose of those multitudinous navigation aids. I suppose all the ranges exist to help bring big ships up the river to Wilmington in fog and night. After all, nothing equals the in-line markers of a range to demonstrate whether the current is shoving your ship off course or not—if only you know which is which and don't get one range marker of a pair mixed up with some group of black-and-white slats marking a sandbar, or a line of telephone poles marching across a shallow, or even a bunch of abandoned pilings that should have been pulled out years ago.

Charting busily and following the buoys, black to port, red to starboard, rather than the ranges, we flew along happy as kids. It

34

made such a difference to get the main down that it was a different world, and often since then we have run whole days in a big wind with a jib up there hard as sheet iron. Soon we turned off into Snows Cut, where wind was nonexistent under the high sand-banks, under a lofty bridge, and then hoisted main again in a magnificent beam wind through Myrtle Sound behind the Wrightsville beaches. Many people in sailboats travel the waterway using auxiliary motor only, no sail, because it's too narrow and too twisty and too much work to be trimming sheets all the time. But that seems to us too dull.

Kay was wonderful, the way she never got scared and always steered for me while I pulled down the main or jib, or gassed up, or got the anchor ready. How she managed the commissary I do not know. It was very exacting, very cramped, required great simplicity, great skill.

Myrtle Sound is one of those pleasant places where the waterway is only separated from the ocean by low dunes and a beach. As we had done so often in the Penguin, we anchored, waded ashore, and crossed the dunes to swim in the ocean breakers on a miles-long beach that contained not a soul, not even a footprint. We had a run on the beach to loosen up atrophying legs.

On this our first cruise, we had no intention of going outside Cape Hatteras, "the graveyard of the Atlantic," where the ribs of hundreds of ships lie buried in the sands. Various authorities say that if you are going outside Cape Hatteras you should be at least three hundred miles off, for seventy-two-hour-long northeaster storms have shoved many a schooner into the Diamond Shoals surf from farther out than that. Still, we wished we could go outside. In these tea-colored rivers and cuts and swamps there was no room to tack or maneuver, and the main thing we did was pour gasoline into the outboard.

Morehead City is a seaport where the tide runs hard past the municipal docks and the moored ships.

The breeze fell off and the day grew hot. We were behind schedule, thanks to a month of interior work, rigging details, and shakedown cruises at Hilton Head. But you can't have everything and the boat was performing nobly. We had the mainsail furled and a white cotton duck awning that we rigged to two spinnaker poles that are lashed across the boom amidships. Under this creation we sat in the shade while motoring through the breathless cuts at five miles an hour toward the Neuse River. Or if the breeze was light and fair we often set the biggest masthead genny (red and white) and still motored and sailed while steering in the shade. Kay says we look like a bumboat in a tropical port.

It was not all roses. On the Neuse River we thought we'd turn inside out. All you could do was crawl from handhold to handhold, even down below. We were rolling along with only the No. 2 genny, and sometimes we almost dipped the spreaders. The buoys were sometimes about five miles apart and could barely be picked up by compass courses. It was wild, with lots of shoals about, and land far, far away almost out of sight. I picked up the most difficult point as the afternoon wore on—a not-too-big marker. And then in my concern for sailing the boat I made for the largest marker in sight, about three miles off, only to find when we approached that it was thirty degrees off our course, the wrong one and backed by miles of breaking shoals. Fortunately the wind was still fair and we could beam reach on a compass course for the correct one, which Kay, glued to the tossing binoculars, eventually picked up, to our extreme relief. It was a wild, woolly afternoon, and when we came into Gale Creek and anchored behind a point, near Hobucken, we felt as though we had rounded the Horn.

Next day, where the waters widened, we sailed a compass course out of sight of land—for the first time. Luckily, a fair wind blew us across Pamlico Sound, glinting with sunshine and white-caps. First we poled out the genoa, and then as the wind came directly astern up went the bosomy blue-and-white spinnaker, which made *Sunrise* jump. "Oh, this is what we came for," said Kay. The markers were miles apart but we made them all okay, and by and by the far shore began to lift up in a blue blur. The sun burned so hot that, sitting at the tiller, we kept covered as much as possible, collars up, hats on, long sleeves, long pants, a shade over the ankles.

Late in the afternoon among these endless shallows we found our route marker and hurried on toward a just-visible buoy in the distance, without checking the chart. Something told me it was wrong. Sure enough, the beacon marked the edge of a mudflat miles wide and I was all but plowing into it. We altered course to the westward, directly into the low sun, and could not look at those gleaming waters even with black glasses on. So then it was compass course again, and, lo and behold, toward sunset the Pungo River buoy appeared ahead.

Here we would leave the limitless inland seas for a spell and find rest and shelter in a quiet creek where no night winds could wreck us. We had seen no one all day except two professionals taking fast sportfishermen to New England from Florida, white gashes across the bay.

37

In an elbow of the channel, near a big flashing beacon, we came to a broad fork and an island. Seeing that the chart showed water enough to float us, we turned out there and dropped the hook in an opening behind the flasher. Sitting in the cockpit, resting on our laurels watching the sun go down in a magnificent display of purple clouds, we were comparing knees to see whose were the sorest. It seemed pretty funny that we should both get housemaid's knee on a cruise, but it was a fact that our knees at this point had become blue and bruised from so much kneeling, to crank the motor on the small afterdeck, to change jibs on the foredeck, to get sails out of the forepeak, or remove food from the little icebox, also in the forepeak. It seemed as though we spent half our time kneeling on the cabin sole to get tools or supplies or clothes from their storage compartments under the bunks. People who feel sorry for us in such a small boat are always sorry for the wrong feature. What they should commiserate about is the lack of stowage space—in every locker, nine things on top of anything you want. Kay next day made a foam-rubber cushion to kneel on, and it saved us much grief.

Just then we heard the drone of a motor. In this land of water and grass, no house, no boat, no sign of man except the silent beacon flasher, here came the ubiquitous outboard. In no time at all it was upon us, circling, two people staring at us. The pair in the boxy outboard skiff were very young, children in fact—the boy about fourteen, the girl around seven. They didn't look very bright, the boy a skinny creature with bedraggled hair and a misshapen mouth, triangular like a fish. The girl, in a tattered pink dress, had an animated face, in an undernourished way, but never spoke. She acted as though she'd like to but couldn't.

Curiosity getting the better of them, after shouting unintelligible questions they turned off their roarer and would have banged alongside hard had we not fended off. We pushed their bow away and let them drift. There was no breeze, and thus they floated, only a couple of feet away.

"You lost?" asked the strange boy, looking us over carefully.

"No."

"You ain't lost?"

"No, not lost."

"You out of gas?"

"No."

Not lost, not out of gas, we were an enigma, I don't know why I didn't feel more charitable. His blank eyes went blanker. Kay came up from below with cups and saucers. "We're having a cup of tea," she said brightly.

"Cup of tea?" he repeated in slurred, bewildered tones, as though this confirmed his suspicions.

In the manner of the quite young, he seemed to feel that speed was a good way out of unsolvable confusions, and consequently pulled the cord of his motor and began throwing spray. As they screamed away, with a roostertail spouting from their wake, the quiet, motionless girl came to life. Then ensued the strangest picture of all. She seized their rope painter, leaned back on it making horse-driving gestures, and began swaying from side to side as she galloped around imaginary curves, straightening up with concentration, a Ben-Hur charioteer lost in her own thrilling pantomime. She was suddenly transformed into a diminutive Winged Victory with fluttering draperies.

Thus they raced away, as they had come, trailing their wake far up a marshy bay. Watching with the glasses, I saw them disappear into a wooded creek, and then they became one more buzz in this lonely, drowned country.

At this point we bestirred ourselves and rigged the screens with dispatch, for the mosquitoes and gnats filtered down on us like fog as the swirls of sunset died away. At the very moment the sun dips, they all pounce at once, and this happens every evening.

Something about those two strange children who had come so many miles to look at us made me apprehensive. When darkness arrived, I saw a light glimmering way up that creek, winking in and out among the trees, and we smelled wood smoke. So they lived there; well, they had to live somewhere, didn't they? Yet as I hung up our anchor-light oil lantern I could picture six villainous uncles, in black hats, squatting around a stone fireplace chinked with clay. They were loading up their guns for a swift and practiced robbery, leaving no trace, you may be sure.

I loaded up my own Smith & Wesson revolver and put it under my pillow.

But nothing disturbed the night except a tugboat with two barges that came down the channel curve and found us dead ahead, a little pinpoint lantern shining steadily inside the blinker beacon. Surprised as she huffed through the blackness, she pinned us in the glare of her searchlight. I was standing in the companionway watching through the mosquito net, thinking, *More people! What a busy corner!* when, satisfied that here was a little yacht anchored for the night and no menace to two bargeloads of pulpwood, she jerked her beam aside.

The searchlight hopped away as though apologetically, making me laugh. The pilot seemed to be saying, "Sorry I woke you, but it's no joke running all night. We gotta work, and you're only playing."

# CHAPTER IV

# PAMLICO SOUND— WESTERN PART

# CAPE HATTERAS—WIMBLE SHOALS TO OCRACOKE ISLAND

WE WERE ANCHORED FOR THE NIGHT in a very lonely bay among the endless swamps and estuaries of Pamlico Sound. Three or four counties out there in eastern Carolina are so wild and faraway it's unbelievable—cypress swamp, vast shallows, only three or four roads in all those counties, thirty-mile stretches without a house.

The fisherman's name was Harold Harris. He was a pleasant, good-looking young fellow with brown hair and nice eyes, in a big old cypress skiff with an outboard motor on it, and he stopped and told us of a row of pilings just under the surface of the present extra-high water that we'd better look out for when we departed. It had been a dock, sticking out from a considerable settlement, but when the railroad went to Belhaven, this little town fell in. That must have been a long time ago, because the buildings had tumbled down and disappeared. We were very grateful to him. People don't usually come out in a boat to warn you of hazards that don't appear on the chart. If we had anchored a little farther toward shore, we might have banged against those pilings in the night.

Harold Harris, who was tending crab pots, pointed out to us his little green house in a cove, the only house in sight. He said he used to be a policeman in Greenville, South Carolina, ". . . and it was killing me." His wife was making good money as cashier in a super-market. She kept on with it while he went down to the wildest country he could find and learned to be a crabber and fisherman— lived all winter in his little cabin motorboat. "It was cold." Got hold of this house, learned about oystering and fishing for scallops and whatnot, then the family came to join him, three children, too. His wife now helps with the fishing. They are very poor but very happy. He gave us nearly a bucketful of crabs, and when I pressed money into his hand he refused, saying, "It's nothing; I only get ten cents a pound for that size." He floated alongside, holding to the rail, and wouldn't come aboard. The evening was calm, so calm the setting sun reflected swirls of red and gold in the miles of quiet water. In that brooding, faraway country the sunsets are pictures you remem-ber for a long time. He looked at the colored sky and then just before he shoved off and disappeared into a channel among the mazes of watery forest, he said quite simply, "People don't know what they're missing."

Leaving Harold Harris to his solitary fishing, we hadn't far to go to the fleshpots of the River Forest Manor in the town of Belhaven. Here we hoped to get a bath and an air-conditioned room, which would give us a brief rest from the burning July sun. Kay was look-ing forward also to a respite from the galley.

At that time the manor's docks were somewhat broken down from storms, and their wooden-fence breakwater built to shield the docks from a fetch of several miles was practically nonexistent. It looked like poor shelter. Fortunately, the weather was settled and calm.

An old black man told us where to tie up at the far end of a row of pilings—which put us immediately on the rocks of some ancient breakwater. He must have been saving all the good berths for big motor cruisers. At any rate, we got off the rocks and tied up four ways in one of the deepest berths regardless of his advice. One more lesson: When docking at a strange marina, you have to take the shoreside advice with a grain of salt.

The manor management assigned us a little cottage that didn't have air-conditioning. But at least our high-ceilinged apartment was cooler than the boat. It didn't have a shower or tub either. However, we found it a treat to be able to walk around in our sleeping quarters and to stretch out on a real honest-to-goodness bed. A bath took a long time because each person had to sit halfway up the broad manor stairway waiting for somebody else to finish his ablutions. That wasn't part of the plan, but the hot bath was a sybaritic rite when at length it could be achieved.

River Forest Manor is a huge old mansion with extensive grounds, built in this watery low country by a tycoon who made a fortune from native cypress timber. It is a favored hostelry for duck and goose hunters, as well as waterway cruisers; many famous people have visited there. It is especially well known for its food. People in the Piedmont cities of the Carolinas think nothing of driving a hundred miles or more to sample the delights its Negro cooks prepare. Buffet-style, we were presented with shrimp, soft-shell crab, fish, fried chicken, beef, candied sweet potatoes wearing a dab of whipped cream, the inevitable grits, okra, asparagus, beets, green beans cooked with pork, wild rice au gratin, avocado salad, pecan pie, and more delicacies than anybody could consume. A parrot in the hallway of the vast old building kept shrilling his wolf whistle at every woman who passed by, while our genial host dished out anecdotes about the surrounding wilderness of bays, swamps, and woods.

Tied up at Belhaven in late June, we looked back on weeks of adventure. We had motored and sailed some four hundred miles and had experienced some of the most gorgeous, shrieking perfect sailing of our lives. Most every afternoon in the open waters the breeze from south or southwest strengthened to about twenty knots, and we roared on our way in a fan of foam, with a big genny pulling like freight trains and the main lugging, too. It was so we sailed the whole length of wide Bogue Sound and into Morehead City—perhaps twenty-five miles that afternoon. We had had our quota of daily emergencies, and that day the bridge tender of a huge span in Morehead City was mighty slow despite the booming wind behind us. We had to come around and tack away or end our cruise right there. Most bridge tenders are very good, but vigilance is the word, and roaring up with a genoa winged out on a spinnaker pole and all pinned down with foreguys and things is next to suicide, we found.

# CHAPTER V

# MOBJACK BAY AND
# YORK RIVER ENTRANCE

You never know what will happen, as our day in Mobjack Bay illustrates. We didn't intend to go near the place.

It seems incredible that I could have been so unknowing, but the tide on that hazy-dim day swept us so far off course I hadn't the faintest idea where we were. When I spotted a buoy with a number on it, the number didn't correspond to any buoys within miles of my charted course. Headed north, I didn't know whether we had been swept to the east or the west. In those days I had a dumb faith in my compass, just hoping we'd truly make the course we were steering.

We had been engaged in a long "straight" course up the Chesapeake headed toward Stingray Point, to be passed to port if it ever showed up in the mist. I had an idea that the tide didn't amount to much in the Chesapeake, where the rise and fall is often two feet or less. However, an immense quantity of water is moved, and to move it in, then out, generates considerable current, especially at the mouths of the York and Potomac Rivers. The flood in

45

this case was not only running up the bay, but also filling the broad York River, which we were passing. I didn't know that in the haze we had come to some invisible fork and been nudged to the left up the York instead of to the right up the Chesapeake Bay.

Once again, I should have been studying my tidal current book and drawn some sort of appropriate vector to ascertain leeway. Always after this I would remember that when the wind is light and the boat is moving through the water slowly, tidal set becomes a greater factor. For instance, suppose you were crossing a mile-wide river; if you took one hour for the crossing, you'd be swept down a certain distance. But if you needed three hours to cross, you'd be swept down three times as far.

I thought we were out in the middle of the bay, and that we were favoring our port hand, or the western shore. Consequently, I was confused and panic-stricken when I suddenly saw land close aboard to starboard, the wrong side, consisting of a long point and prominent white tower. Knowing that that white tower must be an important aid to navigation, I searched and searched the chart, but found nothing at first. At length, scouring the small print, I discovered it was the abandoned Coast Guard lighthouse on New Point Comfort. The Coast Guard had its funds so cut that it gave up most of the outstanding stone towers it used to maintain at strategic points, and has substituted instead some automatic steel-grillwork monstrosities that are practically invisible by day, though they may be all right at night when their modern lights are shining. Kay said one time, "It seems to me we're finding our way to New England by abandoned towers."

While I studied the chart's possibilities, we let the sail flap and just drifted, the wind being extremely light.

46

The day was too late and the breeze too faint and the sun too hot for us to find any other anchorage this Sunday afternoon; we steered, therefore, toward a cove on the northeast shore of Mobjack Bay, there being few sheltered spots in this shallow bay with water enough to float us.

As that was error day and the haze still quite thick, I picked the wrong cove, which resulted in our going aground hard and fast. I told Kay we had been aground so many times, I wasn't going to get excited this time. Coolly and quietly I took off my glasses, removed my shirt, put my stainless-steel jackknife on the cockpit seat, and jumped overboard with my precious billfold in my back pocket. The licenses, cards, papers, all became a trifle pulpy, but seemed to be still legible. I threw the billfold aboard, got my shoulder under the bilge and shoved us here and there, the keel leaving grooves in the hard mud and grass. But it soon became apparent there was nowhere to go, all the area being shallow, and the tide falling. From a man and his children who came along in an outboard we learned that we were in the wrong cove. "It's the next one you want," he said. "The two look very similar. All the sailboats that come in here go aground."

His offer to pull us off was a cordial gesture, since obviously we were beginning to list already, and any such hope was impossible. We thanked him, and improved the shining hour by drying out the contents of my billfold and sleeping four hours on a decided slant while the tide finished ebbing and rose again. The outboard man returned from his outing on the bay and waved to us. He had been gone three hours. There didn't seem to be anything to say. People miles away can see by the tilted mast that you are stuck, and, having suffered similar tribulation themselves, they usually indulge in delighted chuckles. Your swift courser, your responsive seagoer might as well be a rotting barge on some backwater mudflat. You cannot go anywhere, you cannot do anything. You simply endure and try to look cheerful.

And then our luck changed. The breeze came up, the tide came up, and we sailed away for cove No. 2, which was the spitting image of cove No. 1 except slightly larger and somewhat deeper. Since we were almost out of gas, we circled (under sail) a white outboard boat that was anchored and fishing at the entrance, and asked them—a man, woman, and pretty girl—where we could please get some fuel in this harbor. We told them we had been aground, and asked if there was water enough for our three-and-a-half-foot keel.

They directed us to a well-kept new marina a mile or so upstream, where nobody was about, but at length we woke up the proprietor, who had been having a nice, quiet Sunday-afternoon nap in his pleasant house surrounded by green lawns and flowers. While he was filling our tanks, along came the outboard. They were the Reverend and Mrs. Carnan and their daughter, Val. To our surprise, they wanted us to come to supper at their summer cottage by the shore a little farther in. "I'll be out in a rowboat showing you where to anchor, and will take you ashore," the Reverend Carnan told us. "It isn't quite deep enough at the dock for you." Their kindness and savvy concerning water depths was more than we could resist.

It was a charming point they lived on, right across the water from a little boatyard where a considerable vessel was under construction. Carnan was as good as his word, meeting us, directing us, and rowing us ashore. It was only when he scrambled onto the dock that we saw he was extremely lame. As we followed him along a little path through the woods, he told us he had been a flier in World War I.

After the war he continued private piloting, and had a bad crash. "I always try to remind myself I was lucky to get out of it alive." Having taken up the ministry, he became chaplain of a bomber group in World War II, an outfit of Flying Fortresses whose losses over Germany were appalling. "Our group knew I was a flier, and that helped a little. I wish I could have done more for those men."

We had no sooner been shown around the cottage than Mrs. Carnan produced two big bath towels, one red, and one blue. "There you are. We know about cruising people. Now, make yourselves at home, and when you've had your bath, the drinks will be ready."

The hot running water and the civilized luxuries were a glorious treat we made the most of.

We sat in a cool, shady grove of trees above the water, refreshed by our blissful bath, having an iced drink, watching the steaks brown on the outdoor grill, and decided that these wonderful Carnans, who already seemed like close friends, had saved our day. If I hadn't been so inept we should never have met them, and thus, making a virtue of necessity, I did not feel quite such a bumbler by the time my second drink was down the hatch.

Everybody helped with the supper, which included crisp salad and fascinating tales of both the Virginia countryside and the Chesapeake. These people were native Virginians and knew the folklore as we never could. Daughter Val, a girl of about eighteen, carried dishes in and out, helping serve everyone, being very friendly and considerate to us oldsters, not a bit standoffish as some teenagers are. At the same time, she was not wholly there. She was to be married in a few months, and that's what she was thinking of.

The Carnans told us they were soon moving from here to a church at Accomac, on the lower Eastern Shore. They begged us to come and see them next year when we should be going up the coast again.

A look at the chart showed me that the picture puzzle mazes of water and land over there are even more beset with shoals than Mobjack Bay. I suppose it is inevitable we'll run aground hard and fast as we go poking up the crooked channel toward the town. Here's hoping we'll not get stuck on a falling tide, but on the flood, when we can float off like old-timers. One of the oddities of cruising is that you have your deep-water friends and your shoal-water friends. You have to be earnestly devoted to the latter.

# CHAPTER VI

# COVE POINT TO SANDY POINT

THE CHESAPEAKE'S MAZES ARE ENDLESSLY EXCITING—a bay within a bay, then you round a point, twist behind an island into a river, the river bends and opens into a big cove, then a niche, a cove within a cove. There we might anchor among the great spread-armed oak trees, among birds and flowers, or perhaps houses, or fertile fields of waving grain. Or maybe we are so isolated we see the ripple of a muskrat as he swims across the black-mirror water when night comes down.

Oxford, Maryland, is like this. You get a preview of the place as you sail past its outer beach, its town park. Then you round a point in the mouth of the Tred Avon River and keep turning into Town Creek, a tributary arm of the Tred Avon, and sail along behind the town past its yachts and docks.

The place to tie up in Oxford, I think, is Wiley's yard. Ralph Wiley, the great craftsman-boatbuilder, is now retired, and the yard is run by Ed Cutts, a craftsman-boatbuilder of rare skill and integrity himself. Oxford is one of the most beautiful towns we have ever visited. With its green lawns, snug harbor, quiet village streets of white Colonial houses, its town park by the bay, and its neat, seagoing air,

it would make you think of New England at its best, New England
in the old days, New England in the fall, New England in the summer sunshine with a tinge of blue haze on the hills. But there are
no hills here beside the alluvial Chesapeake. Oxford was destined
once upon a time to be a great metropolis, the New York of the East
Coast. It was a big tobacco port in early days and point of departure to England for agricultural products from up the Tred Avon and
fertile Maryland farms nearby. But as ships grew bigger, Oxford
began to look smaller, and could no longer handle the deep-draft
freighters. What a blessing! They went on, to stink up Baltimore.

Now Oxford is a yacht harbor par excellence. As you make the
U-turn entering Town Creek you see on your starboard hand a forest of masts—big sloops, yawls, ketches, cutters, with scrubbed teak
decks, gleaming winches, blue cockpit covers, all spit and polish,
yachty yachts obviously built and maintained on a basis of no concern for cost.

When we were there at the Wiley-Cutts boatyard, Cutts had
eight men working in his yard and his big building shed, where he
specialized in turning out racing sloops of such beauty it made you
gasp to look at their curves. The place smelled of cedar. All fastenings were bronze, and every joint a work of art, fitting so close
you could hardly see the hairline crack. The office was full of half
models, plans, fittings designed by Wiley and Cutts, compasses,
draftsman's tools, sextants and charts, more boat plans, steering
wheels, orders—the fifty-year accumulation in a working studio—
very heartening, making you know once again that true, develop-
ing, never-ending art is alive and vigorous, this waterside hideaway
being one of the many odd corners where it lives and thrives, even
as it did in the Renaissance.

52

Outside, in its cradle, on the north side in as much shade as possible stood a deep-keel wooden hull thirty-four feet long, almost finished. It was badly dried out, seams opened, caulking showing, even gaps letting the light through its planking. "There you are," said Cutts. "A man spent fourteen years building that. Then he got a heart attack and died. We moved it here and we're finishing it up for his heirs."

Kay and I both felt like saying something. But what was there to say? This dream had gotten well broken, sure enough. So often a man can't get a good boat until he's too old.

It just happened that *Wiley Fox* and *Wiley Vixen* were both at the dock, forty-foot double-enders with varnished mahogany hulls, sister ships having unusual cross-planked decks in the Wiley manner and a thousand original features you'd never see in any other boats. They are slim and graceful, having such slippery hulls they do not need large motors or big sail plans to push them. They are centerboarders, like most Wiley boats, and in shoal harbors their owners, standing at the tiller, hold the centerboard pendant in one hand, using the centerboard as an "echo sounder," touching with it, pulling it up, and skimming over the shallows by feel.

Wiley's yard is far and away the best-protected hole-up in Oxford, a hooked-in niche within the harbor creek. It looks as though he got there first and for his boatyard long ago chose the most sheltered spot. It's odd when you've been cruising how "geographic" your eye becomes. No matter how quiet and sleepy the harbor looks, you realize that the wind can probably funnel in from some direction or other, making everything grind and pound and bang and tear loose. You look at each harbor with a cold, appraising eye, not to be fooled this time, having rolled and plunged all night in so many other anchorages that looked smooth until the wind veered and began to whistle. Is there a sandbar to shut out the swell? What about passing traffic and wakes? Where is the high land, the bluffs to give protection from the wind? What about the holding ground or moorings or pilings? Tidal range and currents are almost nonexistent in Oxford. The rickety old staging at Wiley's is jolly good proof that it's snug and well protected no matter how boisterous a wind may blow.

In Oxford we also found a very fine waterside restaurant, great for boats combining a weary cook and a ravenous crew. People arrived in their dinghies, or tied up in front. The place served huge platters of fried shrimp, broiled flounder, chicken, beef, salad, rolls, vegetables, dessert, coffee, all the fixin's.

On a sunny, balmy June morning, sweet-smelling, bright with flowers, the harbor seemed good enough to eat. We turned ourselves around, bow to stern, with warping lines, hoisted jib and mains'l, and went for a day sail up Tred Avon River. Creaming out Town Creek, drawing a long ripple behind us, we had time to study the Bermuda racers in the forest of masts as we sailed gently by. I have stood on the shore summer mornings and watched so many boats sailing out that now I can almost put myself on the beach and see us leaning away into the distance, the man at the tiller, the graceful hull, the pretty woman, the polished bronze cabin ports, the curve of sail, no wrinkle, no flutter. By Jove, that must be me!

Outside the creek, as we heeled to the wind we saw the little two-car ferry crawling across the mouth of the Tred Avon to the village on the far shore. It runs about every half hour, one of the few ferries left, supported, no doubt, by some village improvement association determined to keep Oxford pleasant.

We had a fair wind up the river past the green lawns and flowers, the beautiful houses, fields of grain, each mansion with its own dock, its own boats. Some had their own tennis courts and stables, many had their own sandy beach where children splashed and dived. There was no pollution. Clouds of birds soared over the acres of young oats and around the magnificent trees. We sailed on and on till the river narrowed and the shoals began to get troublesome. Then we realized we would have to tack all the way back against the strengthening afternoon wind. But what did that matter; we had our berth at Wiley's to return to, and no sweat, no wondering where to lie, not even a supper to cook. Sometimes it is great fun to day sail for a change, around some big harbor maze and not go anywhere, as though you lived in one of those impressive, stationary houses set in place on thick stone walls, set solidly on generations of earning power.

The sweet smell of clover hay blew over the river. We cocked up our bare feet and leaned back in the cockpit like lords of creation. No doubt we would soon start dragging our keel, since we couldn't expect to go on up this little river forever. But just now the going was too good to break.

Oxford is one of those rare places that cause you to say as soon as you enter, "Oh my, I want to return to this place again and again. In fact, I don't want to leave, and why haven't I been here before?"

We hated leaving, but the thought uplifted us that now we could look forward to real sailing, broad waters, and a relief from the restricted waterway. Really, when you come right down to it, the Intracoastal Waterway is mostly motorboat country. It has its charms (especially when gales are blowing outside), but running aground in a keel boat is not one of them. We were glad to be on the broad Chesapeake, where it seemed a blessing to be able to make tacks ten miles long if we wanted to, and not have to go down a straight-and-narrow lane from buoy to buoy with a finger on the chart all day, and shoals close aboard on both sides.

As though to chide us for all this exultation, the breeze next day fell off to nothing. As a result, we left Oxford behind very slowly. Finally we cranked up and motored down the Choptank past Black Walnut Point, where a big schooner lay dead in the water a mile away, her sails not even flapping. The busy, top-heavy motor cruisers ground along by the dozens—it was just the kind of hot, flat, monotonous day they're built for. We were bound northwest from there diagonally across the Chesapeake for Annapolis. In the haze both shores of the bay faded out as we progressed, but we had our compass and were quite accustomed to being out of sight of land (so I said to myself). We even allowed for a bit of set on the tide flooding up the bay. My leeward drift allowance would have looked more professional if I could have calculated how much, but I guessed it might be two miles during our slow crossing and let it go at that. The haze being thin, piloting was neither very precise nor very exacting.

We rather object to motoring hour after hour in calms. The temperature began to soar. We stuck washcloths in the cockpit drainpipes and poured buckets of water on our feet to cool them, then sat with our feet in the water till it grew too warm, whereupon we repeated the process. The sun was so hot we went into our desert-Arab routine, with towel around the neck, hat pulled way down, sailbag over the knees, and a jacket to keep the sun from burning through. We took turns sitting in the shady, quiet cabin.

But then at length came the breeze, slamming us into South River with a foaming wake, fast when we didn't know where we were going, past the sandbar entrance into Harness Creek, up the creek among houses, narrow bends, pretty trees, boats at docks. We twisted and turned between the land, staying in the middle, and around a bend saw what we thought must be the house of our friend Bill Blanchett. It didn't look the way we thought it would; it looked a lot better, with lawns, little piers, and the water winding out of sight.

Bill was on the dock, clasping his hands over his head and dancing up and down. He showed us where to tie up, at a small float that squeaked every time we stepped out on it—a friendly protest. We had a big reunion. He is a much more experienced coastal pilot than I am. In the evening we went over charts together, he pointing out some special hazards of Delaware Bay and the Jersey coast, also the few harbors of refuge.

He had often sailed from Long Island, through New York City, down the Jersey coast, up Delaware Bay to the canal, and down the Chesapeake to Annapolis. Like most experienced cruisers, he was convinced that the small inlets along the Jersey coast are dangerous, with shifting sandbars, to be tried only by a person having local knowledge, and not even then in stormy times. "Just when you most want to get in, you can't. The only real harbors in that 120-mile stretch are Cape May, Atlantic City, Manasquan, and Atlantic Highlands at the edge of New York Harbor. Never try Barnegat, Little Egg, Great Egg, or any such inlets as a stranger in a keel sailboat, or you're liable to find breakers on every side of you."

He emphasized dead reckoning all the time, with log and compass course, plus lead lines and fixes on prominent landmarks by

57

means of hand-bearing compass. He showed me how to figure distance-off from lighthouses, using charted height and a handy table in Bowditch. "You want to practice all this stuff on clear days when you don't need it. You need to practice it till you can do it in your sleep, because some day or some night you'll be so damn tired you'll have to do it in your sleep."

He was full of fun, too, and told us about a weekend sailor who was heading out of New York for the Chesapeake with a crew of two when he ran aground on what he claimed was an uncharted shoal in New York Harbor. "Can you imagine, an uncharted shoal in New York Harbor? He busted his rudder, so he went over to Sheepshead Bay. As soon as the boat touched the dock, his crew took off running."

In the morning I asked his wife, Marian, to take me to town and leave me there. She and Kay went picking strawberries at a nearby farm.

One of cruising's great joys is to be a sailor ashore in a strange port—Annapolis, for instance—to wander its narrow streets by the waterfront, alone, unknown, remote from all the fascinating hustle and bustle, the traffic, the shops, the city harbor basin with its true vessels, its oystermen, its rubbernecking tourist craft and fake antique boats with signs, all tied up together along the stone walls, surrounded by the oily water and the noise. You are not of it, but you are drawn to its variety. You are accustomed to holding on, or setting a jib, pulling the tiller, far out on the water with your mate, a long distance from people. Yet here is a policeman talking to a taxi driver. You have to watch them; they seem so strange and at the same time so familiar. They notice you are watching them, which makes them suspicious, and so you hurry on, to nowhere in particular.

I found myself looking through an obscure doorway, at a bar with eighteen men belly-up to it, at eleven o'clock in the morning. On the streets, Naval Academy cadets were everywhere, some in white gloves. Instead of the horizon and the wake and the chart, here was a pantherlike girl slinking by on bare feet, no bra, and sloe eyes with dark lashes.

Here was a bookstore marvelously tolerant of browsers, who stood about on one foot like cranes, reading whole chapters. Here was a ship's chandlery so crowded its wares, including wheelbarrows and anchors, spilled out across the sidewalk. The wide bay you can't see across is very different from these sights and sounds and smells. Most of my pleasure in this colorful antheap came from being no part of it.

In a circular, grassy park, slightly raised above and aloof from busy Compromise Street, great trees were stirring their leaves in a cool breeze off the bay. I sat in the shade and watched the heavy foliage, while below on the brick walks the traffic went past. To be sitting on a park bench seemed amazingly stable and safe and relaxed.

On my way to the nautical shops, I encountered some more Naval Academy cadets, straight, military, chins pulled in, precise from years of habit. They carry their coats just so, their uniforms meticulously in order, shoes whitened, creases accurate, and it is all automatic; they have been trained until it is second nature.

Weems's second-floor sanctuary was like a chapel—nautical instruments, chrome, polished brass, sextants, barometers, chronometers, charts, old ship's wheels. It had an air of scholarship, navigational skills, world voyaging, scientific niceties. The crowd didn't come to this place; it was for steamship skippers, naval officers, students of navigational guidance systems, Omni, Sat Nav, and the stars. People's lives depend on these gleaming aids.

Bacon's was nearby in a welter of alleys and tiny streets, and at Bacon's they have acres of secondhand sails for all the racing classes, all sizes, half price, some almost new. Everything here was Dacron, cringles and sail slides, jibs, mizzens, colored spinnakers, battens, sailbags, rigging and rigging gear.

Fawcett's came next, a dream world of deck jewelry, bronze, chrome, cleats, blocks, genoa-track slides, snap shackles for spinnaker handling, miles of wire rope and halyard line on huge spools, depth finders and electronics, signal flags and bilge pumps, all beautiful as the Queen of Sheba's gems, and almost as expensive. It is perhaps the most complete source of yacht supply equipment on the East Coast. The place was full of racing sailboat buffs (a thousand sailboats dot the outer reaches of Annapolis Harbor on a fine Sunday afternoon), happy, young, looking through bins and racks of twist shackles, cam cleats, sheet winches, rigging toggles, spreaders, and fair-leads. I passed a jolly girl on her knees on the floor pawing through a keg of bronze turnbuckles and shackle pins. She looked up and confided in me, a complete stranger, "If you can find it, it's the wrong size and won't fit." With a silvery laugh that would steal your heart away she saluted this amusing impasse.

I felt that I would like to give her a hug. But that would be most unseemly, so I nodded as though I were Queen Elizabeth waving to her subjects, and passed on.

I headed back for Bill's like a child who's had too much circus, too much spun candy, too many elephants, tigers, and acrobats. I was thinking, Thank goodness we sail in the morning.

# CHAPTER VII

# ANNAPOLIS HARBOR

# SANDY POINT TO SUSQUEHANNA RIVER

# CHESAPEAKE & DELAWARE CANAL, SALEM RIVER EXTENSION

# DELAWARE RIVER—SMYRNA RIVER TO WILMINGTON

BEATING OUT OF HARNESS CREEK, down a winding water lane of trees, green lawns, long shadows, and sunlight in a gentle breeze, we were saying good-bye, good-bye to Bill and Marian, arms waving, hands waving, fingers waving, clinging to them, until at last the point shut them from view. Then all of a sudden came the unavoidable, to-be-loved-and-endured plain hard work of sailing.

Bang in the face like a blow smacked the wind, with a dipperful of cold water added, the moment our sloop poked her nose out of the creek. A villainous wind was tearing up South River from the bay, heeling us to forty-five degrees before we could catch our breath, we cityfolks, we shoregoers. It hardened the mains'l, stretching the sheets thin, tuning up the windward shrouds. Good-bye to the easy land-security, the languorous lying around. I tried to haul in the sheet of our working jib so that we might point up a little closer, but couldn't budge it without the aid of our sheet winch, whose handle and gears multiply my strength to that of eight men. It is bronze and beautiful, and we have two of them, fastened down so securely with bolts and epoxy to oak pads beneath the deck that I reckon the whole side of the boat would have to come off before our winches tore loose.

*Whooo* sang the wind, and *hiss* seethed the spray. We hadn't prepared ourselves—as usual. We were hauling in the sheets, hauling on the tiller, squirming into our oilskin pants, pulling on our foul-weather jackets, soaked already, everything in a mess. We specialize in locking the stable door after the horse is stolen. I wish we could remember that oilskins were invented to keep you dry, rather than to enclose wetness.

For a few minutes there was some doubt whether we could tack out of the river against the fierce, short sea kicked up by wind versus tide. The channel being none too wide, its frill of sandy shallows, as customary on the Chesapeake, lay waiting on either hand to entrap our three-and-a-half-foot keel. It was "Ready about" and "Hard a-lee" every few minutes, and if you have your oilskin pants only half on, that's too bad; we haul sheets, let the pants fall where they may, and go about with snapping lines and thundering sails.

It was cold and soggy, a familiar condition. The spray flew halfway up the mains'l. The sun went under, turning the seascape gray. All that warm world of friendship and easygoing land life was gone in a twinkling. The decks streamed, boat beaten almost flat, strapped down, everything taut as a bar. You do your stuff or get wrecked, and it happens so quick you can't believe it. Fortunately, we have become accustomed to these lightning transitions, the bent tiller, the wet sheet tugging, and spray whipping over the cabintop.

Tacking well in the heavy air, our tough little *Sunrise* made good use of her thousand-pound keel and rapidly ate out to windward toward the Thomas Point Lighthouse, which stands on a shoal a couple of miles offshore. And what a lighthouse! It is one of the few old-fashioned Chesapeake types left, a large, circular dwelling house on spider legs, with a cupola light surmounting the house. Like ships glimpsed at sea, lighthouses have distinct personalities, and this one personifies Sweet Domesticity, with a red roof and a veranda that goes all the way around. It has chimneys, and open windows with curtains blowing, just the same as any house. The wash on the line, including a fine big array of diapers like a string of horizontal flags, signals, IT'S A BOY (or maybe a girl). And, being a Coast Guard installation, Old Glory, of course, flies over all. I pointed out to my captive audience the lively symbolism—a strong, proud nation protecting its happy children, the bravely rippling flag portending an even braver future. But she has washed too many diapers to be impressed.

If we could round the lighthouse, we'd be able to bear away and run up the bay with the wind on our tail instead of on the nose. Keeping well off Sweet Domesticity, we rounded at last, freed sheets, and were off in an exhilarating burst of speed. What a difference! The boat stood upright, the decks were dry, we took off our oilskins, and we opened the cabin slide. Life was better again, in fact super.

Three big tankers lay at anchor out in the bay, one half empty, the other two loaded. It seems to be a favorite place where they wait for a dock or a cargo in Baltimore. Something about tankers seen from a small boat is so monstrous, so uncompromisingly, unutterably ugly you'd have to rise early in the morning to even think up anything so hideous.

We galloped and surfed, leaping, pitching, surging, slowing between waves and gathering ourselves for another and another toboggan down the backs of hurrying combers. First the stern kicks up and the bow is depressed as we fly in a whirlwind of speed that sings; then the stern sinks and the bow rises as we slow in the trough. The sails are engines hurling us through the world, strong, light, so fragile and yet so successfully coping with nature's savage forces they resemble a bird's wings riding the gale. I kept jumping in my mind from birds to horses, our motion like riding some fleeting steed hour after hour, pursued and among the white horses of the sea. We cannot quite plane as we used to in some of the centerboarders we have owned. That is because of our keel, with its bulb on the bottom of the fin; also the weight of cruising gear. But we feel as though we are soaring faster than the speed of sound, and we take joy in the knowledge that our keel boat stands up to very strong winds in a way no racing centerboarder can possibly equal.

Of Annapolis and the Severn River we have a harbor chart that is three inches to the mile. While our bucking bronco goes galloping past the square Naval Academy buildings, Kay combines *Blanchard's Cruising Guide to the Chesapeake* and the chart to educate me concerning the almost irresistible Severn River. We ought to be exploring all that. It is inviting and we are missing it, a stunning area that we shouldn't bypass, perhaps a little like the Tred Avon but bigger, with bolder shores. "Annapolis is said to have the largest concentration of boatyards of any harbor in the United States." The chart shows Spa Creek, famous home of famous yachts, and the book runs on enthusiastically about Weems Creek up the Severn as a convenient anchorage. Here is the familiar Chesapeake pattern of bay within the big bay, a river, creeks running into the river, and coves around bends of the creeks—wheels within wheels. Luce Creek, Salt-works Creek, Chase, Clements, Brewer, how enticing they sound as we read of their "high banks, thickly wooded." And Round Bay sounds most inviting of all. But perhaps Forked Creek, almost at the head of navigation, would be best. Blanchard writes:

> This is one of the most perfect, interesting, and attractive anchorages into which we have ever poked our way. It could have been a fine hideout for American vessels from marauding parties of British in the days of the War of 1812. Perhaps it was. The entrance is hard to find but it finally appears beyond a sandy bluff with several private wharves on the north shore of the Severn, just to the right or north of a wooded point with hills 40 and 60 feet high as shown on the chart.
>
> Favor the port shore on entering, as a sharp point to the starboard has a shoal which projects further than the chart indicates.
>
> Inside you will find around to the starboard a splendid landlocked anchorage in 14 feet. Further up, in 10 feet, good-sized sailing craft can moor among the trees.

We could spend three days blissfully meandering around the Severn if we didn't have Maine on our minds, if we weren't blessed by this commanding wind that blows us by at our top speed of six knots.

By the time we finish our vicarious cruise up the Severn, our ship is roaring and soaring under the Bay Bridge, which seems so vast and spiderwebby from a small boat at water level that we can scarcely comprehend its arc above our heads. Already Annapolis and the Academy buildings are sinking into a clump, and the tankers are diminishing to black bits of formless charcoal.

At this point I inadvertently took the wrong side of a large square area marked on the chart SPOIL AREA. I suppose they have to dump the dredgings somewhere, but it seems odd to dump them at this junction where the sea road forks to the left for Baltimore and to the right for the head of the bay. No depths were marked on this blank square, so I was scared to cross it, though later I learned it had plenty of water for us. We didn't care. In this nautical extravaganza and romp, the longer the voyage the better. Such sailing repaid all the work and worry. The breeze in our hair; the salt on our lips, the far, far shores and winking water, another lighthouse going by, the boom just clearing the waves, the curve of the sail and the surging, lilting boat spreading a white fan astern as she rushed on and on and tirelessly on—what could ever be better than this! To be so free, on our own, so happy in the wind's arms—no one who has ever experienced it can ever forget it or cease loving it. We were eating up the miles toward the head of the Chesapeake.

By early afternoon the bluffs of Worton Creek were swinging back, disclosing a whole packet of surprising details inside.

Worton Creek is a pretty little harbor, well sheltered and thus much liked by cruising skippers. We sailed past high bluffs into a smaller bay from the big bay, past a long, uncluttered beach, around a bend, and followed a tricky course where you can't go straight from one buoy to another because a shoal bulges out midway. A lot of keel boats have been aground on the sand along that crooked course, I suspect. When we had rounded a little sand point, the narrow harbor between woods and houses lay before us. Like so many Chesapeake harbors, it was full of boats on permanent moorings on both sides of the channel. Centerboarders use the shallow areas by both shores, and keel yachts the deeper waters near the center, leaving little room for visiting yachts. Now and then you see a big visitor, maybe a seventy-foot schooner, that gets disgusted and just anchors plumb in the middle of the channel, as much as to say, Go to hell.

We've become accustomed to all that. We cruised slowly among the silent, empty yachts, and our outboard scarcely ticking over. We made several passes, picked the biggest opening that would give us most room to swing (and mighty cramped it was, too), circled, came back to it, and dropped the anchor. We're getting quite professional, so I made the anchor line fast, asked Kay to put the motor in reverse, and we dug the hook in before shutting off the kicker. Then everything became marvelously silent and restful, no sound but some children swimming and playing inside the miniature Sandy Hook at the entrance. We got the ladder over and had a swim ourselves. The swimming ladder is our companion ladder, which, like many other things on this small cruiser, does double duty.

In the morning we went to the yacht yard at the head of the harbor, where I explained to the foreman that I wanted some work done on my masthead electric light. "I can't go up the mast that high on my own bosun's chair," I told him, "because the boat is so small I'll turn her over if I do." It is a general rule that one pound at the masthead has a turning force equal to seven pounds on the keel.

He understood at once. "We've got a good crane here," he said. "Bring your boat alongside. You can crank me up in the bosun's chair. I do it all the time."

It was a simple boom hoist for unstepping masts. He brought out a bucket of tools, hung it on the seat, hooked to the cable, and sat there saying, "Grind away."

The affair had an iron crank, a pawl and brake. The cable wound up on a drum as one turned. It seemed to me this jolly fore-man had great faith in me, to allow a stranger to winch him thirty feet into the air. How did he know I wouldn't get mixed up about the pawl and brake and drop him with a crash?

Anyway, I was extremely careful while he was working up there. It didn't take him long to attach my new masthead twenty-point "steaming" light, legal for use when motoring. Wires were already through the mast and protruding at its top. I didn't know at the time that I could have installed a two-way masthead white light, one for motoring that shines two-thirds of the circle forward, another that shines all around, for use as anchor light or emergency. Sailboats have a bad time with their lights, since the jib often masks the low, dim, red and green running lights: "You can always tell a sailboat at night because you can't see it." Sailcraft aren't allowed a white all-around masthead light except at anchor; just the same, it's good to have one for occasional use under way. As somebody has said, "I'd rather be illegal than run down."

With extreme caution I lowered my new friend. It was a treat to get the work done so efficiently and cheaply.

Beyond Worton's Point, one approaches the head of the Chesapeake, and the great bay begins to narrow. One hears the thud and crash of artillery shells—even hears them screech—being tested far across the water at the Aberdeen Proving Grounds. We passed the broad mouth of the Sassafras River. It is beautiful country, fertile, rich, with waving fields of grain. Then we turned from the Elk River into Back Creek, toward the Chesapeake & Delaware Canal. This great thoroughfare, much used by coastal oil barges and oceangoing ships, is twelve miles long and has five bridges. It would take us across country to the upper reaches of Delaware Bay, where we would turn and sail seaward forty-eight miles to Cape May, at the southern tip of New Jersey. The canal connects Baltimore on the Chesapeake with Philadelphia and Wilmington on the Delaware, and most of the ships we saw were plying between these ports.

All the buoys were numbered wrong for us as we approached the canal, because improvements have been made, new ones added, and our chart was a year old. But we could manage all right by comparing landscape features that don't change, and by keeping the black on our left and red on the right, guessing where a marker had been removed or inserted. Boats, cottages, and ships grew thicker. Motor cruisers by the dozens passed us. The great freighters, many half empty and showing their red underbellies, crept up astern of us, while others coming down loomed over our bow. We felt ill-equipped to cope with the thickening traffic after being so long among the watery coastal spaces where the sun goes down in the marshes and comes up out of the sea. The day began well enough, with a light, fair wind, but ended badly.

All around us civilization was closing in, yacht clubs, sandy-beach summer resorts with hundreds of cottages and campers, chimney stacks and oil tanks. This is a funnel, and we were headed into its narrow neck. The Chesapeake tides pouring into the canal produce currents of five knots or more, currents we cannot buck, though ships stem them well enough. The canal is operated by the U.S. Army Corps of Engineers, who have checkpoints here and there, tugboats to assist vessels in distress, and there are motor launches for putting pilots aboard foreign ships. One of the rules of the canal is that ships with the current behind them have the right-of-way—a sensible arrangement.

As usual in such situations, we were studying the *Cruising Guide to the Chesapeake.* Of the five bridges, three are fixed structures built high, with a clearance of at least 135 feet. For the other two, which are lift bridges, we must blow three blasts. "If the span is to be opened immediately, the bridge tender will answer with one blast. Two blasts means there will be a delay." In other words, a train is coming, and, brother, you'd better go into reverse, or something, but how do you stand still in the current? There are also signal lights and many other regulations.

It is hard for a little boat to manage the tides: If you have a fair tide through the canal, you meet a foul tide when you get to Delaware Bay. And tides up and down Delaware Bay run very fast also. Then, too, there is the coming of darkness, which doesn't help, and there's no quiet place to anchor at the Delaware end.

We made good progress, with fair wind and current, having no trouble. At Chesapeake City, three and a half miles in, we paused at

Schaefers', the famous one-stop cruisers' marina. It had at that time a restaurant, bar, fuel, ice, groceries, liquor, and marine supplies. The tide runs so fast there, it is quite dramatic to watch cruisers riding down the current as they circle to come in to the dock. No sooner do they turn into the current than they stop in midstream. When they get to the dock, they make fast a bow line quickly or quickly get in trouble. Even more dramatic is to see the great freighters coming around a bend through the green fields and looming overhead as they pass.

Schaefers' store was famous for beefsteaks, so we bought a good big one, with ice for our little fridge. We also stocked up on groceries, topped our gas cans, and laid in extra quarts of motor oil. Across the channel is a mooring basin that has been dredged out by the engineers. We should have spent the late afternoon and night there. But the tide was still running in our favor, and I thought we should use it to transit the remaining miles of the canal.

So we pushed on, finding that the lift bridges are railroad bridges that nowadays stay open most of the time. By five o'clock we were at the far end. There a headwind with fierce squalls beat us almost flat, and obviously it would be foolish to sally out into Delaware Bay with darkness just around the corner. Near the Delaware Bay entrance are clusters of pilings known as "dolphins," in an expansion of the canal, but if we tied up there we'd roll madly all night in the wake of passing ships. I ran back, therefore, to the Pennsylvania Railroad bridge and anchored close by the shore in its lee. The abutments of the vast black structure jutted out into the channel, narrowing it and making a little sheltered corner in the angle of bridge and shore.

It just happened that at the time of our transit the C&D Canal was in process of being widened. This extensive operation had

71

been completed from the Chesapeake end as far as Chesapeake City. The broader, improved channel compressed the narrower, unimproved part, vastly increasing the velocity of tidal currents in the stretch from Chesapeake City to Delaware Bay.

Anchoring under the bridge was a great mistake, and indeed quite illegal. One salves one's conscience with the thought that such regulations are for ships, not for little twenty-foot sailboats.

We had our supper. It seemed like an ominous place. Close by on the canal bank, cars whizzed along a gravel road. Two fishermen hunched over their poles near our stern. The railroad bridge above us remained at its lift position, apparently abandoned for the night, no trains, no watchman, and no bridge tender.

The ships kept passing close beside us. The tide gurgled evilly, so strong it was almost like a rapid. Our anchorage was far from satisfactory: If we swung in, we were too close to the bank; if we swung out, we might get hit by a ship. The night seemed eerie among the long lines of canal yellow lights, the red and green bridge lights, and the lights of great ships. I wished I were somewhere else.

I put out a stern kedge anchor to hold us close to the bank. Unable to sleep in such a risky place in the fierce current, we took turns at anchor watch, and it was well we did. I was on watch when the tide turned, and we went broadside to our bow and stern anchors. The stern line was stretched so tight I couldn't pull it in. So I fastened another fifty feet to it, and while the line was paying out I quickly took its end to the bow cleat so that both anchors held us bow-on.

The ships continued to roll us. There seemed to be more of them at night than in the day.

At one-thirty a car stopped nearby on the canal bank roadway, snapped off its headlights, and a drunk staggered on the water's edge. "Lookit a goddamn sailboat!" he screamed. I unlimbered my Smith & Wesson, and a boathook in case he should decide to swim the short distance. All he did was smash a bottle on the rocks, get into the car with three other sinister-looking individuals, slam the door, and drive away.

At four A.M. a big Presidential Lines freighter was approaching from the west, our side of the bridge. Like the others, her high sides resembled cliffs. She was going fast, with tide and wind behind her. We could hear the hiss and throb of her engines, smell the hot oil. She got her nose into the drawbridge aperture, the narrow opening, when her whistle exploded in emergency blasts. Only then we realized another ship was coming up. They were going to hit, there wasn't room to pass, and the lights on the water seemed to reflect imminent doom. Those great black towers 180 feet above our heads—I didn't even dare look up at them.

The Presidential freighter sheered over even closer to us, shaving the bridge abutment by inches. The other ship coming up seemed to give way very little. I could not see very well into the darkness below the bridge. We were in a panic. I was trying to haul the anchors up, to get out of there at all cost.

At this moment the two ships crashed, a horrible metallic grinding, two monsters rearing up against each other in a war of the worlds. Sparks flew. It sounded like forty freight trains colliding head-on. Searchlights jumped out of the darkness. Foreign voices shouted. They had been going at about eight knots, but the shock stopped them dead. The American ship was thundering full astern, and still she couldn't keep off, for her bow ran hard and fast aground in the canal bank mud not far below the bridge. The other ship, a Greek freighter, was out of control, trying to get under way in order to avoid being swept ashore in the heavy current. It was his fault, since he had the current against him and could have slowed instead of meeting in this impossible spot. The crazy fool! He would probably succeed in knocking the towers down on us yet. I had hauled in the Danforth and was struggling with the kedge, feeling that life itself depended on getting out of there. But the anchor was stuck under some sunken timbers or ancient iron left over from the bridge building. One should never anchor in such places. I could raise it a foot or so off the bottom, but then it sank back again. So I slipped it, buoying it fairly short with a pneumatic fender, not wanting a long line to swing out into the channel and foul somebody's propeller. We were getting under way when the Greek came up through the bridge, HELLENIC LINES on her side in letters four feet high. And right in the middle of the printing was a huge dent like a crease.

Lights on the bridges near and far had flashed bright red, a signal for all traffic to stop. Since the American freighter was blocking the channel, it was important to avoid a further pileup. Searchlights were playing along her stern, where a U.S. Army engineers tugboat and patrol boat were passing lines. To get away from the hideous bridge and the grounded freighter, we slowly followed the Greek, backward, to the westward. Patrol boats loaded with engineer personnel were roaring through the canal exceeding their own speed limit. Another army tugboat passed us rapidly. The Greek slowed and came to anchor about half a mile from the bridge. Not far away, near the opposite bank by a grassy place, we anchored, too. Looking at the dent in his side, I wondered whether anybody had been killed. I could imagine the engine room crew being thrown flat on the plates, slung off ladders, banged into hot pipes. The impact must have thrown everything off tables, pots off stoves, bodies out of bunks, slammed doors, and hurled people across decks.

The tide kept coming in strongly. No ships moved, although how a tug with four barges or a great ship coming down on the current could stop, I didn't know. I just wanted to get out of there. These black industrial complications were not what I came for.

The Presidential Lines ship got off the mudbank with the rising tide and the help of tugs. She went on down the canal, probably to dry dock somewhere. Traffic resumed, and as dawn was breaking we followed her. I swung in by the bridge pier, trying to find my buoyed anchor. But the tide had risen higher than I calculated, and our buoy was sunk and invisible. We could not endure tarrying in that ominous spot, so left it, lost it, wrote if off, my beautiful five-pound Herreshoff-design yachtsman's kedge and its chain and fifty feet of Dacron line, all of which had served us well for many a year in the Penguin. I had planned to use it as my present dinghy anchor.

Out in Delaware Bay we had a fair wind and a fair tide down the channel toward the sea. The sun came up. Kay made coffee despite the chop. And we flew like some winged Pegasus, our trouble behind us once we were free in sailing waters again, with room to maneuver and the land far away.

Because we had missed some of the ebb, only three hours of fair tide remained on our forty-eight-mile course down the bay. Most tides run six hours in and six hours out, but in Delaware Bay the flood up the river advances with you (if you are going up), so that you can carry a fair tide not only six, but seven, eight, or even more hours. Conversely, going down the bay you have four hours or less of fair, ebb tide. When the tide strengthened, it would run five knots or more against us. And the *Cruising Guide* had some extremely ominous warnings concerning Delaware Bay.

Thus when the tide went slack and began to turn against us, we swung into the Cohansey River on the New Jersey side, one of the few sheltered spots along the whole windy estuary. Extensive shoals ran off, but markers were prominent, and inside the river's mouth we anchored inside the marshy hook at the entrance, not far behind Cohansey Light, among green marshes stretching away to the horizon.

Right away we found the place alive with biting greenhead flies, voracious monsters in clouds that wouldn't take no for an answer. We were accustomed by this time to insect pests, however, and quickly rigged our forehatch screen and companionway netting, thus keeping most of them out.

It was only ten o'clock in the morning when we quit for the day and went to bed. But we had had no sleep during the eventful night. Often we have fun quoting to each other some half-remembered verse, for instance, one of Stevenson's *Child's Garden of Verses:*

> *And does it not seem hard to you,*
> *When all the sky is clear and blue,*
> *And I should like so much to play,*
> *To have to go to bed by day.*

This day it did not seem very hard. In fact, sleeping there at anchor was blissful in the cool breeze among the marshes, and we slept till three P.M., when we woke up and cooked that magnificent steak.

76

# CHAPTER VIII

# DELAWARE BAY

# LITTLE EGG INLET TO
# HEREFORD INLET

# ABSECON INLET

IT WOULD HAVE BEEN POSSIBLE to go up the winding Cohansey
River through the marshes to a little marina at Greenwich Pier. But
the biting flies deterred us, and you can't go everywhere. Most
important was to catch all the ebb tide available for going down formidable Delaware Bay to Cape May. Having done our charting and
homework as thoroughly as possible the night before, we left early,
picking our way carefully over the shoals and out to the channel,
where a surprising number of ships were going up and down.
Unlike the channel, the river was very broad and getting broader, its
low shores scarcely visible.

In all our travels we never met a cruiser who didn't dislike the
Delaware Bay passage between Cape May, New Jersey, and the
Chesapeake & Delaware Canal. Because the bay is shallow, with

strong tides running up and down, a wind against the current can kick up steep, short seas. The low, faraway shores seem gloomy and featureless. Even the names on the chart are ominous: Murderkyll, and Joe Flogger Bank, for instance. The *Cruising Guide* warns yachts not to attempt it at night because of dangerous shoals, ship traffic, and confusing lights, as well as tidal sidesweep.

We found the channel's many doglegs marked by old-fashioned lighthouses, many of circular steel, round and red, that had once been lived on, with balconies all around. But all were automatic now. One called Old Tower was in ruins. It would be very easy to get confused on the southern end of Cross Ledge Shoal between Miah Maull Shoal Light and Elbow Cross Light. We were following compass courses and trying to stay at the outer edge of the dredged-and-buoyed channel because big freighters often passed each other abreast of us, one bound up, the other down. What the hurrying tugs and barges would do was also hard to predict.

East of Brandywine Shoal, we cut away from the channel and its traffic to head for the invisible Cape May Canal that cuts across Cape May and would save us many miles on our course along the New Jersey coast toward New York. The ships went on down the channel that leads through extensive shoals off the mouth of the Delaware and so out to sea.

By this time the ebb had gone slack, with the flood commencing. How much should I allow for leeway as we sailed diagonally across the increasing current that was coming in from the sea? In my Power Squadron piloting courses, in a tidy, well-lighted classroom, we used to figure such leeway quite accurately, drawing neat little triangles called vectors. It was all very precise—your speed, let us say, 6 knots, the side current 2.7 knots, your distance 7.3 miles. But here the lee-bowing current was strengthening minute by minute, the distance was depending on whether we made our mark or not, and the wind (our speed) was fluky. What it boils down to is that one makes an educated guess. And as it turned out, I didn't offset enough for the strength of the flood, so we came to the low, sandy shore a considerable distance above the canal. We could then follow down along shore till we saw the great ferries that dock in the canal entrance. They carry scores of automobiles and hundreds of passengers across the broad bay mouth from the New Jersey side to Cape Henlopen on the Delaware shore.

The Cape May Canal is narrow, made more so because its sandy banks have been sloughed off by the wakes of fast motorcraft. Taking down our sails, we motored through the cut, coming at the far end to the Cape Island Marina. I couldn't be sure of its entrance because of three pilings there, marked neither red nor green. No doubt I had grown unduly apprehensive about marina entrances, since numerous ones along the waterway advertised eight-foot depth but didn't have three. Wondering what to do, we circled about, having a look at the harbor anchorage, where many boats were swinging peacefully. We'd have anchored there, except that we had our minds set on a bath.

As often happens, a local motor cruiser went swishing through so we'd know which sticks to go between. And a magnificent, big, well-run marina it proved to be, with hundreds of motor cruisers and sportfishermen at a maze of slips and walkways as big as a city block. The shoals off the Delaware provide such sport that fishermen come there from all over Pennsylvania and New Jersey.

After the pleasant dock master had assigned us a slip among the forest of upturned outriggers and broad transoms, the *Sunrise* complement bundled up their soap and towels to try out the shower baths at the excellent facilities. Quantities of hot fresh water! What a treat!

The weather continued to treat us nicely as we came up the coast, forty miles from Cape May to Atlantic City. This was a blessing, as we were not accustomed to long stretches on the open ocean. On the other hand, we weren't apprehensive concerning ocean sailing, for our solid little keel sloop had proven rugged and tough, and we could now handle her with some confidence. Also, we had discovered that "sheltered" inland bays often consist of shoal water in all directions, narrow channels, fast tides, and obscure or nonexistent navigational aids, all of which can be extremely hazardous and difficult for a keel sailboat. We were glad to get out into the ocean, where we had plenty of water under us and not so many worries. In fact, I have had a letter from an aged single-hander who has been around the world, sailed to Gibraltar, the Mediterranean, and many times to the Azores and England. He says, "I'm too old for harbor-hopping along the coast, getting the sail up every morning, heaving in the anchor, charting all the time." Kay and I have pondered a great deal about his words. The other side of the picture is that, aiming for harbor each night, we have a good chance to miss three-day northeasters and other gales at sea.

As usual, we left early, after our solid breakfast of fruit, scrambled eggs and bacon, toast, marmalade, and coffee. Kay sits on the after end of her bunk preparing it and dishing it out. The forward lid under her bunk is open at such times, where most of the food is stored. The stove and its hinged-down shelf are immediately before her. The utensils and dishes are in the cupboard at her left hand. I don't know how she manages in such a small space, sitting at the center of her culinary domain, but that is her secret. I am across from her on my bunk, keeping out of the way, as there is scarcely room for two pairs of feet on the diminutive cabin sole. Or I am on deck preparing for departure, getting down the dew-soaked mosquito bar, unlashing the tiller, seeing to the motor, taking down the tie-offs that keep the halyards from drumming against the mast, hanking on the jib, undoing sail ties from the main. One of the advantages of small size is that the sails and gear are so easily manageable.

It was a calm day with light wind. We could just sail, close-hauled. It was so slow we mostly motorsailed, and thus accomplished the forty miles in nine hours. It was lovely on the ocean, out of sight of land, a hazy day, visibility only about two miles. My compass courses worked out so well we picked up a sea buoy nicely after a blind run of eight miles. I was practicing with my radio direction finder, too.

What a collection of hotels Atlantic City is from the sea, with domes, minarets, cupolas, towers, and ten thousand windows! The entrance to Absecon Inlet is a lane of small low buoys that look like little square old-fashioned coach lamps. Waves break on the beach to starboard. *Sunrise* sailed and motored up the main channel, past an extension of the boardwalk and around to the vast municipal marina, where thousands of motorboats rocked in their slips. Amazingly, there was no room for us in this teeming place, no tie-up, no slip, nothing—because a tuna tournament was in progress. The dock man suggested we retrace our course to Continental Yacht Harbor, a small place in the old fishing harbor of Gardner Basin.

It was here at a nearby slip that we became acquainted with meteorologist Mack McLaughlin, his wife Joyce, and their *Galatea.* Being a trifle rusty on our mythology, it took us a while to find out that *Galatea* long ago in Greece was one of the Nereids, a daughter of Neptune. The ancients also applied the name Galatea to a statue so beautiful that her creator fell in love with her, whereupon she came to life, and in a touching scene returned his love. It is the theme of the Pygmalion myth, from which were derived Shaw's play and *My Fair Lady,* and has no doubt recurred in many civilizations. Both fancies seemed appropriate when Mack came to name his boat, for she is supremely at home in the sea, and he also created her with his own hands and brought her to life. His boat is a thirty-six-foot ketch, of the Nereia class, designed by that master craftsman L. Francis Herreshoff. A remarkably complete and skillfully drafted set of plans, specifications, and directions was first published in *Rudder Magazine,* and many have been built. She is beautiful, fast, seagoing, and very simple in the way a work of art is simple. Herreshoff pays no attention to the handicap rules, which he says have spoiled so many modern ocean racers designed to take advantage of the rules' special characteristics. He thinks of the sea and its ways, not the racing committee, and proved his point by designing the world's fastest ketches. *Galatea* has a six-foot bowsprit, an outboard rudder, and carries twelve thousand pounds of lead in her long straight keel. She has eleven feet of beam. We walked around down below as though in a ballroom, overwhelmed by her spaciousness. She is planked with inch-and-a-quarter African mahogany framed with white oak; it took Mack four years of spare-time work to build her.

We stayed over an extra day in order to go sailing with him and Joyce on his day off from the Weather Bureau office.

What a vessel! She shouldered aside the ocean swells as though they were ripples, her bowsprit rising and falling like a dance. I strolled to and fro on her wide teak decks à la Horatio Hornblower or Lord Nelson. They let me take her tiller and sail her over the horizon while we all sat in the cockpit and they told us of the building. To us it seemed an epic.

The McLaughlins were living then in Burlington, Vermont, near Lake Champlain. Mack was a year gathering materials and drawing the plans full-sized on a makeshift lofting floor. He got white oak from mountain sawmills, Sitka spruce from Boston for his hollow masts, had the keel lead poured at Fairhaven, Massachusetts. The exquisite varnished tiller I was holding, curved and carved, was the first component he made that winter, and many a time he wondered whether the boat to go with it would ever be completed and launched. He had no shed and few machine tools; built her in the open in his backyard, improvised a steambox, hauled heavy tarps on and off his frame as it rose. In the winter he continued with his planking, sometimes at twenty below zero, and would come into the kitchen to thaw out his hands after getting on a plank.

Joyce had heard it all before, and proudly lived it, too. She went below to light up the Primus stove and make tea. Mack told us of the trip they made in their ship to Bermuda, their first ocean voyage, and his blue eyes shone at the memory of their landfall, the loom of Gibbs Hill Light one eventful night in June. They were only six days on the way. "Once we had a forty-eight-hour spell of running before a near gale, when we averaged seven knots."

You could see by the long curves of her wineglass stern she was made for running. She would be a boat for rounding the Horn or circling the world.

"Tea's ready," called Joyce.

"Come on, we'll all go down," said Mack, lashing the tiller. "She won't go anywhere."

We sat on settees at the bolted-down drop-leaf table while *Galatea* sailed herself, steady as a church, right on course. The cabin was full of wonders: big bunks back of the settees, chronometer, barometer, eleven bronze portholes that could be screwed shut, bookcases and lockers everywhere. Forward were a big chain locker, two comfortable bunks, toilet, and hanging locker for shore clothes, coats, blankets, and gear. Then came the main cabin, aft of which was a galley that even included a Shipmate coal range (with oven) for those clammy nights in Maine. She had a thirty-six-horse engine, the finest of hand bilge pumps, a sixty-gallon freshwater tank, and stowage galore aft for sails and spares.

I examined her not as a stranger, for the Nereia had long been my cruising dreamship, functional in her rig, deck layout, shroud attachments, anchor winch, every detail, not too big, not too small. As a creation in the yacht world, I thought there was nothing quite like her, with her long waterline and her bow that has evolved from centuries of seafaring experience—just as there has been nobody like L. Francis Herreshoff, third generation of superb yacht designers.

Subsequent investigation disclosed that the cost of having one built in a good yard could run as much as one hundred thousand dollars. Thus ended my romance with Nereia.

*Sunrise* didn't say anything, she just buckled down to work next morning as we beat along the coast against a cold blustery wind. The sea was lead-colored and purple, no joy in it, the tops whipping into our faces hour after hour, and water crawling on the cockpit seats, cascading off in little waterfalls to gurgle down the drains. I hadn't been sure we should try it, fifty miles to Manasquan against a wind and sea like that, but we decided to give it a go.

Zigzagging out to sea, in toward the beach, out to sea again, we had sailed about sixteen miles but made good only about eight by noon. Thus with forty-two miles still ahead of us, a long, dreary afternoon and night seemed in prospect. I was cold and wet despite oilskins and boots. "How will you like another twenty hours or so of this?" I asked Kay. "Perhaps entering Manasquan Inlet in the dark?"

She knew what I was up to. "I won't like it."

"Let's run back and try another day, shall we?"

"You bet!"

As soon as we eased sheets and swung off, the boat flew over the waves like a happy child. Where had the wind gone? As always, it seemed to have dropped in the most amazing way when we turned and ran, no longer fronting and fighting it. All of a sudden that formidable enemy became our ally. The sailing was dry, too, and not so cold, and the sun came out.

The wake seethed, the bow tossed, while we ran back to the Atlantic City harbor mouth in slightly more than an hour, a most delightful sleigh ride.

When Mack came down to the docks that evening to do some work on his *Galatea,* we wondered whether he would scoff at us for having caved in. But he is an old hand. "You must expect to change your plans in a little boat," he told us. "That way you avoid trouble. I was hoping you'd turn when you found what it was like outside. You did right."

His words soothed our pride. We walked on the boardwalk, staring at the shops, auction rooms, orange drinks, eating counters, flashing signs, amusement pier. Looking into the darkness of the raging ocean, I was glad we weren't out there. Kay gave me a loving punch in the back and said, "You were so good to turn back just on my account."

# CHAPTER IX

*Interlude*

## About the Jib

CHANGING JIBS, a smaller one for a larger one, or vice versa as the wind diminishes or gets up, is one of my principal jobs when we are cruising. I go to the foredeck—one hand for the ship and one for myself—unsnapping one jib from the forestay and snap on the piston hanks of the other. These spring-loaded bronze hanks often get stuck with salt and have to be worked loose with pliers. Several times the boat has gone out from under me as she tosses, and then I find myself in midair hanging on to the grab rail. I sure am glad I made that grab rail strong. Kay at the tiller is worried about me, afraid I'll go overboard, afraid most of all she might not be able to pick me up. I should wear my safety harness, I really should, snapping its big hook onto a cleat or the rail or something. But once I was wearing it and tripped over its tether, so it seemed like just one more hazard. I wear it often for her sake. At the same

time I operate, rather, on the principle that the rearing prow will
pitch me overboard if it can, but I won't let it.

Is it better, I wonder, when changing jibs to head downwind
or what? Robinson and Hiscock do. It is good also to keep headed
roughly to windward but have your helmsman luff and jog as slowly
as he can. Certainly the worst plan is to punch to windward at
maximum speed, throwing solid water all over your foredeck man.
What a joy it is to hoist it at last, wet though you are, to see it fluttering up, sheeted home, and feel her taking off again with zest,
the way she was meant to. Sloops without jibs feel as though they
were crippled.

There are many fancy hooks and double-pulley rigouts for fastening the sheets to the jib clew. But that afterpoint of a jib flaps like
a whip every time the boat comes into the wind. Like many people,
I tie the sheets into the jib clew with a bow line and don't have any
hardware up there to beat me black and blue.

If ever I think it is work, I have only to remember the old-
fashioned yachts with their heavy gear, the gaff to complicate
mains'l hoisting and lowering, their tops'ls, their reefing tackle. The
great heavy booms that were common in 1900 were so clumsy and
difficult we can't even imagine such things. Some schooners had
main booms seventy-six feet long and as big around as telephone
poles. Looking at pictures taken around 1910, one is amazed at the
heavy tackle and blocks even on small boats. Many had three head-
sails to handle: Aftermost was the stays'l, with boom appropriately
termed "the club"; next came "the jib"; and ahead of that the topmast or flying jib. The club swung athwartships by itself on its own
traveler (and you'd better keep out of the way of it), but the other
two pairs of jib sheets had to be handled every time you came

about. Quite often there were running backstays to be hauled and loosened also. And yet they did it, those men of fifty and a hundred years ago, and they in their turn thought it was simplicity itself compared with the hundreds of lines and the tons of gear required by a square-rigger.

One of the impediments on my foredeck is my pole. This pole has always been a joke to most people, including my mate, but I cling to it because it is so useful. My pole is fourteen feet long, and difficult to stow aboard a twenty-footer, so I lash it on the deck as best I can and stumble over it forever. I used to stand it up and fasten it in the rigging, but that meant too much of a job getting it down. It is wonderful as a whisker pole for the genoa, a double rope sling around mast and pole serving as length adjuster. Many's the little boat we have beaten on a broad reach because we could wing our big genny out, and they couldn't. It has a boathook end, and often when I am making one of my less professional landings at a dock, I seem to be drifting away and not going to make it, when out reaches my fourteen-foot boathook, and I make it after all. Its best use is as a sounding pole in shallow water, especially when we are feeling for an anchorage out of the channel. If a rock suddenly appears, I can shove off with my pole and go somewhere else. Once, way down in South Carolina, in a shallow, narrow part of the dredged waterway, we were aground in the mud, trying to sail off and push off at the same time. Along came a breeze and heeled us and freed us, but as a result of my vigorous pushing, the pole was stuck in the mud about four feet. As we began to sail away, I had to let go of it, and there it stood, nodding forlornly behind. I thought I had lost it that time, but almost immediately we got stuck again, at which point a shallow-draft motorboat came along and asked

"Can we help you?" I felt quite beyond help, and was convinced that if I could ever get five hundred miles out to sea I'd stay there. But I did manage to say in desperation, "Yes, you can fetch that pole for me." So they did, and by and by we got clear, taking the famous pole with us. It is a piece of laminated spruce, and it is worth its weight in gold. I've banged my toes on it so many times, I feel a deep affection for the thing, somewhat as a mother for a wayward child.

# CHAPTER X

# GREENWICH POINT TO NEW ROCHELLE

# LONG ISLAND SOUND'S SOUTH SHORE—OYSTER AND HUNTINGTON BAYS

# STRATFORD TO SHERWOOD POINT

# LONG ISLAND SOUND— EASTERN PART

# BLOCK ISLAND SOUND AND APPROACHES

IN A LIGHT BREEZE, and quite hot again, little *Sunrise* entered Mamaroneck Harbor, which we found filled to bursting with boats, like most of the harbors along the New York–Connecticut shore of the sound. The spinning Seagull took us slowly up a narrow channel past hundreds of sloops, cutters, motorboats, ketches, and schooners to the harbor master's float. Usually, you can't find the harbor master; he's off somewhere. But this one was right on tap.

"Can you possibly find us a mooring or a slip for the night?" I asked.

"No slips, no moorings. A dozen people want every opening. You can try the marinas. But they're full."

"Well, we'll anchor out somewhere then. Can we haul up our dinghy on the float while we go to buy groceries?"

"You can if you want to. But the boys will steal your oars. Maybe the dinghy, too." He retired to his office.

No room at the inn. After the easygoing friendliness of the South, the cold shoulder of the metropolitan area came as something of a shock.

While we were thinking about all this, in from the sound sailed a pretty blue racing sloop under main and jib. She was about twenty-eight feet, slim and graceful, with long overhangs and a very small tucked-up transom, all varnished, with gold lettering. Apparently she had no engine, which made things look precarious as she roared up the jam-packed channel under full sail, inches away from boats both sides. Mamaroneck Harbor is a Y-channel, with its base toward the sound and its arms extending inward almost to the Boston Post Road. At the V point of the Y a little round basin of open water still existed. Here the skipper smartly rounded up into the wind and commanded, "Down main." One of his two crew, with the halyard in his hand, let go, while the other pulled the sail down in a twinkling. Still with way on, the captain spun his boat off down the right-hand arm of the Y with his jib drawing in a beam wind. Fifty yards down that narrow lane of moored craft, he pronounced,

"Down jib," and it fluttered to the deck while he slid on at reduced speed. But apparently he was still going too fast, for he began to waggle his tiller vigorously from side to side to slow his progress. On he drifted till he was opposite his slip, whereupon he did a right-angled turn with just way enough to steer and nestled into his dead-end slot as softly as a feather. Casually the three of them made fast their four-way hitch.

It was such a sailorlike, masterly performance we felt like clapping.

Motoring out, we anchored by the edges of the sound in a not-very-protected spot. But summer nights are usually calm there-abouts. I resolved that if a thunderstorm got to growling in the night, I'd tail onto a big moored schooner along the inner channel. One simply can't lose one's boat for the sake of politeness in a place where the locals have appropriated all the water. Being a transient, and knowing that nobody owns the water, one feels, rightly or wrongly, that transients should have a few small rights, just maybe space for an anchor.

We rowed ashore to Mister Friendly Harbor Master's float again, and I sat by the dinghy while Kay went uptown shopping. She came back in a taxi loaded with goodies that would surely keep us going for a number of days' voyaging toward waters more far-reaching. Most people we had met in our travels had been ever so kind to us, so I shouldn't complain.

Eatons Neck Sand Hole on the Long Island shore not far from Huntington and Northport is a popular anchorage for the sound's thousands of yachtsmen. It was dug out long ago by dredges devel-oped for work on the Panama Canal, as a trial to see what they could do. A basin in the sand, it is many acres in extent, but when we went through the narrow entrance channel its charming expanse was well filled with anchored cruisers, even though this was a weekday night. Up near the head of the harbor we cruised slowly, looking for a spot with room to swing. There was none, of course, but plenty of dirty looks from people who expected us to drop our hook and bump them in the night. That didn't appeal to us any more than to them, so we wended our way back to the entrance end of the basin. A hook of sand was there, with a steep beach and plenty of water directly astern, so we put our anchor down.

Pretty soon we swam ashore to the steep beach. Climbing over the barrier of sand and gravel, we walked a mile or two along the edge of the sound looking for shells and driftwood, seeing flocks and swarms of sails far off over the blue water. The skyscrapers of New York just barely stuck their points above the horizon, seeming pleasantly remote. When we had gone almost as far as the Coast Guard station, a large establishment on a sand bluff looking over the sound, we turned back, swam aboard again, and started supper.

Everything was blissful, including a swirling copper sunset that colored the water around the quiet fleet of boats. No blaring radios, no trouble. Not yet.

In the night the wind veered suddenly to the north, a shift of nearly ninety degrees, and blew straight from the head of the harbor, a screaming, knockdown blast of great power. I had checked the anchor, of course, before going to bed, and at that time we were tailing off toward the steep beach in plenty of water. With the wind's change we had swung off, not toward the steep beach formed by the shank of the hook, but into the encircling sandbank arms. At three-thirty in the morning I felt our keel bump on the sand, and rushing on deck found us broadside in the breakers. The waves were white and frothing in the darkness. I should have realized that as the fast tidal current swept in and out of this harbor an eddy would form in the angle of the hook, depositing sand. I should have sounded all around us in the dinghy, making sure we had room to swing in all directions. In fact I never should have anchored there in the first place. I should have jammed in among the crowd of boats in the good water near the head of the harbor, or anchored in the channel even, and put out a kedge astern to haul myself to its edge if the Coast Guard patrol boats came by and objected. One simply cannot allow politeness to endanger one's boat.

All these might-have-beens occurred to me in about three seconds while I was hauling on the anchor line, putting it around a sheet winch and cranking. But our boat would not come off. Kay was pushing with the pole. I jumped overboard and pushed with all my strength; the thousand-pound keel was stuck fast in the sand, and the wind was driving us on, not off. *Sunrise* was banging me as well as the sand. The low shores of this harbor hole were little protection from the wind whistling five miles across the sound onto us.

It seemed we might lose our boat in the pounding as she rose and fell, thumping heavily. How could any boat stand that? It was all so sudden, I had a sense of betrayal, as though the wind and darkness had sprung a trap on me, lulled me, and then struck. But it was my fault. I felt so ashamed and disgraced, too. Being extra careful, I'd put out too much anchor line, so I did not have room to swing without grounding on the sandy hook. The most ignorant lubber knows better.

Meanwhile we kept on banging, and it looked worse every minute as the waves grew bigger. The clothes we stood up in might be all we'd save at this rate. "Put on your warmest, driest socks and sweaters and pants," I told Kay, thinking of the two-mile walk along the beach in the cold wind to the Coast Guard station.

In the reeling cabin we struggled into sweaters, slickers. "Now jump overboard." Over we went, and standing in the breakers tried once again to dislodge the pounding hull. But our beloved boat would not move. Quite the contrary, she was on even harder, she was heeling toward the beach, and the tide was ebbing fast. Indeed, she soon was not bumping anymore, just lying there in the sand, her mast pointing way off down the sky, looking like a wreck. Obviously, the tide would soon leave her high and dry.

We stood on the sand in the pouring rain and looked at our stranded craft. "Why did you tell me to put on dry clothes and then to jump into the water and get them soaked," asked my shivering wife. I replied that walking to the Coast Guard station in her nightie hadn't seemed appropriate.

"I'm going aboard again," she said. "I'm not going to stand here and freeze. This boat's not going anywhere."

The fact was becoming more and more obvious. All the outer beach was roaring beyond the low barrier. It was a good thing we weren't on the outside edge where the waves were slamming the sand with a thud you could feel. Powerful squalls whistled through, and the night was black. What could anyone do? The water level continued to fall, our keel now exposed, only its bulb still covered. At least we weren't going to lose our boat. If this had happened on the outer rocky coast of Maine where the great combers come shouldering in from the Atlantic with a fetch of some three thousand miles, we would be dead and our *Sunrise* a mass of splinters.

I climbed aboard, where a gleam of yellow showed through the portholes. Kay had lit the gimbal oil lamp, which looked very incongruous standing upright in our down-on-its-side cabin. We were so far over it was easier to stand on the sides of the hull than on the cabin sole. Kay had leveled up the stove with the copy of Bowditch and an old plate, and was making a cup of coffee and a sandwich. I was glad to see that her bunk was on the down side. Mine was uninhabitable.

Having drunk our coffee, eaten a huge slice of bread and marmalade, and changed our clothes again, warmed by the stove, we had a sleep, she in her nest against the side, padded with life preservers, I on the floor between the bunks.

In an hour or two the dawn's cold light woke me and I went out on the beach. One could go ashore dry-shod now. No other boat, it seemed, had been blown ashore, only me. But then, as the dawn came, I saw that far across the grass a huge catamaran had been blown into the marshes. While I was examining my fellow sufferer through the binoculars and feeling a little better, a Coast Guard patrolman came along the beach. He was quite young, as most of them are these days. And judging by his twang he had been born in Maine or New Hampshire.

"You got aground, eh? Well, you're not the first one to get stranded here, nor the last, I reckon. Name please." I gave it. He had a clipboard and a walkie-talkie. "Boat's name?"

Then he surprised me by speaking to headquarters via his radio telephone. "The owner says his name is E. T. Merrick. Name of the subject vessel is *Sunrise*. Yes sir, aground."

It sounded as though I was going to be booked, fined, and jailed. And rightly so, for I deserved it.

He turned to me. "Do you want a tow off?"

"No, no!" I was horrified. I had heard too many tales of powerful Coast Guard craft ripping the decks off boats, tearing them to pieces, towing them under at speed. High and dry, with the whole keel exposed, how could anyone tow me off?

"The owner of the subject vessel says he doesn't want a tow."

"The owner of the subject vessel would like to know the exact time of high tide, though," I told him. I had looked it up already in my tide book, but thought I might get confirmation from the experts. It came just as I had figured: "Three-sixteen P.M." Not three-fifteen, not three-thirty, but three-sixteen on the dot. An offshore or onshore wind will change things as much as an hour, but I suppose you can't predict such realities a year ahead.

So we would be here till afternoon, on view all day. A great blessing, however, that we had gone aground an hour and a half after high water. Suppose we'd gone on at the top of the tide!

"You'll be okay," said the boy, walking away. And then, as though he were my grandfather, he turned and added, "It blew fifty knots last night."

By breakfast time we could walk all around our slantwise wreck. It showed no damage. Its side was lying in soft sand. Using a dinghy oar for a shovel, I dug a foot or so of sand away from the bulb of the keel, thinking it might float us a little sooner when the tide came. I took the anchor and walked it to the water's edge, setting it firmly among the shells.

Boats left the harbor one by one, not saying anything, not asking, "Can I help you" or any such trivialities. They scarcely looked at us. The land was bearing us up bravely, and they could see we weren't sinking. This was the metropolitan area, I reminded myself, where too many people have seen too many people doing too many things—including getting their boats stuck on sandbanks. By and by they were all gone, the harbor empty, and I was glad to be alone with my sense of shame. Captain indeed! At the big marinas they say, "Want fuel, Captain? Tying up for the night, Captain? Take your lines, Captain?" Always before, it had bucked me up after a day of many mistakes to be addressed as Captain.

About two-fifteen in the afternoon we floated off, placid as a toy duck in a bathtub. I decided it was too late to go anywhere, so moved up the harbor and anchored near its head in better shelter and with lots of water all around. On the rest of our cruise to Maine, I made a point of circling and sounding before I anchored. At high tide the catamaran kedged itself out of the marshes and came flying up the harbor with all sails set. A man and woman aboard made a great show of whizzing past us, coming about with rattling blocks and flapping sheets, jumping hither and yon as though coping with a national emergency, and roaring out again at tremendous speed. Finally we saw them disappearing far across the sound. I guess they were demonstrating to themselves that they really could sail. I had to do the same next day.

I was feeling better next morning and thinking how fortunate we Americans are to have so many tens of thousands of harbors, even though some incompetents get wrecked in them. Daniel Webster called Long Island Sound "the Mediterranean of the Western Hemisphere." And the Chesapeake is a wonderland all its own. Think of the rivers for cruising—the Cape Fear, York, Potomac, Delaware, Hudson, Connecticut, Housatonic, Thames. There's Narragansett Bay, where you can sail for two weeks in and out of

Rhode Island's irregularities and never see them all. And beyond lies Maine. All these treasures lie dreaming (like the "dream time" the Australian aborigines speak of, the old, old days before we changed), waiting to be seen from a boat. Just suppose we had a long straight shore like the West Coast, where there isn't a decent harbor between San Francisco and Portland, Oregon. And even Portland isn't good, judging by the number of boatmen who have been drowned on the breaking Columbia River Bar.

Long Island Sound in summer is supposed to be a placid lake where sailboats lie becalmed for days in the mirror water, but it didn't treat us that way. The breeze we got was nearly thirty knots, tearing the bruised-looking water to foam. Nevertheless, we had to go, even though the blow was ahead. I felt I had quite a slate to wipe clean. We tightened our oilskins, put on the storm jib and a reef in the main. "We can always run back," I said.

The squalls laid us practically flat, but our stiff little ship lifted up her head and pounded on up the center of the sound, just barely able to make a course for Stratford Shoal Light and the far Connecticut shore. When we were heeled forty-five degrees the sail spilled about half the wind's weight, which was a blessing. And of course, the keel is a pendulum whose righting movement is stronger the farther it goes from vertical. For this kind of going you need a boat that was built to sail, no compromises, no shallow draft, no blocky shape that enables you to "sleep five" or sport a large cockpit suitable for cocktail parties. All emphasis must be on hull and shape and rig, rather than rose-colored wall-to-wall carpeting. It seems silly to mention such obvious truths—except that many mass-built, mass-marketed boats are built for sale instead of for sailing.

The wind kept shrieking till we didn't even hear it. The squalls frequently stood us straight up in the cockpit, giving us a chance to look the foamy suds right in the eye. Kay rested in the cabin on the leeward bunk or took the helm to relieve me. I did not see why she should have had to suffer. But she is a real traveler and did not seem to mind. Often she says, "I don't care where we go as long as we go." So we thrashed on, always marveling at the seakeeping ruggedness of our boat, always remembering how impossibly swamped the Penguin would have been in anything like this. Few boats were on the sound, none visible for hours. The wavetops reared up against the sky, frequently obscuring both the Long Island and the Connecticut shores. We were alone, and that was the way it should be. For lunch we had peanut butter crackers and a swig of milk that the wind blew away if you didn't drink it quickly.

After many hours we won past Penfield Reef, where waves were breaking furiously, and into Black Rock Harbor, across the sound on the Connecticut shore. We really hadn't done such wonders—only about twenty miles made good, after all that stiff beating. Black Rock Harbor, near the city of Bridgeport, turned out to be also near the city dump. Evil-smelling fires that flickered all night meant we didn't like our anchorage much.

Next day the wind, though still ahead, was not quite so strong. On long tacks we beat past Stratford Shoal and fought our way abreast Falkner Island with its radio beacon and green grass and faraway look. At length *Sunrise* came into Clinton, Connecticut—a long stone breakwater, a "made" harbor that was once only a narrow tidal stream and marsh, one of those nooks where fishermen with oars and sail used to poke in and out solely at high water, hoping they wouldn't get caught outside in a blow at ebb tide when their "harbor" was nothing but a mudflat; then along came the U.S. Army engineers (plus the chamber of commerce) and dredged out a long, crooked, narrow channel, and scooped out the marshes behind the beach, so that, lo and behold, we have a yachting center where a thousand motor cruisers can lie among acres of finger floats flashing their window glass in the sunset. Such harbors are usually crammed and crowded with boats, squeezed in by shoals. There is no "good" water except the "made" water, and they are as different from spacious natural havens as night from day. We were tired from the long beat and glad of this one in any case, glad of its entrance avenue beautifully marked, especially at the elbows of its narrow channels, by red nuns on the right and black cans on the left. We creamed into the harbor under sail, disdaining motor, around all the bends, flying fast, the hard, implacable sandbars rearing their gray shoulders close on either hand, the wind strong, no room for any misstep—and this a strange harbor we had never seen before. But we had a good harbor chart, three inches to the mile. On our port hand was a vast expanse of inviting water, except that our chart showed its depth as less than a foot. A motor cruiser was coming up fast behind us as we neared the narrowest channel bend of all, where we would have to jibe around a nun with inches to spare. I'd need all the room there was, and if he tried to pass me at that point there'd be bad trouble.

He politely slowed down, following me at a respectful distance, understanding the situation perfectly, as though he'd once been a sailor himself. Later, where the channel widened out, he went by slowly, with a pleasant hail, and I could see he was explaining to his wife how smartly we were handling our windship. My wife said, "They seem to be a pleasant couple."

The vast Clinton marina doesn't like sailboats much. Here again, it is motorboat country. The owners of these powerful craft like to maneuver skillfully in tricky little basins, surrounded by similar boats and owners, demonstrating twin-screw performance, one ahead, one astern, spinning the cruiser in place, backing into slips with inches to spare, then full ahead to stop her just before her transom crashes the pier. Sailboat auxiliaries simply cannot do such things; they don't have the quick bursts of power, having been built for something else. So at Clinton, sailboats are required to lie outside the basin, at long floats bordering the channel, where they get banged and rubbed by passing wakes, which are many and boisterous. "We don't allow sailboats in the basin," the dock boy told me. "They do too much damage. Their skippers don't seem to know how to handle them, that's all there is to it."

I was proud of myself that I did not tell him how much farther they go, even around the world. We put out our two big fenders and our two little ones, rigged two spring lines against the fast tide, made fast breast lines and bow and stern lines. Then we took off our oilskins and looked around.

We were four transient sailboats on the outside versus about a thousand resident-permanent motorboats on the inside. The permanents pay dockage on an annual basis, many of them coughing up a thousand dollars a year. Naturally enough, in crowded harbors the transients have to take what is left. In such places as Mamaroneck and dozens of others there isn't anything left at all. When you're in a different harbor every night, you're always at a disadvantage—except that you're having more fun than anybody. I was beginning to find out you have to take care, too, that you aren't squeezed out of the good holding ground onto rock or very soft mud where your anchor will drag.

One of the sailcraft belonged to some jolly boys from City Island who, though bound for Gloucester, were so inexperienced as to ask advice from me: "Gosh it was rough out there today. We stayed. How did you manage?" I forget what I answered, but I know I thought, *The blind leading the blind.*

Ahead of them was a twenty-five-foot sloop on charter to a young couple who had three little boys. The oldest couldn't have been more than six, and the woman sure was busy, washing, cooking, minding her brood. "Courageous, I call it," said Kay, and immediately struck up an acquaintance with the courageous one and took the small fry for a long walk along the shoreside.

Just astern of us was a ritzy yawl with a fashionable-looking man and woman aboard who seemed a trifle cool. He was extremely efficient, a sailor's sailor apparently, lines flemished, boat all scrubbed with fresh water to get the salt off, brightwork rubbed with a chamois, chrome freshly polished, mains'l furled in such a neat tube it made us look quite messy. We probably wouldn't be having much truck with them. "How do you do," they said, pleasantly enough, in their Breton-red shorts and striped jerseys.

Darkness came, and the wakes quieted down and the boats ceased passing. The fast tide gurgled by, while we slept the sleep of the just.

In the morning all barriers among the sailing crews disintegrated. The man and woman with the three little boys had a stopped-up toilet. We did not mention that our special bucket seldom gets out of order. The little family's cruise was at a standstill, and the sky seemed to have fallen in on them. Like a herd of elephants we all rallied around the stricken members of our band. A plumber had been sent for; he was on the way; he arrived; smiles all around.

The plumber turned out to be a small, very wizened, dark creature with frizzy hair, who should have been old but really was young, and looked like a monkey. He had that curious, perverse New York City manner of making good out of bad. I fancy that when you come from the slums of New York City, you make a wry joke of life's tribulations—a form of courage. At any rate, all was trouble here, so he whistled and sang and grinned and frisked like some gnome in a fairy tale or a goat in clover. Everyone was very hopeful as he worked away at the stopped-up pipe. But he had no luck, which pleased him mightily. He told us with a cheery laugh that we'd all have to tug at a masthead halyard to heel this Islander sloop while he worked overside from a dinghy to see if he could get a wire in from the outside.

All of us men from the four sailboats were happy to be able to help, as we certainly didn't intend to be outdone in cheeriness by one of the Seven Dwarfs. We lined up on the dock, including Mr. Standoffish, the well-dressed one, and pulled our hearts out, practically singing chanteys. She was a stiff little sloop, and didn't heel very far despite our best efforts. Anyway, the angle was wrong—we were too close. The plumber-dwarf was happier than ever to find he could do no more from the outside than from the inside. When he crawled out of the dinghy onto the dock I asked him about it. "Women will never learn," he said with a joyful sigh, and disappeared shoreward in search of reinforcements or more tools or those mysterious aids plumbers are always disappearing in search of.

Mr. Standoffish was on his knees on the float looking decidedly humble. In the scramble of the tugging bee he had knocked off his glasses, which had fallen through a crack into twelve feet of murky water floored by mud the consistency of thick soup. His Mrs.

popped her head out of the cabin of their boat and explained, "Now he can't read the charts." She seemed sympathetic and very pleasant. "I'll read them for you, dear," she said, and that seemed to make him feel worse than ever.

Apparently their cruise also was now at a standstill. "I can get along okay except for those charts," he confided in me.

I had a sudden brainwave, remembering two pairs of spares I carry that came from Woolworth's. They are simply magnifying lenses that you try out from rows of different gradations along the counter until you find a pair that suits you. I dived below and came up with a pair. "Just on the chance, try these," I said. He put them on and was overjoyed. They suited him fine; he was farsighted like me. He wanted to pay me, but I told him they were only cheap things, and felt very magnanimous—also very warm to think that he wasn't such a stiff stick, not cold or distant at all. We exchanged addresses, parted bosom friends, and doubtless he felt good to discover I wasn't cold or standoffish at all. Quite a nice chap, I could almost hear him telling his wife.

Kay and I decided this socializing that goes on endlessly at dockside everywhere is all very well, but we had come to sail. So we got our outboard warmed up and we hoisted our main and started taking off our six dock lines. Our hearts were not very heavy to be saying farewell to beautiful Clinton, Connecticut. The three lads came along and recommended the blind-leading-the-blind discourse by asking, "How can you leave now, how can you find your way in the fog?"

Visibility was about a mile, and I figured I wouldn't get lost too badly if the mist didn't close in any thicker. I said, feeling like an old-timer, "Well, we study the chart very carefully. We have our most likely course marked off already, and we'll go for the best whistles, gongs, bells, and horns. We have a good compass, you know, and we'll run our compass courses and keep our time and distance so that usually we can find our way from one marker to another. Not always, of course."

Sure enough, we made it to Mystic and tied up there at eight o'clock that night, tired as usual after a long day's run, but pleased to have threaded our way among the shoals off New London and the various hazards that decorate the entrance to Fishers Island Sound.

# CHAPTER XI

*Interlude*

## ABOUT OUR COMPASS

OUR COMPASS IS A BEAUTY, and I ought to know, having spent so many days steering by it. It has a five-inch face, is on gimbals to stay level, and I placed it under a plate glass window in the bridge deck, right in front of the helmsman. You always wonder about a compass—whether it's reading correctly or not, whether something temporary or permanent is giving it error or has put it out. And especially you wonder in fog and obscurity, when you and your crew are utterly dependent on that little swinging needle. If it should be out five degrees, you'll probably miss the buoy you're heading for, and when you've run your distance you'll have to search around and around, or, better, in squares whose sides are of calculated length. If you can't find the marker, you'll have no point of departure for the next marker, which, in turn, gives you a slim chance of finding No. 2. Then you will be well and truly lost.

Knowing how supremely important the compass is, I tried to check it and correct it before we set out. At Hilton Head I warped the boat around till it was headed north, then compared the boat compass with my very fine hand-bearing instrument. The theory is that a handheld compass can be six feet away from any local attractions that may deflect the steering compass, and so you can use it as a standard. It all sounds so easy, but never is, for errors of judgment creep in. Anyway, we had a small north error, which I corrected using a nonmagnetic screwdriver on a compass set-screw (half, as per the books). Next, the boat was turned south, and seemed about right. I tied her up heading east and heading west, correcting a fairly large error on those courses. All summer I kept checking it against courses we were running from buoy to buoy, and as compared with my hand-bearing compass and the chart. Sometimes I thought it was just right; sometimes I thought it had eight to ten degrees of easterly error, at other times westerly. The side currents, the leeway, make every day's run different. I made a fancy deviation card, but it didn't check out, so I threw it away. You don't always know what is pushing you sideways, or how much, or for how long. For instance, you are crossing a big bay that has marshes, islands, and a big river in its upper end. You know that the ebb will push you seaward as you cross, and, conversely, the flood will drift you landward. But how much? And when will the tide go slack where you are? Moreover, when will your side drift begin to decrease, or even reverse itself? We know that in a tidal river the current runs usually at its fastest about three hours after high or after low water—that is, at half tide. But two miles offshore no books tell you what it's doing, and all you know is that the shape of the land or islands affects it plenty.

Once we found that we had put two empty, ferrous cans in the trash basket under the bridge deck. We were some eight degrees off course that day, and it was a good lesson to us not to be so careless again. I decided late in the summer that to compound the mysteries, we have a heeling error. A heeling error caused by our thousand-pound iron keel right under the compass, swinging out, let us say, to the eastward or the westward, thus attracting our north-pointing needle to the right or to the left. Books claim to tell you how to correct heeling error. However, this will vary on different courses, and besides that, we're heeled rail-down one minute and practically upright the next.

I very much envied a big-boat skipper I met who proudly proclaimed, "My compass has no error." Sometimes I felt ours was perfect, and at other times, I had an almost uncontrollable urge to tinker with it. But I knew I mustn't, for I wouldn't be sure what I had done. When we are tossing about in a big sea, we can hardly steer within five degrees of the course anyway, so we just do the best we can. One of my best checks is to run from buoy to buoy maybe two or three miles, on a magnetic course I have drawn on the chart, picking a calm day, at slack tide, to see whether we make our mark or not.

There is one simplification. In this coastal piloting we use only magnetic, taking our courses via the parallel rules from the magnetic compass rose on the chart—not converting to true, as we would have to do if we were offshore and navigating by celestial.

Here again I find fault with the impractical emphasis on precision in the Power Squadron piloting courses. They don't say anything about the pot buoys and which direction they are streaming, or the bubbles and ripples going by them, or whether maybe the pot buoy is bobbing half under. They are motorboaters, much more likely to be on an even keel, in an enclosed wheelhouse, running at a calculated speed, much less subject to the vagaries of the breeze. The skipper of a small sailboat, on the edge of a jibe, may have his hands too full of sheets and tiller to be studiously poring over a nice dry chart table with rulers and distance measurements and accurate vector diagrams. You may say he should have done all that ahead of time, and probably you're right. But he wasn't quite sure whether he was going to the west of that rocky island up ahead or east of it, because he was having to tack to windward and, though he preferred to go to westward of it, he was sagging off and making an awful lot of leeway.

To have seen waves breaking on a reef dead ahead on a hazy afternoon did not raise my faith in *Sunrise*'s pilot (me).

When I spoke to him about it, he took a defensive attitude, saying, "Well, for heaven's sake, we knew you were lost, didn't we! And we knew the reef was somewhere around, so we were keeping an eye out for it."

"We sure were."

"And so we saw it. So what! It happens in the best of families."

"But if you'd only had faith in your dead reckoning—"

"How can I have faith in my dead reckoning when you're chewing your fingernails off?"

# CHAPTER XII

# NARRAGANSETT BAY

# CAPE COD CANAL AND APPROACHES

TOWARD THE EASTERN SIDE of the estuary of the Sakonnet River we beat in past the tall white shaft of the abandoned Coast Guard tower that had so blessedly oriented us, past the nearly invisible new and scientific Coast Guard spiderweb that takes its place, and anchored a couple of miles up the Sakonnet River in Sachuest Cove, where beaches surrounded us on three sides and magnificent mansions surmounting the distant hills looked peacefully down. I thought their attitudes bespoke a mild disdain for the arrival of a twenty-foot sloop. But it's hard to be sure about magnificent mansions, especially when they are silhouetted against a setting sun. After all, they were only half the size of some of the magnificent mansions in nearby Newport. In this place we were snugly sheltered from all winds except north. The evening radio report out of Newport gave no word of north winds, which was comforting or deluding, according to one's viewpoint. One of the few forecasts you can depend upon is advance warning of a strong cold front as it comes sweeping over eight or ten states from the northwest.

Just before dark a forty-foot yawl with white topsides and varnished masts came in, luffed up to windward, smartly lowered sail, and anchored with skill and dispatch. No motor for them. Watching cruisers moor, you can always tell whether they are experienced or not. This was a heavy, able craft, run solely by an elderly man and his white-haired wife. They knew how to do things right; no lost-in-fog for them. The woman went below immediately to mix the drinks and start supper, while he was making a neat furl in the main and mizzen, frapping the halyards, taking down his ensign, bagging the jib, and lashing antichafe guards around his anchor line. Then they sat at ease in the rocking cockpit, in the cool of the evening, looking at the sunset, as they no doubt had done a thousand times.

Late that night came the wind, cold and strong from the north. It woke me at once as our motion changed and we began to pitch and yank at our anchor. Waves on the beach behind us broke with a deepening roar. I undid the lashings on our spare storm anchor, a twenty-five-pound plow, and overhauled its twenty feet of heavy chain and two hundred feet of half-inch nylon. Should we put it down? Weren't we already pretty close to the beach? We didn't have two hundred feet of leeway. The shifted wind blowing into our erstwhile harbor had a fetch of four or five miles down the broad river. It was piping up every minute. How black it seemed outside, how ominous and shivery! I stood in the companionway watching, deciding what to do, wondering whether it was bad or I only thought so.

Lights glowed in the cabin of the yawl. Soon two figures in oilskins emerged with flashlights and began tying in a reef.

"If they're getting out of here," I said to Kay, "it must be time to go." There was no doubt the wind was continuing to rise, and the sooner we were gone the better. This breeze might turn out to be nothing; but then again, if the wind should blow sixty miles an hour we'd be practically helpless on this lee shore. While our anchor continued to hold, we put on our oilskins and set to work reefing the main and hanking on the storm jib.

The night seemed bottomlessly black with all those white horses marching out of nowhere. What is most disconcerting is that you pick a sheltered harbor for your night's rest, among the fields, so to speak, and then the wind shifts 180 degrees and you find yourself wide open to the elements. It's a shock to be reminded once again that there is no security.

At least we were doing something, not mouthing gallows humor while having another beer. As we worked with our flashlights on the tossing deck I was glad. I always knew that some night sooner or later we'd get blown out of our anchorage. And now it had come and this was it. The wind was blowing too hard for our little motor to do anything against it. That beautiful little motor whose smallness keeps us pure! We would sail off this lee shore as sailors have always had to do, or get wrecked.

Our friends in the yawl took off smoothly, the old man on the foredeck getting the anchor in, the woman at the wheel ably conning her out.

I hoped we could get off on the right foot, on the offshore tack, as she had. We saw to it that our sheets were free, everything in order, and hoisted the madly flapping main, blessedly diminished by its reef. The wind was whistling a truly high note in the rigging. We must have no repeat of the Eatons Neck wreck, for this was a pounding, exposed shore, not a harborside sandbank. Our handy little boat can beat to windward moderately well without its jib, so I bundled up the hanked-on storm sail in order to keep it from whipping me while I was hauling the anchor on the foredeck. Fortunately, we had practiced sailing out the anchor. We'd have no time for getting the mud off its flukes this night. The east was turning gray.

"Ready?"

"Ready." Dear Kay at the tiller, steady as a rock, the flapping main sheet in her hand. I hauled in to shorten up the scope, wrapped a turn around the sampson post, and put my foot on it. She sailed off on the correct tack, which yanked the anchor free. I was determined that if we got off on the wrong tack toward the beach I'd raise the peak of the jib in my hands and back it to force the bow offshore. But that wasn't necessary. She luffed the slightest bit, to give me some slack, and the anchor came aboard smoothly. With mains'l drawing hard, *Sunrise* gathered way, and we were off.

As soon as the jib was hoisted and sheeted home, we rushed toward the river's far shore doing fine, charging through the waves, the reduced sail making this wind seem not very fierce.

We were pleased to have chalked up one more experience in the cruiser's book. Dawn was breaking, spray flying, and the wine of life flowing fast in us. I had thought I might beat up the river looking for a sheltered cove. But we were doing so famously and the daylight seemed so encouraging, we ran right out of the Sakonnet River for Buzzards Bay and the open sea. We almost tripped over a fishnet nearly half a mile long at the river mouth, but luckily saw its orange buoys in time to reach out around and past the buoy marking its end.

Along about midmorning, out toward Buzzards Bay Light Tower, miles offshore, we encountered our friends in the yawl again. They had apparently jogged out for a spin and were bound back again toward Sakonnet and Newport.

I have the greatest respect for some of the elderly cruising people we've seen, people who are often very much more seagoing than we. This yawl couple were the type, reserved, experienced, and I had an idea they enjoy cruising as much as we do.

In the late afternoon we came to islands blue on the sea, the outermost one being Cuttyhunk. These are the Elizabeth Islands, a remarkable group that adds much to East Coast cruising delights.

The Elizabeth Islands belong to the Forbes family; they just plumb own them, in a feudal sort of way.

How can anyone characterize Cuttyhunk Island, so wild and at the same time so overpopulated? High on the spine of the island, far above the blue ocean, looking off to Gay Head on Martha's Vineyard, we experienced a sense of aloneness and discovery that made us say, "This is what we came for." A similar atmosphere prevailed across lonely paths through the moors to Gosnold Pond at the far end of the island, waves breaking down below, while we read the sign telling of a colony here in 1602. The village of Cuttyhunk itself was folksy also, with a post office almost part of somebody's kitchen, complete with crying baby. And nearby stood a little cottage where a woman named Mildred baked fresh, crusty bread every day that you could buy if you got there before too many other cruisers.

That was the trouble—too many other cruisers. Cuttyhunk is just a nice, challenging weekend cruise from dozens of Connecticut mainland harbors, whence whole fleets set sail. I often say "Why don't they stay home!" to which my mate replies, "Why don't you stay home?" The harbor is small and dredged, bounded by sand shoals you can get stuck on. You come up a narrow, tidal channel into the square, dredged basin, and before your eyes are the huddled masses of yachts, fifty, a hundred of them, with barely room to swing on their shortened anchor rodes. Comes a gale, and they all drag and end up in a snarl.

We had sailed there in a fine fair breeze, with our genny wung out on its long whisker pole. Partway, we picked up the Buzzards Bay Tower, noting again how like a running deer those navigational towers look when seen from a distance, especially if the day is hazy. The legs stand in the sea, surmounted by the oblong house that is the body (flat-backed to form a helicopter landing pad). At one end is the raised lighthouse structure forming the deer's head.

Approaches to the island were strewn with rocks, shoals, and reefs, and at the harbor mouth, lo and behold, we came upon our friends the spinnaker people. They had passed us halfway, but were now in trouble. Somehow in the tossing swells they had achieved the father and mother of a spinnaker wrap. The loose folds of the upper ten feet of their silky balloon had wound themselves around the forestay in several directions, while the bottom ten feet had wrapped in opposite twists. In the middle, between the two wraps, a bulgey bag was filling and collapsing with sharp bangs, shaking the whole boat and threatening the mast. They couldn't get their chute down, and they dared not leave it up. A man in a bosun's chair was sent aloft to wrestle with the beast, fruitlessly it turned out. At last, in despair, they sent up a big sheath knife, which he used to cut the cloth to pieces: streamers in the wind, desolate, colored rags signifying another thousand dollars gone.

While we were giving the galley slave a rest and eating dinner in a pleasant inn high on the hill, not paying any attention to the clustered yachts swinging at their anchors in the crowded harbor, some so-and-so in his so-and-so boat knocked a piece out of our rail without leaving his calling card. Cuttyhunk's lovely beaches, its moors, its lookouts above the sea, thereupon lost their charm for us. The crowded loneliness, the congested solitude! Must be, we decided, everyone was looking for the same thing we were—not finding it.

But then we were at sea again, leaving all those shoreside troubles astern, our dear little boat scooting fast in a commanding southwest wind, bound for Marion, Massachusetts. On the way I learned another lesson, to wit, don't try to pass in front of a tugboat-and-barge unless they are so far away as to be practically invisible.

We had been sailing so rapidly I thought surely we'd get ahead of a distant tug battling to windward, throwing spray clear over her pilothouse. Surely that headwind would slow him. But by and by we had to turn up, and up, practically to windward, to have more room, to hope to get ahead of him. I should have changed my tactics, been adaptable, gone astern of him, except that by this time it was too late. The great broad barge was churning white breakers ahead of its bluff front as it plowed; yet the tug's immense power was eating up the miles to windward just the same. One thing you can count on: A tug does not change its course, and if they run over you, they run over you. And they are so big, and we are so small! We got across, just barely in time and were then miles off our course, with all those miles to make up. Fortunately, a fair wind still filled our sails on the new course.

It was rough, so we thought we were quite hardy sailors when, having passed Cleveland Ledge Lighthouse, we came to the narrow entrance of Marion's harbor and had to think again. In the harbor channel were six little girls on six little Sailfish sailing boards, tipping over, capsizing, righting themselves, and whizzing off again with delighted giggles.

As usual, the harbor was chock-a-block full of moored yachts, so we asked a passing club launch (manned by a fairhaired girl) whether we could take one of the empty moorings marked BARDEN'S. Barden's is the boatyard at the head of the harbor.

"Yes, you certainly can," she cheerily replied and came neatly alongside. "That will be six dollars. Six dollars a night."

It was worth it and more, as Marion is a grand place for the traveling cruiser. The harbor tends to be quiet, no streaking motorcraft or skiers. Pretty cottages line its well-kept shores, the whole place dominated by the green lawns, piers, and striped awnings of the Beverly Yacht Club. The town dock, with water hose, had a dinghy float. Just a short walk from the shore, the main street was lined with shops of all kinds including a grocery and liquor store, and a post office.

Intending to thread the base of Cape Cod via the Cape Cod Canal, we were very apprehensive as we approached this water road, remembering our troubles in the Chesapeake & Delaware Canal. Sometimes it is hard to fight back the fears and suppress the worries.

Beyond Cleveland Ledge Lighthouse a long row of buoys on each side marked the entrance to the canal. With tide and wind behind *Sunrise,* she practically flew into the dragon's mouth.

There were red and green lights, regulations, signs, army engineers' headquarters, and patrol boats. One of the patrol boats rushed up alongside, opened its pilothouse window, and an official shouted, "Do you have an engine?" to which I nodded.

"Well, turn it on then!"

It turned out that you are not allowed to sail through the Cape Cod Canal without an engine.

There is an old story about the designer Francis Herreshoff's method of outwitting the authorities. He was such a purist sailor, he often sailed in boats without an engine. Once while sailing with a fair wind through the canal, he had his paid hand banging regular strokes on a frying pan down in the cabin, while clouds of blue smoke came up the companionway from another pan of salt pork frizzling on the stove. After all, an independent-minded genius has to have a little leeway for his quirks, doesn't he?

This canal looked much the same as the other, with stone-lined edges, a roadway along its banks, arc lights as though it were an avenue, little parks, an occasional house or industrial area, an open railroad bridge, heavy tide, and now and then a ship. What if two ships passed just where we were, making three of us?

Partway through, we met two ships, one behind the other, so we had room to squeeze over. And then came the East Boat Basin, which we ducked into from the fast-flowing tide, making a short day of it because tomorrow when the current spewed us out past the jetties at the far end of the canal we'd be faced with Cape Cod Bay, Massachusetts Bay, and then the open ocean and a long trek to any harbor.

The basin was crowded with yachts and fishing craft, all waiting to go east (north), or west (south). Fully expecting to get another piece knocked out of our rail, we motored slowly among the ketches, yawls, sloops, schooners, lobster boats, and trawlers, looking for a hole. Finding none, I let go the anchor near a sloop to starboard, a schooner to port, a big catboat ahead, and a trawler astern. Generally, Kay motors astern to dig in the anchor while I tend the chain, but that was impossible here because of the short scope. I thanked my lucky stars that we had chain, with its weighted sag to help our holding.

Every hour all night I was up, watching the boats as they shifted relative positions. The shore surroundings were black and sooty, the lights yellow, wavering, and unfriendly. Railroad cars were banging somewhere in the distance. I wondered why I was so apprehensive. Maybe it was uncertainty about the long sail tomorrow to Isles of Shoals, off the New Hampshire coast. Would we be able to find that small clump of rocks in the broad sea?

CHAPTER XIII

# PORTSMOUTH TO CAPE ELIZABETH

# CASCO BAY

ISLES OF SHOALS, nine miles off the New Hampshire mainland, are a wild collection of rocks and grass, especially when the fog closes in. We put in there on account of the fog. Even on a sunny day they seem lonely and far away, the surf forever breaking, and the anchorage none too secure. Perhaps this forsaken quality is a result of the offshore distance. At any rate, they are in reality much more inhabited than many coastal clumps. There is a lighthouse on White Island, an abandoned World War II Coast Guard base on Appledore, many buildings stand on Smuttynose, and the summer home of the Reverend Frank B. Crandall is built on Lunging Island. Nineteen Spanish seamen wrecked one wild February night in 1813 lie buried on Smuttynose, and doubtless many another poor wretch has been beaten to pieces since then on the barnacle-encrusted rocks. The always fascinating *Cruising Guide to the New England Coast* states that the Reverend Crandall's cottage is kept supplied with food and clothing throughout the year for the possible relief of people

123

marooned or shipwrecked on the island—which could easily happen in the winter, when only the lighthouse clump of rocks is
inhabited. On Star Island the Oceanic Hotel is filled all summer by
large groups of Unitarian-Universalists holding conferences. And for
this hostelry a motor vessel runs daily between the Isles of Shoals
and Portsmouth, New Hampshire, ferrying guests and bringing supplies. We had hovered alongside this craft as we came in, asking
whether we could buy a few gallons of gasoline, but the ferry captain told us, "You can get gasoline over in Portsmouth," waving
toward the distant mainland. As if we didn't know that!

In Gosport Harbor, the only anchorage, we put down our
Danforth in three to four fathoms among some lobster boats belonging to summer fishermen. This rather exposed cove is formed by
Star, Cedar, and Smuttynose Islands, with rough stone breakwaters
linking Star to Cedar and Cedar to Smuttynose. Quite near us on a
rise of ground stood the large old hotel with its flying wings of gingerbread porches and many outbuildings, but the fog erased them
most of the time. Through the tumbled rock breakwater ahead of
our anchor the sea surge gurgled. In gales it would surely crash so
heavily across as to make this spot untenable.

On Smuttynose in the early 1800s (there were at one time nearly
a thousand fishermen living on these islands) old Captain Haley had
a mill and a ropewalk. To serve ships at sea, he kept a lighted lamp
in his window. It was he who picked up the drowned Spaniards and
buried them. When digging for a well, he found a fortune in silver
bars, probably left by the many pirates who frequented this hideaway, and with the hoard he built two breakwaters that form the so-
called harbor. I can imagine the old-time fishing smacks fleeing from
this precarious spot to Portsmouth Harbor when the autumn storms

began to shriek. But in the 1600s and early 1700s the coastal island fishermen feared the Indians over there on the mainland almost as much as they dreaded the gales from the sea. A brave and desperate lot they must have been, those early sailors who came across the ocean from Cornwall, Devonshire, Brittany, the Hebrides, and heaven knows where else.

Modern coastal cruising folks are fond of these islands, and three more yachts came in out of the fog before night settled down. With darkness the visibility shrank to slightly beyond the end of one's nose.

But sometime in the night the wet soup blew away, and just before dawn when I poked my head out of the scuttle I could see the lights of mainland Portsmouth twinkling in a row. We were ecstatic. Imagine being able to see nine miles!

At daybreak we were first out of the harbor. It was looking a little rainy by then, but the breeze was fair, fair for Portland Lightship fifty miles across an indentation of the coast. To hell with this ducking in and out of harbors all the time. The lighthouse was flashing and the hotel all lit up. Visibility is almost as encouraging and stimulating to us as fair wind.

Our first reference point was to be Boon Island Light, also far offshore. We sailed well at first in a moderate wind that soon became a close reach. Before long we saw it, a big stick 133 feet tall, dark on the horizon. As we approached close enough to make out the surf frill, the island looked grim, a low, rocky mound of perhaps three or four acres, a tall tower with dwelling houses and outbuildings crouched below it. There is no harbor, nor any tree that I could glimpse. This is the kind of lighthouse you read about, where winter seas thunder so loud the keepers don't talk about it. Reefs extend nearly four miles to seaward. I'd prefer to keep strictly away from there, but on this day of increasing haze we needed the lighthouse as a sure point of departure from our compass course on the long crossing to Portland.

Kenneth Roberts once wrote a story of shipwrecked mariners starving on Boon Island. From his home on a hilltop near Kennebunk he could see the island far out to sea. In his later years when he was writing *Oliver Wiswell* and *Lydia Bailey,* he looked at the distant light first thing in the morning and last thing at night. "It's good for the courage," he said. As for me, it was good for my courage when we put it behind us on a course of fifty-one degrees for Portland Lightship and were no longer in any danger of striking those off-lying ledges.

The straight pencil line on the chart looked fine and direct. I wondered how we would fare, since this was the longest ocean crossing we had made. Visibility was becoming poor, the wind fickle, and the sea so rough that in the faint breeze the sail slatted unmercifully. I took down the main after a while to keep the boom from thrashing around, and then put up a bigger jib. The jib slats less violently, having no boom to bang and snap around. Sometimes nothing would draw, the breeze went so light. The lumped-up sea popped into pyramids and threw us about as though in a storm. Mount Agamenticus, that blue hump mariners first see on the horizon as they approach the coast of southern Maine, faded out, and all the shore with it. I started the outboard, for we had a long way to go. Our first six-gallon tank soon went empty because we couldn't get it filled at Isles of Shoals. So I shifted to the second. The day seemed gloomy as the fog drew close around us.

Kneeling on the cabin floor between the reeling bunks, I got to work with the radio direction finder, headphones on and watch in hand. Portland Lightship is a powerful beacon station, and we were homing on it. If ever the fine new British radio direction set was going to earn its keep, this would be the day. Sure enough, the signal came loud and clear, on one minute, then off six minutes, then on again for that all-too-brief minute. A couple of those periods are spent tuning the set, then a couple more searching for the most accurate null. By then twenty-four minutes had slipped away. I could pinpoint it within about five degrees, which is as good as I usually do. The pitching and rolling accounted for perhaps another five degrees of guesswork. Pretty good for me. The null seemed to show at forty instead of the fifty-one degrees ideally drawn on the chart. Some books say a side-on current plagues navigators in this great bight between Portsmouth and Portland. I decided, therefore, to alter course ten degrees to port and told my mate, "Steer forty." I kept trying and checking at the six-minute intervals, and that seemed about right, so I went on deck and put up the mains'l, then hauled it down again. If we'd only had a decent breeze, it would have steadied us and speeded us on our way. Where, I wondered, were those famous southwesterlies that always waft the Boston Brahmins Down East on summer afternoons in their Alden yawls?

There was no sign of anything now in this pea-soup fog. All we had, perhaps twenty miles from land, were the compass, the radio direction finder, and the faithful little outboard motor. I went forward and put up the big genny, leaving the No. 2 lashed to the bow rail. As a safeguard against being pitched overboard I was now using my safety harness, clipping it to the mooring cleat.

To cheer ourselves we would have lunch. I took the tiller while Kay sat on the cabin sole between the bunks and prepared the grub in her usual miraculous fashion. It was extremely difficult, I could see. She laughed and groaned, "The side of the cabin house just came down and hit me on the head." It was a solid thump, too; I could hear it. The plates slid, the coffee slopped from side to side of the mug, but it was the usual good lunch, delicious, crisp salad with cabbage, onion, tuna fish, and Italian dressing, peanut butter crackers, pickles, canned fruit, cookies. As soon as the meal was cleared away, I went to work on the RDF again. I wished we had more gasoline for such a long crossing. Half the second tank was gone. It was going to be touch and go, with the wind failing us this way. According to my figuring, at four and a half miles per hour we'd scarcely arrive at the lightship before four-thirty.

As always, I had great confidence in the boat. It didn't leak, it was strong, a wind would come sometime. Suppose we missed the lightship, we'd be offshore for the night, so what? I was determined that in a bad jam we'd follow the experienced cruising precept, which is to stay well out to sea clear of dangers in a confused time. "When in doubt, stay out." Trying to make harbor in fog and storm is what wrecks boats and does people in.

So we churned along through the obscurity, getting a little help now from the genoa. The sharp dot-dash of the beacon signal was again ten degrees off our course. It was worrisome, and furthermore I'm not accustomed to finding my way by my ears, headphones on, beeps blasting my eardrums, the hand-bearing compass held as still as possible, this compass-aerial turned to that elusive "null." Where is it, that lowest tone, that least sound?

There was nothing to do but to alter, so we shifted ten degrees again to the left. Why should we be so far off our original course? One never knows. I wondered for the millionth time whether our compass had some ghastly error, and I laughed at myself, too, since the classic boner of the landlubber lost in fog is to mistrust his compass. This compass and I were old friends, well tested on many a critical sail, and if I couldn't trust it now, what could I trust? We had altered course a full twenty degrees since we'd left Boon Island; there must be a current shoving us sidewise. At this rate, we were proceeding in a crescent rather than a straight line.

As we rolled on in the obscurity, I told myself this was what we came for, to really manage, to learn, to experience. Just the same, the tossing was getting oppressive. I didn't have sense enough to go down in the cabin and have a nap. You've got to take turns resting, that's all there is to it. But we hadn't yet reached that milestone in our nautical development. We were still in the transition stage, locked in the reflex cramp, believing that in a difficult time maximum worry brings maximum results, though nothing could be more idiotic.

I kept looking at my watch. According to my timing we had run our distance down. Our fuel wasn't going to last much longer. I throttled way down, to listen for the lightship horn, but could hear nothing, so turned it off entirely. Still nothing. Perhaps we had passed it and were getting a backward bearing on the RDF. Stranger things have happened. I had a look at the gas tank. We should save a little for coming into harbor, for emergency if about to be run down by a steamer.

"It must be quite a powerful horn," I said to Kay. "Portland is a big seaport. You can always count on it that the aids to navigation are much bigger and better in harbors used by oceangoing ships."

The RDF showed us to be right on course. We cranked up and motored on. It was so thick now you could hardly see fifty feet. The sail dripped, slicing through a curtain of moisture, and to make everything worse daylight was fading. I decided I mustn't worry, which is always a sign that things are getting critical. We turned off the motor to listen again, tossing there in the gloom, ears strained, mouth half open.

WAW-W!—a gigantic bellow, right dead ahead. We couldn't see it but it was there. We had found it, far out in the ocean, at the end of thirty miles and six hours of seeing nothing. We had managed it, on our own, a really difficult crossing, for the first time, in fog.

Motoring on, we made out a shadow, the lightship, red, plunging on her anchor chain in the chop. And on its side in huge white letters, instead of the PORTLAND LIGHTSHIP we had expected, it said, appropriately, RELIEF.

Her mast was a turretlike tower surmounted by a powerful circular light. As usual, nobody aboard was visible, that being the way of ships. We meant nothing to her, though she meant so much to us. We skirted her, pretty far away because it was rough and the waves were slamming us around. The harbor was still eight miles away, and we were planning to get the lightship dead astern as a new point of departure on a compass course for the harbor bellbuoy.

Suddenly out of nowhere loomed a giant Esso tanker. She was bound in, too, just taking on a pilot. She must have been eight hundred feet long if she was an inch.

The monster headed right for us, accelerating as soon as the pilot was safely aboard. A bass blast, BAHP! like the voice of a mechanical bull, jumped from her stack and scared us. "He is blowing one,"

I told my mate, recalling Power Squadron piloting classes. "That means, you see, he's going to put his port side to us. We, being the overtaken vessel, as well as a sailing ship, have the right-of-way. However, it takes him three miles to stop."

BAH-H-P right in the middle of my know-it-all explanation came the hideous blare again. Did he mean to run us down on purpose? It looked that way. How could he put his port side to us without a wide turn? It mystified me, so I jibed over and went way off course to get as far away from him as possible. That's all a little sailboat can do about ships. It's absurd to think they will budge one inch for you.

As changeless as the ticking hours, he held his course, his overpowering bulk sliding by on our left, his starboard side to us, and when he had passed, he blew again. Then and only then it occurred to me he wasn't blowing for us at all. "It's his fog signal!" I shouted. "How stupid can I get?"

He was on our course, naturally, being bound for the same place. He disappeared in the thick fog, and after a while we saw our bell dead ahead. Of course it was dead ahead; why shouldn't it be? Hadn't we come thirty miles and found our marker despite an unpredictable side current? If we could do that, I reckoned we could find a little old harbor buoy.

But I hadn't allowed for our nemesis, the tanker. As we went up the harbor, from buoy to buoy, always on compass course, groping in visibility of less than fifty yards, we came upon her again, anchored in an offshoot cove of the channel. Her pilot must have thought it was too thick, or maybe they were waiting for an inner harbor oil dock to be cleared. Or maybe they were waiting for us. Whatever the reason, she upped her anchor and started after us. She soon caught us and shouldered us away over onto the starboard side of the channel. Once there, it was pleasant to know we were in twelve feet of water, where she couldn't follow because I knew by her Plimsoll mark, which I had seen all too close, that she was drawing thirty-eight. I was so sick of the tanker by this time I hoped the pilot would ram her into the mud. To look at her bow-on was an amazing sight, broad, squat, like a crocodile's face.

We later discovered that Portland is an important oil port with six overland pipelines to Montreal, built so that ships can bypass the stormy Gulf of St. Lawrence and its winter ice. A tanker comes to Portland almost every day, we were told, from Venezuelan oil ports or around the Cape of Good Hope from the Persian Gulf, and they are big ones.

Inch by inch we crept across the chart up the great natural harbor of Portland, which I had never seen but always dreamed of entering from the sea some sunny day when the spruces were green and the ocean blue and all the islands of Casco Bay spread out like cookies on a platter. We were thinking, as we have a thousand times, how wonderful the Coast and Geodetic Survey is to make such unbelievably accurate charts. You can put a ruler on a chart and find the distance scale is accurate to a hair's breadth, and the ranges are right and the buoys and lights and landforms and symbols. Rocks awash at low tide are distinguished from ledges that remain submerged at low water. Here we were, complete strangers, surrounded by rocks where the ocean swell was surging, unable to see them, unable to see anything except an occasional nun or can, but because of our chart we knew exactly what the harbor was like, where the channel lay, where the dangers were, and we could draw off the compass courses we must follow from one invisible marker to the next. And then, as though by magic, the dim shape of the buoy appeared, rocking on its mooring chain, dripping fog, nodding like some friendly lunatic in the mist.

Suddenly, halfway up the sky above us blazed a light. It would be Portland Head Light—no cliff, no buildings, just the bright yellow eye hung in the fog. The day was fading completely now, getting dark, visibility approaching zero. We were sailing as well as motoring, thinking the gas would give out any minute, and at length found ourselves among a collection of moored boats. The silent craft reminded me of dark mourners at a graveside in the rain.

The chart indicated a ferry landing. This must be Peaks Island, directly across the harbor from the city. In this quiet, well-protected haven, our boat one ghost among other apparitions, we dropped our hook, furled our sails, and went below with a sigh.

Because we couldn't see the shore, I had a feeling we didn't know where we were. But the fifteen-foot depth corresponded with the chart, and we had glimpsed the end of the ferry pier. To confirm, one of the little Portland Harbor ferries soon chugged in and out again, for all the world like a city bus, loaded with teenagers going to the movies. We had one cupful of gasoline left in the tank.

Very tired, we sipped our bourbon. Rain pattered on the deck to emphasize our cozy warmth, the stove going, the gimbal lamp gleaming yellow. We couldn't have made it without Kay's ability and grit. She'd steered for hours while I was below with the radio direction finder. But for the RDF we'd be out there still, looking for the lightship, and we might not find it for a week.

Somehow Kay still had strength to prepare supper of clam chowder, followed by canned beef stew marvelously "reinforced"

with celery, carrots, onions, Worcestershire, and brown gravy, con-
cluding with fragrant coffee. More than fifty miles we had come, our
ruggedest day to date, and our most successful piloting venture so
far. We looked at each other and said, "We did it, we did it! We're
getting to be real cruisers at last."

A tanker moored in the roadstead was giving periodic blasts
on her earthshaking whistle, afraid she'd be run down. Far away,
other ships seemed to answer. Bells rang, too, the traditional fog
signal of ships at anchor. We were part of all this, a real part. I
remembered the first time we'd gotten caught in fog, three years
ago, in a chartered boat. Her compass was no good; its needle
went around and around every time we started the motor; we
had no radio direction finder, and didn't know how to use one
anyhow. Not even a lead line. We were panic-stricken and ill-
equipped to cope as we crept along a rocky shore. But today was
different. To an old salt it would be nothing, but to us this finding the lightship and the harbor was victory, victory over ourselves mostly.

"Perhaps we won't be so scared of fog another time," I said. She
answered with a special smile.

The diaphone on Portland Head kept blasting out its singing,
deep, two-tone chord. A great happiness filled my heart as I rolled
into my bunk and slept, quiet in the ferry cove of Peaks Island,
Casco Bay, Maine.

In the morning the fog parted sufficiently to reveal a row of cottages and large wooden dwellings on a bluff above us. Some of them
even had Victorian gingerbread fretwork around their porches. In
the other direction we looked out across the harbor, where two

tankers were at dockside and another in Diamond Island Roads against a background of the city's tall buildings. Then the rain and gray curtains closed about us once more.

We didn't care. We were happy to stay at anchor, resting, reading our books, while the rain drummed on the cabintop. Squalls blew up, too, with a wind that lashed us not very playfully. We could look through the Plexiglas companion hatch and see sheets of water bouncing off it. I thought how fine to have a tight deck, not one single drop coming through the portholes or anywhere. We lit up the pressure mantle lamp, which burns kerosene and gives a fine lot of heat as well as light, swinging from its hook near the head of the bunks.

About noon the rain slacked off. I heard a bumping nearby and went out on deck. We had put our anchor down among the usual collection of lobster pot buoys, there being no clear space, and here was an old man pulling his pots from around our anchor rode. He was smoking a cigar, sitting in a battered square-ended punt. It had no paint, but many deep gouges. A board on end had been nailed against the side to patch the gunwale, and this patch itself was almost sawn in half by the friction of ten thousand pot warps. The punt was a quarter full of water, but its occupant had on a good pair of rubber boots. These were in glaring contrast to his blackened, ragged oilskin pants.

"I hope I didn't foul you up too badly," I said, forgetting that unnecessary verbiage is out of place in Maine.

He puffed his cigar and made no reference to my wordiness. "Come from the westward?"

"Yes, from the Isles of Shoals yesterday."

"Hm-m." He thought about this for a while.

"We come here fifteen years ago," he told me. "A hard bunch in harbor. They stole twelve of my traps. Couldn't buy stock last winter. Only got a hundred left."

The cigar smoke smelled fragrant in the wet air. He seemed contented and competent.

"Lobsters scarce here," he went on. "Higgin Island we had closed season all summer. Plenty there. One first haul I got fifteen hundred pounds."

"Oh," I said. "I have read that they have a closed season in Monhegan Island, too, and it seems a good idea."

"That's what I'm tell' ye, M'nhiggin Island, that's the place."

"Didn't it almost kill you, the cold, hauling pots in winter?"

"You get used to it. I been lobsterin' since I was fifteen and I'm seventy-six now." He went on baiting his traps with old fish, rapidly, expertly, hardly looking. Then, almost as an afterthought, he looked up from his broken-down punt. "Where's your home port?"

"We've come from South Carolina."

He chewed on this, working meanwhile. His lobster pots were hitched together even here in the harbor, in the Maine fashion, four pots to one buoy. Fishermen frequently have more than that tied together. His pots looked dreadfully old, his oars worn thin, his lines frayed, his boat almost as ancient as himself. Yet somehow he seemed to have won a victory over time, wet, cold, poverty, toil. Maybe it was his courage. As he hauled his traps closest to where our anchor lay buried in the bottom, he was thinking about our voyage along the coast. "I got as far south as Block Island," he said. "With the mackerel seiners I was."

He picked up his paper-thin oars and rowed away. Like so many magnificent human beings we encounter on our travels, he vanished and we will never see him again. I hope when I'm his age I'll have his stamina and backbone.

We decided we must stir our stumps despite the rain, and go ashore and get some gasoline and groceries. So we tied a float on our anchor line, cranked up, and went off with our last cupful for a gas dock near the ferry landing. Here again was the Maine fortitude, this time in youth. No sooner did we creep in to the float than down came the rain. The dock boy was about fourteen. He had no foul-weather gear, only a shirt and pants, no hat. He helped me with my two six-gallon tanks, pint of oil in each, paying no attention to the rain, which was running off his hair and down his neck. "That's a nice boat," he said, flashing his white teeth.

The little house on the dock had obviously been the pilothouse on some defunct dragger. I paid my bill and pressed half a dollar into his hand, saying, "Here's something for you." He looked at it dubiously. Had I done the wrong thing? But it was all right; he flashed his rain-drenched smile at me, and I felt I must be okay even if I am rich.

"I'd like to fill my five-gallon water can."

There was no hose on the dock, but his little brother, Harold, led me up a long gangway to a faucet in back of their dwelling house. Battered trucks stood here and there. Apparently the boys ran the gas dock while father labored at other jobs. Harold was an appealing kid, with brown eyes and a friendly air. About eight years old, he hungered to be a man, working and useful. He wanted to carry the forty-pound jug down the slippery gangway, but I couldn't let him. He wore a hand-knit red sweater with white stripes, which caused me to remark, "Your ma won't like that sweater's getting soaked."

"Twunt be the first time," Harold replied. When Kay appeared from the grocery store with a disintegrating brown paper bag, he ran to take it from her. He stood by our lines, waiting, dripping, imperturbable. When we had stowed and got the motor going, he cast us off, bow line first, just right, stern line last because it was blowing hard from astern. "Have a good trip," he said, putting his hands in his dripping pockets and strolling away.

And the rain came down and the rain came down, as we lay at anchor all that night and half the next day, till by and by the books began to pall. So we hoisted sail and roared over to a place called Diamond Island in gusts and heavy squalls.

We were bound for a marina described in the *Cruising Guide* as belonging to Ted Rand. It didn't seem to be much of a marina, having no sign, but we tied up to long floats anyway, and lay there in the chop. We were told it would be one dollar a night. The water was too shoal for us to lie inside the floats, so I put out a kedge to hold us off from banging.

It was a Sunday afternoon. Rand's three boys came skylarking down to the float and set off to fish from a rowboat in the cold rain. Rand himself, a pleasant, hardy man, wearing a soaked sweater and no hat, pumped gas for several lobster boats that chugged in. We decided these were hardy people, and no mistake. An Italian couple were aboard a motor cruiser nearby, with three black-haired little children, and they also slopped around in the rain quite unconcernedly. It developed that they ran a restaurant in Portland and were just here for the weekend, friends of the Rands. We were quite happy reading, snug in our cabin, keeping our clothes dry, since almost everything we owned was wet already and we didn't want to saturate the last dry garments. But our little boat tugged heartstrings as usual, and about four-thirty of that dismal afternoon along came Rand, chipper and hearty, knocked on the cabin and said, "We're having a few people up to the house for supper and we want you to come."

We demurred, told him we were about to cook up some hash and have a drink and that we were just fine. But he wouldn't take no. "You've got to come, you've been cooped up on the little boat all afternoon in the rain and my wife says if I can't get you to come up she'll be down on the wharf and make you."

So that was how we came to have a lobster supper with the Rands. There were five couples of summer cottagers present, each person interesting in his way. Rand, we discovered, is a graduate engineer who has taken up lobster fishing instead of engineering, because he likes it better. The house is an abandoned Coast Guard station he bought just after the war. One of the guests ran an oil dock in Portland Harbor. Another was a bright young fellow who had just sailed a trimaran up from the Caribbean to Maine. He seemed an experienced navigator, and told of a gale they had encountered, with winds of nearly seventy knots. It got so bad the owner of the trimaran came to him and asked whether they should radio the Coast Guard. Our newfound friend advised that in the storm the Coast Guard could scarcely be expected to find them, and even if it did, what could the CG cutter do for the plunging tri? They survived okay and the advice was good. Like most trimaran enthusiasts he believed that a steamer must have run down Arthur River, lost at sea, the famous builder, designer, and world's greatest advocate of trimarans. On the other hand, trimarans have had so many breakdowns at sea that some people dislike them for ocean crossings. As with other sailor arguments, it is an endless source of controversy, never silly because it involves survival. Since then Eric Tabarly, the redoubtable French naval officer, has proved in the Atlantic and the Pacific that trimarans can be as tough as anything else.

The boys came and went with plates, the women laughed and chatted in the kitchen, and there was a boiled lobster for each person, or two or three if desired, plus mountains of additional Maine fare such as golden bantam corn. We had a wonderful time. They could hardly believe we had come so far in such a little boat, but we tried to soft-pedal that subject, having covered it so many times to so many people already. The men got to discussing civic matters, especially plans to make Portland a "great" oil port, with more tanker docks and a huge array of tank farms on harbor islands. Most of the men were opposed, on the grounds that such developments hire comparatively few people, bring little revenue to the city, demand much of city services, and ruin the vacationland business of this picturesque coast. I had supposed that Maine, which is obviously so poor, so in need of new industries, would welcome anything. They spoke of Machiasport, with its eighty-foot depths right up the harbor, as being under study by oil engineers and oil magnates. They were opposed to that, too, and seemed to have no fear that Gulf, Socony, American, Atlantic-Richfield, or anybody else could pressure Maine into doing anything it didn't want to.

I was ashamed to think I had forgotten what rock-ribbed, sterling characters Maine-ites, are, people who put many values ahead of money. Rand, it turned out, was a member of the Portland mayor's committee appointed to report on pros and cons of more tank farms in Portland Harbor. When it came time for us to leave we felt very much in Rand's debt. The party, what with children and second helpings, must have accounted for at least twenty-four lobsters, and lobster is a dollar a pound or more. "Oh, that's nothing," said Rand. "When you're a lobsterman you get a lot of odd ones with one claw and such that won't sell, so we save them for a do like this."

One couple decided they must go with us down the long boardwalks to the glistening dock and climb aboard in the rain and sit in the cabin dripping sociably to see our staunch little cruiser. They liked our boat so much they wished they had one like it. We were ever so grateful to them that they could share our enthusiasm and not ask, "Where's the toilet?"

Next day, still in the rain, we went walking on Little Diamond Island along leafy lanes among wide-spaced cottages. The land smells were so fragrant, wild mint in the dewy grass, balsam, clover, violets, we felt as though we were wandering in some luscious fairyland. Having come to the dead-end ferry landing and been thus reminded this was an island, and not a very big one, we turned the other way and came to crumbling pine-plank walks beside the road, then massive open gates and a high fence of chain link enclosing an impressive property. Inside, expecting to encounter a château, we soon came upon weedy tennis courts, fields, baseball diamonds, swings, playgrounds, and several large, gray-shingled buildings looking like abandoned hotels. Two black-habited nuns who were standing on a porch beckoned to us to come in out of the rain.

They were Sister Mary Amata and Sister Mary Teresa. This had formerly been a Catholic summer camp for children, and for the children's families, too, if they wished to come. "But now," said Sister Mary Amata sadly, "institutional care is looked down upon by everyone, and the children are farmed out to various families one by one."

"Will they be as well taken care of as here?" we asked.

"We do not inquire about that," said Sister Mary Teresa with demurely downcast eyes. "But we miss the children. They seemed happy, and they made us glad."

The sisters learned we were off a boat, a sailboat, and were overjoyed. They were starved for someone new to talk to, and did not want us to leave. They themselves were here on their yearly ten-day vacation from teaching work at schools. "Some of us are nurses. Come, you must meet the other sisters."

They led us to an adjoining building, where three more smiling nuns were busy in a big old-fashioned kitchen complete with wood range and newly baked bread. They plied us with slices of the crisp, warm loaves and blackberry jam; they gave us fruit, and baked beans that were homemade. They wanted to know about the boat and where we had come from and where we were going. They were overjoyed to find that Kay was a nurse, too, and that I had once been a teacher. They told us of their work and of the books they were reading.

The rain continued falling in silver curtains, making their kitchen seem warm and secure. The oldest of them, Sister Mary Lucille, was the liveliest, with bright blue eyes and a ready laugh. She gathered us around her in a corner, where she sat with the conspiratorial air of a born raconteur and told us that she had been sailing once. When she was a senior in high school, the father of her best friend owned a big schooner, and she had been invited to sail with them all the way to New York City. They carried a cargo of lumber, and when they arrived, they anchored in Jamaica Bay and she went ashore in the ship's boat. "It was the finest trip I ever had," she told us, with her eyes shining. That eventful voyage had taken place in her eighteenth year, and she was now seventy. The rest of them listened respectfully, though I felt sure they had heard about it many times before.

They talked and talked, making every second of this brief visit count. "Where do you sleep? What do you eat?"

We countered with, "What do you teach? Where do you nurse?"

We couldn't drink any more coffee or eat any more of the delicious bread and baked beans no matter how we tried. We donned our oilskins again and started making our departure. They fixed up some of the New England baked beans for us to take in a jar, and wrapped half a loaf of the new bread to press upon Kay. They came out into the rain with us and exchanged addresses and asked us to write (which we did).

They were so hopeful in their hopelessness, so strong in their weakness, so friendly in their loneliness, we left them with a mixture of regret and gladness. It seemed to us we had so much, and they had so little. Not being devout, we were unable to understand. Imagine, we said, their being denied even the children they love to care for! Aren't private summer camps "institutional"? A kid doesn't care what you call it so long as he can play on a sandy ocean beach in the summer and get wet. Do the much-vaunted private homes provide beaches, tennis courts, baseball fields?

The sisters stirred tragic contradictions within us, as perhaps we may have within them. I wished I could take all those jolly nuns sailing, not for a day or a week, but for three months so they could really get the feel of it. They have made their choice, I said to myself, a very different choice from ours. And yet it seems as though the development of these intelligent and capable women had been arrested in some ways at an early age. I decided they have a different freedom from ours; at least they are free from the continual necessity of making important decisions. I had to remind myself that we dumb men make a great mistake when we get to sorrowing over the pitiful females of this world, whether they be unselfish sisters or ardent feminists, for in reality the "frail" creatures outlast us ten to one.

# CHAPTER XIV

# CASCO BAY

WE THOUGHT WE HAD TO SEE EVERYTHING in Maine. First of all, it was necessary to poke into Falmouth Foreside, very carefully, studying the chart as always, to avoid knocking our keel on a rock. There we had a look at Handy's Boatyard, and next was South Freeport, past tiny Cup o' Tea Island, entering to port of it via the main channel, though we saw a local boat cutting inside to starboard. It looked like a well-protected harbor, much better than Falmouth Foreside.

The day being yet young, quite clear and no fog, we made for Jewel Island Harbor. The entrance is tricky, not far from West Brown Cow. This latter is a reminder that almost every man along the Maine coast in the old days was a farmer as well as a fisherman, and thus the prevalence of such agricultural terms as Bull and Pig, Haystack, Horse, and so forth, for harbors and islands.

In Jewel Island the chart showed a good harbor between a point and a nearby small island. We anchored there and went ashore looking for the Punchbowl, which the *Cruising Guide* describes as a rock basin at just the right elevation to fill at high tide and be somewhat warmed by the sun as the sea recedes at low water. Sure enough, at half tide when we were there, its water was slightly warmer than the ice-cold sea, so we had a swim. It takes quite a while to get accustomed to Maine's chilly water, but people do, and some hardy souls will swim and float and bathe in it for twenty minutes, though it turns a newcomer's ankles blue.

We walked on a path to an abandoned Coast Guard station, relic of World War II, and thought how blessed that those tragic days are gone, and how blessed also to be stretching our legs on a real Maine island of rocks and ledges, grass, juniper, wild roses, cool breeze, and even a little beach.

Next day we went out across Casco Bay, with its hundreds of islands, to the tip of Whaleboat Island, where the light breeze faded and left us drifting. A place there is so steep-to that a keel boat can lie alongside the rock at high water. Two lobstermen in a powerful thirty-five-footer were hauling pots with a swing and a swish, long-practiced partners, or perhaps co-owners of this well-equipped boat. One man handled the wheel while the other baited. But as soon as the screw quit churning, the wheelman helped with the winch and the pots, while the other stacked pots aft. Then away with a rush, yanking strings of six or eight off the stern deck as though they were half-pint baskets. We wondered how many traps they could tend in a day. In any case, they hauled twenty-six while we were watching.

Motoring along Broad Sound, we went through the narrow passage between the nun and can off a point of Haskell Island and made for the triangular monument on Little Mark Island. Being seventy-four feet high, it stands out prominently.

In the afternoon we motored up the New Meadows River to anchor in "the Basin" at sunset, a lovely saltwater lake inside a tidal pass so narrow you wouldn't know it was there unless you had a chart or local knowledge. I remember Alfred Loomis speaks of it as one of his favorite anchorages in *Ranging the Maine Coast.*

Somehow we felt that having reached Maine we didn't have to hurry anymore. As a result, we loitered in the Casco Bay area a little longer, reaching only its farther limit, at Small Point, next day.

As we neared the point we saw its jolly-looking campground, with trailers and tents here and there among the spruces, and children playing on the sand beaches between miniature rock headlands.

I had noted on the chart that going in toward the narrow harbor in the base of the point we would pass a submerged ledge on our port hand. Since it had six feet of water over it, that shouldn't bother our three-and-a-half-foot draft. Just the same, I kept well away from it, and that was a blessing, for here on the open ocean shore as we drew abreast of the ledge and about four boat lengths off, a great swell reared over the rock and broke with a fearsome roar. It gave me the shivers, and made me remember an enormous swell I'd once seen curl and break over a rock pinnacle that was thirty feet under. When a big sea is running, you need lots of water.

Rocks, rocks, everywhere. Just off the harbor was a little rocky island with a basin in it. And then we were through the opening and into the Small Point anchorage, putting the anchor down among seaweedy rocks, a strong tidal current, three moored lobster boats, and a summer folks' outboard. Up above us on the rocks stood an old wooden hotel, in poor repair like so many old ones. Some men seemed to be fixing it, but they soon left, and after that we didn't see a soul. I was going to row over to a tiny beach and have a swim, but it looked awfully cold. And now at dusk the mosquitoes came, which necessitated the cockpit netting, and then we had our evening drink. So that settled that. For supper we had a splendid corned beef hash and lima beans, with nuts and raisins for dessert. The tide ran strongly, then turned and ran strongly the other way. Our anchor rode trembled in the black, silent current. We slept quietly, here at the edge of the sea, where far outside, the horn on Seguin was booming.

In the morning, needing bread, I cranked up the outboard and poked cautiously farther in through a veritable hole-in-the-wall to a small gas-dock float where I could see the bottom right under our keel, and some shells and rusty cans. The clear water was flooding fast, so we didn't worry about the close-up bottom. A long flight of slimy steps led to a little grocery store perched far above. "You have to carry everything up or down," a boy in an outboard informed us.

The store was run by a pleasant, hardworking woman in a pretty print dress who told us her husband had been killed in World War II. She had never been in a sailboat, she said. By the door, bolt upright, sat a big, gaunt woman like a grenadier, noting everything that happened, every word spoken. She made me think of Madame Defarge in *A Tale of Two Cities*. She was the mother-in-law. Suddenly she started asking about our travels, smiled at Kay, and opened up to tell Kay about herself, beaming as we left, and saying good-bye like a long-lost sister. Of all grocery stores by the sea that was the quaintest, stuck up on poles wedged into rocks, fish barrels occupying the high stage, pulley-block hoist, gas pump practically hanging over the water, seaweed rocks right near the door. Here was the smell of sea and lobster and fish and boats, mixed with the old-time grocery store odors of beans and cheese, kerosene, onions, and rope, a store where some newsy conversation would surely salt the transaction.

We picked our way from handhold to handhold down the steep, slippery steps with our bundles. At the bottom, in his boat, crouched the boy, wrestling with his outboard. He was jolly and plump, about fourteen, with pink cheeks, but something of a man about him already. He was taking his motor apart, slapping it together again, cranking, removing the flywheel once more, and occasionally whistling. I could see he knew quite a lot about outboards.

"Yes," he told me, "I've busted three of 'em this summer. I got 150 lobster traps, you know, and that's hard on motors. I'm hard on 'em too. I make 'em work!"

I thought to myself, Is there a male on this coast who doesn't lobster?

He was cranking, cranking, with admirable stamina, fiddling, yanking the rope. The motor gave a cough, almost went, and then died, as so often happens. He took off the flywheel again and seized his wrenches. A schoolgirl came halfway down the steps, an obvious contemporary.

"What's the matter, Howard?" she fluttered.

"Twunt go. Can't you see?" He began to jerk the cord even faster.

"I bet you'll be able to fix it, Howard." She smiled at him in motherly fashion and preened, fixing her hair.

"The damn thing's sick," he tossed up to her.

"Maybe it's got influenza," she said.

"Maybe it's got the pip. I'll take it to the doctor in Bath this afternoon if it don't get better."

"He'll fix it for you, Howard, I know he will," she said, dancing up the steps.

Howard wiped his greasy hands and watched her go, with a serious expression, as though priding himself on his ability to cope with her wiles. Gulls were wheeling, seaweed fronds streaming in the tide rush, high rocks all about this saltwater pool.

"You seem to know quite a lot about outboards," I ventured.

"Some," he replied.

I told him about mine, started it, showed him how it stuttered and staggered. He knew immediately. "Why! You need new spark plugs. That's all! They get fouled up."

Sure enough, when I climbed up to that wonderful grocery store they had outboard spark plugs, of course. When I put one in, my motor ticked like a clock; it throttled way down or sprang to life with a roar. It never missed a beat, and it pulled like sixteen horses.

"Thanks, Howard."

"Twant nuthin'."

To be put right so quickly by a fourteen-year-old boy is a chastening experience. We motored away from the fabulous grocery store and its rock pool, over the smooth waters of Casco Bay in a calm. I wondered whether I'd ever catch up with Howard in the field of mechanical expertise. Blessings on you, Lobster Boy! Long may you wave.

We didn't go far. Casco Bay was calm, and we wanted to have a look at the Small Point vacation campground and walk along its tangle of sandy tracks that twisted among clumps of spruces. Something about cruising lends itself to walking. The change, or just the chance to keep one's legs from atrophying, make climbing little mountains or following paths through the woods a pure joy.

A jolly place the campground proved to be, with many tents and some recreation vehicles as well as modified pickups, each in its sequestered spot out of sight from others, some by the shore, some in the trees. Nearly all the families were from Boston or the vicinity, most of them with children. They were paying a weekly rent for each camp spot with its table and fireplace.

Out toward the end of the point the swimming beaches were populated by elders who were sunbathing while their children romped in the surf edge undaunted by a chilly wind and the cold water.

Kids! We saw a little drama here.

A safari was arriving, Ma and Pa in the family sedan bulging with umbrellas, tents, bedding, blankets, cots, pails, gasoline stove, a cat, and children. They had almost as much gear as we have. And of course, the very first thing, little Jennifer must get acquainted with the ocean, which she has never seen before. Little Jennifer, a blue-eyed, flaxen-haired mite, is so tiny and wispy you'd expect the sea breeze to blow her away. Here she is, pattering her microscopic feet down over the wet sand to the lace edge of foam not far from the thundering breakers, and o-o-o are they big! Her diminutive skirt flutters in the wind as she inspects this blueness as far as she can see, to the end of the world. One toe in it is all she wants at first sight, and then back to Mamma. Meanwhile Pa is busy clapping a two-foot life preserver on one-and-a-half-foot Junior as though Junior were going to swim out over the horizon.

Some of them at the edge of the ocean for the first time are afraid. They hunker down on their little haunches in the sand and glare at the monstrous ocean with a species of hatred. As soon as Ma is gone, such a little one will often turn and run for the camp. But others with a joyful frenzy advance right into the surf and get tumbled flat and come up laughing and get tumbled again and have to be pulled out by an irate parent, still laughing. Most of them don't react in any such ways; they advance and retreat, daring a little more as they learn, being afraid, being brave, trying it out, all their senses a-stretch, even as Kay and I are, wishing to dare, to savor more adventures.

One father plucked his spluttering offspring out of the waves and carried him up the beach. "He didn't know I was watching him," he said, "but I was. Carefully supervised neglect, that's the system."

# CHAPTER XV

# DAMARISCOTTA, SHEEPSCOT, AND KENNEBEC RIVERS

# SOUTH BRISTOL HARBOR, CHRISTMAS COVE

# MUSCONGOUS BAY

# PENOBSCOT BAY AND APPROACHES

COMING INTO BOOTHBAY HARBOR we were beating against the breeze—as so often happened to us—past Squirrel Island, where we furled the sails and motored the last stretch. Boothbay Harbor's roughly circular basin was crowded with yachts and fishing boats, mostly yachts, all its shores lined with commercial establishments, wharves, motels, pilings, floats. Here was a bustling, very civilized place. We threaded our way slowly among the anchored craft to a Boatel at the head of the harbor, where we took a mooring for five

153

dollars a night. They had a little restaurant, and showers—which were fifty cents extra.

Tourists, cars, buses, bicycles, motorbikes, baby carriages, gift shoppes, postcards, popcorn, food shops, hardware stores, beach clothing—all the paraphernalia of a resort were here. Two grocery stores existed, one by the water quite expensive, another, a super-market a mile or so away. Carrying our canvas tote bags, we chose the supermarket, though it was a hot day and lugging all our needed supplies was no joke. Kay loaded up mainly on fresh salad stuff such as lettuce, celery, parsley, peppers, chives, and broccoli, all heavy. We didn't mind any of it, checking groceries through the cashier aisles, jostling throngs along the sidewalks, because all the old boring procedures were quite different for sailors ashore in a new harbor. We did not feel like tourists. Odd as it may seem, we felt quite proud and changed from our at-home selves, to have come here, not by car, or bus, or plane, not by somebody else's doings, but under our own steam in our little boat and mostly via the wind. It seemed as though we had a proud and secret identity, walking along with our heavy bags while the cars whizzed by. Nobody needed to know about it, only ourselves.

After stowing our supplies, what a pleasure to sit in the cock-pit, the dinghy bobbing astern, a glass of beer in hand, watching the bustle ashore and on the water.

Next morning we rowed around the harbor in Rubadub. An Alden schooner was on a mooring, and a St. Pierre dory, about thirty feet, with cabin, at anchor, belonging to an elderly couple who told us they had never been to either St. Pierre or Miquelon, but that the boat was very comfortable. With her cocked-up sheer, bow, and stern, she looked like a good sea boat—but sadly, no mast or sail.

Among yachts swinging on the sparkling chop was a twenty-five-foot sloop with Ma, Pa, and four children. Dinghies propelled by out-boards buzzed here and there, hardly anyone rowing except us. We have seven-foot spruce oars, and I like to row, though the Avon inflatable is tubby and has little "run." On the far side stood a boat-building shop where a man on a little pier was working. Right away he spoke to us, saying, "That's a Carinita isn't it, a Rudder design? I saw you come in yesterday." At his mooring rocked a neat little Sam Crocker raised-deck sloop painted green and red. "She's got a lot of room in her for her size," he told us. "Crocker was a master hand at the raised-deck design, to keep them functional and not boxy look-ing. She goes to windward well, too." This was Roy Blaney. He took us up to his boat shop, where he was building a thirty-foot sloop on order, half planked at this stage, and a beautiful job, done with the skill of a real craftsman. "Takes me about a year," he said. Beside his boat shed was a small stony beach. "The only place left in the whole harbor where a fisherman can haul out to caulk a seam or fix his leaky stuffing box between tides." He had a guest mooring of his own that he invited us to take, and we did. It was a joy to be able to come and go as we pleased, leaving the dink at his float.

I went for a walk along a winding road and came to a big hotel filled with people in colorful clothes who were playing tennis, sit-ting about, even playing croquet. I went up onto the extensive porches and sat in a rocking chair, wondering what it would be like to be staying there. Then I went back and got Kay and we walked out for supper in the huge, clattering dining room seating about three hundred. All of it was new and shiny and wonderful to us.

Mrs. Blaney very kindly showed us how to operate her machine so that Kay could resew a seam in our little mains'l where the threads had been chafed away by rubbing on the shrouds and cross-trees.

Next day we went for lunch to a lobster-roll pier not far from Blaney's and sat in chairs above the water, sipping clam broth and enjoying lobster meat that someone else had caught, cooked, picked, and served. A teenage daughter of the Blaneys had a summer job in the place, a sweet little girl, who told us that when she finished work, at about nine P.M., she generally dived in and swam home.

Nearby was a co-op fish processing and marketing outfit, an enormous two-story, shedlike building with floats and gangways, where lobster boats and trawlers constantly came and went. High up on the roof, along the ridgepole, sat a long row of gulls tightly packed wing to wing. When we went into its mazes of steam pipes and bins to get some ice ("Would you like five hundred pounds?"), we learned that times were hard for the co-op and its fishermen. How sad it is that the once extremely prolific fishing—an abundance hard to imagine—has been ruined at the source by powerful trawlers dragging nets across the bottom-feeding grounds! In the days of sail, when they didn't have the power to wreck the resource, you could sink a dory to the gunnels in one morning jigging cod.

The Blaneys let us have another bath, which didn't cost fifty cents. They asked us about coastal marinas and coastal lore, telling us to take their guest mooring again if we came into Boothbay on our way south. They were already competent sailors, and thought their Crocker a bit small for living aboard. Their dream was to build a thirty-two-foot cruising cutter of their own before long and cruise for at least a couple of years or however long the money held out.

\* \* \* \*

Damariscove was the most dramatic of the Maine islands we touched. Crouched in the sea far from land, it is three miles long— really a pair when you include smaller Wood Island, attached by a narrow neck. It was blustery and cold when we pushed offshore and saw it in the distance.

As we sailed back and forth off the channel that cuts into its middle and forms its harbor, I wasn't sure we should venture in. The bellbuoy marking a breaking reef called the Motions was clanging loudly and tipping in a wild dance as everywhere great waves climbed the rocks and sucked back with a roar. The entrance was so narrow it was almost obscured by breakers on both sides. We had been reading the *Cruising Guide* about this historic island, which sounded so fascinating we were loath to turn back.

"Captain John Smith made it in all right," said Kay.

I had read that Joshua Slocum and his fifteen-year old son sailed in there too in *Spray,* after his around-the-world voyage, and when he got inside, the Great Navigator slid up on a smooth rock at the starboard side of the channel and stuck. "But all hands turned to and got her off without serious dramage." The place looked too lonely to provide any hands to haul us off if we got stranded.

A quartering breeze would be favorable for a swoop through. If we stayed in the middle of the entrance, the chart showed plenty of water. So we let draw and practically holding our breath galloped into the heart of Damariscove Island. Here was another one of those "harbor islands" that are so appealing—and so useful, for how can you live on an island if it has no harbor? This one had been a famous fishing station in the early 1600s.

Continuing on, we veered a little left to avoid Slocum's sunken ledge and then went back into the middle of the narrow channel, passing the abandoned Coast Guard station to port. It was a large two-story building that must have consisted of dormitory, kitchens, and dining hall, in addition to commodious quarters for two surf-boats with their attendant slipways for running out the boats. But the whole gray-shingled establishment was falling into ruin, windows broken, roof leaking, empty, sad. During World War II it housed a considerable Coast Guard contingent who manned the watchtower night and day at the island's highest point, listening, especially at night, for U-boats on the surface charging their batteries. It is said that on occasion they heard several, and summoned planes to bomb the subs or drive them under.

Just inside the Coast Guard station was a summer fisherman's shack and his boat at a log dock, the island's only inhabitant. Farther into the harbor the bottom began to rise up through the clear water glittering with shells. There we anchored in six feet in a slot between rocks where there was hardly room to swing. Although it was quiet as a pond where we were lying, great combers were lashing the seaward side of the island not far off.

Launching the dinghy, we rowed ashore and plowed through a brushy slope to some high rocks where we could look seaward at the thundering surf. A lobster boat just off the breakers was pulling pots in what looked to be dangerous ground. If his engine should fail, he'd be a goner. But he acted as though he fished this place every day. The shore was littered with broken pots torn loose from the rocky bottom by storms.

Returning to the dinghy, we rowed across to speak to the fisherman in his shack, where smoke was curling out of his stovepipe. He was a short, grizzled character who didn't appear to be starving for talk. "Poor holding ground where you're lying," he said.

"Is there any better?"

"No."

Back at the boat, I put out a bow line to each bank, tied around boulders, also a stern anchor. Some such system must have been the way fishing vessels moored in the old days. We could see drilled holes in the sloping ledges that looked as though they'd once held iron ringbolts, long rusted away by three hundred years of salt spray. In the year 1622, some thirty ships rode in this harbor during the summer fishing season. They were mostly from England and France, with perhaps a Dutchman or two. You can read all about it in the *Cruising Guide to the New England Coast*. You could pick lobsters out of the seaweed at low tide in those days—so plentiful they were considered poor folks' food. Cod was the staple, and it was on account of cod that this was the chief maritime New England port from 1608 to about 1625. Heavy evergreen forest covered the land in those days, until the demands for firewood, building materials, and grazing sheep denuded it to a few scraggly remnants.

We stayed three days and could not seem to tear ourselves away. Most of the time was spent roaming over the island. Much of its slightly rolling surface was covered with prickly brush, with here and there grassy expanses. Near the narrow neck connecting Wood Island was a large freshwater pond, thickly inhabited by the largest black-back gulls we had ever seen, sitting formally in rows whose black-and-white dignity reminded us of judges. Straggling across the island were old stone walls that must have required immense labor, for sheep, we supposed—those sheep that have damaged so many islands. In our explorations we came upon massive stone-slab foundations and impressive stone ramps that must have led to second-floor storage rooms of the old fishing stations. These inclined planes were no doubt useful for raising heavy loads, probably barrels and casks and kegs, rolled up by means of the "parbuckle" method. In colonial times, when every village had its cooper—and every whale ship, too—most supplies came in the coopers' barrels. Rocker-shaped, they were their own wheels so to speak, and a small man could easily roll a two-hundred-pound puncheon here or there, then tip it up onto its bottom so that it ceased being a wheel and stayed where he put it. When empty, it could be collapsed into a flat bundle and stored for future use. I could imagine how such barrels were rolled onto two ropes at the foot of the ramp, each rope brought up over the barrel near its middle and taken to the top of the ramp. The ropes the barrel rested on were also brought up the ramp and made fast to something solid in the floor. Men up there simply hauled away, and the heavy cask of beer or salt beef or cod liver oil or sugar or flour became not only a wheel but its own pulley as it rose.

No doubt they dried their salt fish on the rocks—those cargoes for their wives and children and markets. And how fortunate they must have considered themselves to have plenty of fresh water in the impressive pond—a scarce commodity on many a solid-rock island. There might have been a thousand men here once upon a time.

We wandered the rough shores and stony beaches looking at driftwood. Often we sat on the high rocks near the watchtower while we looked off toward Portugal, with the sea crashing below, a lonely, forlorn spot in the sea wind, yet filled for us with the strength of those old pioneers. The place cast a spell on us. I could almost see and hear those long-ago fishermen who came so far across the ocean.

Captain John Smith, the Kilroy of his day, arrived about 1612, and the Pilgrims of Plymouth in 1621 sent a vessel to get food for their starving colony.

As for us, in the cool, almost cold evening we were snug and well fed in our cabin, with the Coleman mantle pressure lamp swaying on its hook from the overhead, giving light as well as heat. The rubbed mahogany was red and gold in the lamplight, a singularly warm and cozy hue, almost like the glow from a fireplace. Once when Kay looked up from her book, I said, "Imagine getting here in our own boat!

"Yes," she said, "it seems marvelously unreal, sort of a fairyland, but a rugged one. I wonder if they had any women here."

The afternoon of our second day the breeze fell light. Just before sunset a small sloop, about twenty-six feet, sailed in and right up the harbor channel flying a blue-and-red spinnaker. Smoothly she slid between the rocks, while the man-woman crew neatly doused the chute, rounded up, and anchored close to *Sunrise* but not too close. The sailing couple turned out to the headmaster of a large New England boys' school and his wife. They were towing a dinghy in which he quickly rowed out to the harbor mouth with his rod, where he caught a fine mess of flounders and gave us some.

On the fourth morning I regretfully took in my lines from the boulders, hoping we could return someday to the seventeenth-century enchantment that pervaded the place.

The schoolmaster's battery was flat, which meant he couldn't start his inboard gasoline engine; neither would it run without an electric spark. Our outboard motor, of course, started with a pull of the cord, and ran on a magneto. A brisk breeze blew directly into the harbor, scarcely a boat length wide in spots, much too restricted

for any possibility of tacking out. In such circumstances, the old sailing vessels must have been warped out by gangs of men heaving
on lines from either shore. I told our friend, "Suppose I lend you
our battery? We only use it for running lights at night, and don't sail
at night if we can help it." There are advantages to a tiny five-horse
kicker after all.

"Great idea," he replied. "We'll give it back to you once we get
out in the clear beyond the Motions where we can sail."

When he had hooked up his cables and cranked off, we putted
out behind him. Outside, the whitecapped swells of the open ocean
made coming alongside something of a crunchy operation but by
both hanging over plenty of fenders we managed the transfer with
no splinters. Waving many thank-yous, this pleasant couple soared
away for Boothbay Harbor, while we set sail for Pemaquid Point
and Muscongus Bay.

We were great friends at this time with Dwight Shepler, a
remarkable artist-sailor who was giving an all-out summer ren-
dezvous party for the Boston Squadron of the Cruising Club of
America, of which he was an active member. He invited us to be his
guests. The affair was to be held at Wadsworth Cove, up the
Damariscotta River, not far from our cruising path, so we sailed up
the river, and were glad we did.

Any goings-on that Shepler had a hand in were sure to be filled
with zest and a robust sort of charm. We had first met him years
before when he came to our house to do a piece for the *Boston
Sunday Herald.* Each week he was then doing a write-up and a charcoal portrait of some author or public figure, and I had just published a book. We had kept in touch ever since. He was full of fun,

very athletic, extremely knowledgeable, and such a good skier that he had been an instructor, and even organized ski tours in the Alps. Aspen and "the Headwall at Tuckerman Ravine" were among his favorites. He now made his living from a yearly Boston show of his watercolors of the New England coast and ski-slope scenes, plus oil portraits of industrialists and educators whose boards of directors could afford such things. Because his parents had owned a stony little farm on one of Maine's rivers, he became acquainted with sailboats and Maine coast cruising at an early age. He and his wife could hardly dish up a couple of thousand dollars for an all-out party, but they had been to so many such gatherings given by their sailing friends, they decided they must reciprocate. They teamed up with a pal who was in a similar box and sent out engraved invitations long ahead. Included were little hand-drawn charts of the narrows in the Damariscotta River and directions for ways of avoiding the ledges among the boiling tides of that miniature strait.

A string of ledges also guarded the entrance to Wadsworth Cove, but these were so well drawn on the invitation, and the members were such real sailors, that not one of the fifty yachts piled up. For us, it was an experience. When they were all anchored in the cove, they included *Gesture, Carina,* many other Bermuda racers, and as fine a collection of beautiful yachts as could be found anywhere. Because we were the smallest of the fleet, many people told us how remarkable we were to have come all the way from Carolina in such a little boat. This was a familiar story, but made us feel moderately distinguished ourselves.

The setting could hardly have been improved on; high above the river on a grassy hill, against a frame of trees and a tennis court, stood the main house and cottages of an estate. The shore where all the

163

dinghies drew up was ideally suited for the outdoor supper-banquet in that it had a parklike series of grassy humps and hollows among clumps of spruces interspersed by smooth gray ledges that made places to sit. The bar table contained cases of Scotch, bourbon, rye, rum, gin, wine, and every known mix. For the children, of whom there were many, barrels of iced Cokes, Seven-Ups, lemon, lime, etc., were displayed on a serve-yourself basis. The young fry, by the way, were singularly well-behaved. Maybe it was that they could go rowing around the cove in dinghies whenever they got to feeling restless.

Busy as Shep and his wife, Hennie, were with their host duties, they found time to point out to us ketches, cutters, schooners, and sloops that had been to the Caribbean often, or to the Shetland Islands, the Med, or Ireland. They introduced us to several around-the-world sailors and their wives, a friendly lot, every one of them.

Shep and his cohost had hired the whole crew from the Goudie and Stevens Boatyard to put on a typically Maine feast. They had had big fires going since morning, now perfect beds of coals. The clams were steamed in seaweed, but there was luscious broth, too, if you wanted it. For everyone there was a lobster, or two, if you could manage. Golden bantam corn freshly picked from a neighboring farm, gigantic bowls of salad, home-baked bread with butter and honey all filled the chinks. We sat on the smooth rocks and feasted. After so much lobster and corn, few adults could do justice to the apple pie and chocolate cake, but almost everyone dipped into the buckets of coffee.

As twilight descended on the assemblage, mostly dressed in shorts and bright tops, a musical member with an accordion went wandering from group to group. He was one of those play-by-ear geniuses who can play anything you care to remember. Pretty soon "Memory

Lane," "Greensleeves," "Down by the Old Mill Stream," and other favorite four-part-harmony songs were in full swing, to which Kay and I added our bit. Nightingales would be no match for this group.

It seemed as if there never was such a lively, charming, and delightful picnic party. After our many weeks of solitary wanderings, poking through lonely Carolina sounds, often seeing nothing but nearby waves or the horizon, or a wall of fog, or maybe a breaking reef, always on our own far from people and in a different world from towns and cities, this warm sociability, and these capable folks who loved the life afloat touched our hearts. After weeks aboard, one grows sensitive to the voices of children, to the smell of spruce and juniper and flowers.

Now that we were cruising, we began to form a cruising philosophy, of course. Mostly, our aim was to be far from people, to be in wild places with only the seabirds and the porpoises, and now in Maine the harbor seals. We weren't keen on marinas except as a necessity for water, fuel, and food. But here again were the knotty paradoxes: We don't like people, but we like these; we don't like marinas, but we like to lay in stocks of water and supplies. We like to be independent, we say. But here we are with an aluminum mast, stainless-steel rigging, Dacron sails, outboard motor, and all the products of a complex civilization. I suppose that, like everybody else, we just do the best we can and follow our ideals at least partially. When you have a boat, you meet such fascinating people! That's because they are boat people.

It was getting dark. As the dinghies pushed off one by one, lights came on in the anchored fleet. Because we were special guests of Mine Host, we and the Sheplers assembled aboard the red yawl Cirrus belonging to Alan Bemis, commodore of the Boston

Squadron. The Bemises and the Sheplers often cruised Down East together. An M.I.T. prof, a great sailor, and an industrial genius, Alan had a summer place in Eggemoggin Reach to which he commuted from Boston in a light plane that he landed on a cow pasture. He said he had seen seventy sail go through Eggemoggin Reach one Sunday. Jim Stevens, of the Goudie and Stevens Boatyard, and his wife were there, too, and his wife wanted to know all about Labrador from Kay, because a Stevens daughter had a summer job in a hospital there. Having spent two and a half years as a nurse in Labrador, Kay was able to supply some details. Alan said he had just shortened the main boom of *Cirrus* and found it gave him more speed. I could hardly believe it, but Shep said it was true.

Jim Stevens told us it is common in Newfoundland villages to see the blacksmith making anchor grapnels, with an iron collar surrounding the clump of hooks that form the best gripper in rocky bottoms. He said the yard was building a yacht with a circular cockpit for Laurance Rockefeller. He said that in Newfoundland outports they have a revealing joke-expression. They say that a clever man goes into the woods in the fall with an ax, and comes out in the spring with a schooner. It isn't true, of course, but it gives some idea of the rough-and-ready character of their boats, that are, of necessity, make-do in all respects, made from green timbers and planks, hand-hewn bowsprits and masts, hand-wrought iron fittings, with Spartan quarters below. "But they always have a stove, you bet, and usually the cook is the skipper's daughter or niece—poor girl in a world of men—and does she work!"

He described how difficult it had been to gather materials from all the world for Rudy Schaeffer's *America,* replica of the famous schooner that won the America's Cup in Queen Victoria's time.

Shepler claimed that friends take a leaf from Schaeffer's beer ads and say of *America,* "It's the boat to have if you're having more than one."

Alan recalled that he had been sailing up and down the reach near his house one Sunday afternoon and not looking what he was doing when he ran up a smooth ledge and got stuck. He knew perfectly well it was there, but just wasn't paying attention. As he sat waiting for the tide, along came one of his sailing buddies, who remarked as he breezed past, "You know, Alan, a little local knowledge is a dangerous thing."

Shep uncorked for our benefit some of his best Maine fisherman stories, all done in the distinctive dialect that made the "Bert and I" records so famous. I must interject that these men have the utmost respect for Maine fishermen and freely grant that Maine's rugged seamen regularly accomplish trips in fog and storm they themselves could not possibly emulate. They know full well what it must be like to haul nets and pots in the winter, as is done in Monhegen, and thus in their stories of Maine fishermen there is genuine admiration rather than condescension. As a matter of fact, in Maine it is the fishermen, standoffish, taciturn, letting down the barriers only for the most capable, who condescend to the yachtsmen.

Shep's anecdotes reflected the struggle for existence, and the ability to laugh at one's own frugality: "If a rop's too shaat, you can always splice it; if it's too long, you can't do nathin' about it."

Seems there were two fishermen chugging Down East toward Cutler in a dungeon fog, when the skipper says, "John, go down and get the Cust Pilot so's we can see where we're to."

John calls up, "The page we want has got water-soaked so's I can't read it."

"Never mind," says the skipper, "we'll keep her goin' till we get on the next page. I had a chaat back aways. Trouble with them chaats, you pay two dollahs fer one of 'em and fust thing you know, your off'n it."

These yachtsmen have been half a dozen times to the St. John River in New Brunswick, where the famous Reversing Falls stand at the river's mouth. So great is the tidal rise and fall that at dead high-water slack (to avoid the tidal whirlpools) a yacht can enter with plenty of water for her keel. Inside, the river soon gets fresh, and much warmer, making good swimming. There are widening lakes and picturesque villages for a couple of days of ideal sailing, without fog. Shep says, "You keep the red cows on the port hand and the black ones to starboard, and you'll be all right."

He went down below to get us the tiniest sip of brandy, "a mere soupçon." Mrs. Bemis told us that Hennie is an expert at picking mussels off the rocks at low tide and making them into "clam" chowder. She said it's better than real clam chowder, and we decided we must try her system at the first chance. We had passed acres of them in Mussel Ridge Channel.

Alan told us what fun it is to cruise with Shep. "He has his own sailing lingo. When we're motoring, we're muttering. The mizzen is always the miserable. If I touch anywhere, he tells me I'd better quit breaking the bricks or knocking the cobbles about. He insults my fancy shock-cord mains'l furler every morning, saying 'How about gettin' the garters off'n 'er and hoisting up some dimity?' When we're passing Pemaquid or some bold headland where a big sea is bursting white and flying halfway up the rocks, he tells me, 'Alan, if we were to get into that, it would be non-habit-forming.'"

Sad to relate, every party must end sometime. No thank-yous could ever be adequate. We finished the brandy and rowed away to our floating home.

Maine, "hundred-harbored Maine." Rather, thousand-harbored Maine, one of the world's most magnificent cruising grounds. People love it from the land, but it is much better from the sea. We were two months on the Maine coast, and it was here that of necessity, we really began to get our sea legs and amount to something.

I don't know what got into us. A day around McGlathery and that maze between Stonington and Isle au Haut. Then (madness) down the reef-strewn eastern shore of Isle au Haut, a horrible jumble of rocks wide open to the eastern swell. Just missed one of them. Good visibility though. To Head Harbor on the south, farthest point of Isle au Haut. Lovely, lonely, wild. Two houses there. A couple in a lobster boat moored nearby called out and told us where there was a spare mooring, and then gave us a whole quart jar full of lobster meat! They had more that they could eat, given to them by a friend on shore. Kay fixed us a gargantuan lobster stew. This harbor is dangerously open to the south. But not many southerly storms in summer. A visit with our friends the Merrills at their salt-water farm in Turkey Cove. The wonderful Georges Islands, Allen, Burnt, Otter, where we picnicked and swam.

It was tricky coming up Mussel Ridge Channel, with rocks and reefs both sides, plus a strong tide. But the southwest wind was fair for us as usual. Far off we saw the oft-photographed Owls Head Lighthouse, and were surprised to see a man waving to us from the balcony high up on the lighthouse tower. Well, isn't that nice, we thought. It was only when we came nearer that we saw his waving hand clutched a cloth, for polishing the extensive lighthouse glass.

Just an example of self-centeredness. But of course, you have to be self-centered when you're poking along a strange, rocky, and unfamiliar coast, peppered with reefs in a small sailboat. It is only by being extremely self-centered that you can, with luck, keep off the rocks.

We embraced somewhat the same sort of delusion when we later sailed to Monhegan Island, a blue lump miles out to sea. As *Sunrise* came creaming into the harbor, we saw dozens and scores of groups of vacationers in their white and bright clothes coming down the walks toward the harbor, and thought again, Isn't that nice; they've come down to the shore to see the beautiful little sloop that appeared as though by magic from the sea. It was only when we looked astern and saw the daily mail boat coming in, with its expected and looked-forward-to mail, supplies, newspapers, and passengers from the mainland, we knew what really garnered all the attention.

To Rockland, Rockport, then Camden, another great cruiser center for supplies, groceries, liquor, a bath.

And now we are on the edge of Penobscot Bay, where everything gets better, and better, as though it hadn't been heaven on earth already. We went up Penobscot Bay to the magic East Penobscot Bay islands, Eagle, Butter, Bradbury, Little Spruce Head, Great Spruce Head, and to Castine. Eggemoggin Reach is called a reach because so often a southwest wind is a beam reach either way. Horseshoe Cove is one of our favorite anchorages.

* * * *

After a short trip to Matinicus, a true ocean island far offshore, we sailed back to the mainland with the setting sun in our eyes. The light wind headed us. Every course we could lay was close-hauled so that we seemed to be barely moving. Beating slowly past the Green Islands, we saw that the middle of Large Green was indeed green, with sheep cropping the grass. There were a few fishing shacks, and a lobster boat in a cove, but the islands looked low and uninviting, having scant protection from winter storms. In fact, they are doubtless deserted then. Ahead of us the chart showed the Northern Triangles, dead to windward, naturally. We made short tacks to keep clear, drawing ranges, figuring courses that we could lay. They are so low as to be practically invisible until you get right on top of them. At length we picked up the first of the three, not far off, in fact too close—black rocks dripping, bared by the swell. It would be hard to describe an uglier, more sinister hazard, lurking miles offshore to gore an unwary sailor. In reality, of course, those seaweedy rocks don't care one way or the other about the unwary sailor. But fallacy or not, they brought shivers to a loose-jointed pilot like myself. We were doing the correct thing; we were tacking a long way to port to clear them. Soon we saw the other two of those black, half-submerged menaces and felt as though they had a way of sliding right in front of us. One can't be too careful with nearly invisible ledges such as these. You decide to give them a wide berth, and then you give them a still-wider berth to be on the safe side. Whereupon they show up quite close aboard, giving me the cold chills. I sometimes think this coastal cruising requires an inordinate amount of concentration. "Do you know where all the rocks are," asked the nervous woman passenger. "No, lady," replied the captain, "but I know where they ain't."

171

To the north of us the chart showed Two Bush and a maze of islands, reefs, and islets, "horrible garbage" we called it. By heading off to the westward past a gong and a nun we would be out in the clear, though to windward, for Tenants Harbor and its blessed entrance tower and bell.

The afternoon was getting late, the breeze still on the nose. We cranked up the outboard and began to make some ground, motor-sailing on a very close-hauled tack. It was great to have been in Tenants Harbor before on our earlier charter voyage, and to have no fog. The bell at the entrance was an old friend. We knew right where to anchor, even without studying the chart; and to be able to see all the rocky shores and cottages, the fish stages, gas docks, and moored boats was a treat. We rigged our mosquito net just before the varmints attacked as the sun went under. Relaxed, in complete command of the situation, we decided that if we could continue to keep from getting wrecked, we'd be old hands someday.

The fog plays tricks on you. We were drifting along in a glarey white mist, groping for Great Sprucehead Island, which has a high rock profile we hoped we'd spot before we hit it. All of a sudden what looked like a big white motorboat appeared. But it didn't move, and had a ripple of tide running past. Then, on close inspection, I made out a lobster pot buoy, a little float of wood not more than a foot and a half long. That's what no perspective can do to you, nothing to compare with in the surrounding murk.

But something truly bigger soon materialized out of the white nothingness—a windjammer schooner with all sail set, ghosting along at about two knots. Kay and I decided he probably had radar that showed every nearby island so he knew exactly where he was.

The passengers looked subdued, as though—like us—they had had too much fog.

We groped on at our own knot and a half until at last we saw the dark shadow of the fan-shaped head that gives Great Sprucehead its name. There we anchored in a rocky cove where a pebbly shore and green grass behind it showed through the wet obscurity. In the thick fog, we were glad to spend a quiet night there.

Next morning, in clearer air and a pleasant breeze we sailed around the other side of the island and into what seemed a private, basinlike harbor, with boat sheds, floats, moored boats, cottages, all belonging to the Porter family made famous by the nature photographer Eliot Porter. What a kingdom! Barns, pastures, hay fields, gardens, a farmer caretaker, shelly coves, forest, their own beaches, clams, lobsters, and paths among the spruces, rocks, and blueberries. It looked like a heaven for children, and for grown-ups, too. When it comes to real estate, that's the ideal—your own harbor island with good freshwater supply, an exquisite fairyland of trees, rocks, fields surrounding your protected mooring pond, and right in the middle of it, your boat.

To be in love with the world you have to be in love with a place, or places, specific ones. You know those old Dutch paintings of a canal, a sail, distant trees looking as though you could step right into them, a church spire, fields. They are nearly always done in slanting light, early morning or late afternoon. They are sentimental, yes. But they are real.

If life grows empty to certain sophisticates who jet from Nairobi to Sardinia to Bombay, that is their loss. Not to be jaded, but instead to go beyond, toward a tempered sort of willful simplicity—that is the important step. A small cottage on the Maine coast, with rocks and surf, with gulls calling, with blueberries and spruces, may mean more than an empire. Or perhaps it's by a lake. It doesn't have to be comfortable or to have running water. It does have to have an aura, a character, a flavor, a uniqueness that makes you work for it and suffer for it, a charm. To love your own fireside, the chipped, blackened bricks, the way the smoke curls, the way the room smells—that's the important thing.

A lot of people wanted something else, or didn't have good enough luck to acquire a cottage, a fireplace, or a boat. That doesn't mean such things are bad. Sort of a movable place is my boat. She's individual, she's a place that gives the world significance for me. Of course I love her good qualities, her ability to fight to windward when the going is tough. But I have a certain fondness even for her faults.

How lucky the Porters are! I hope they realize it.


Bound along Deer Island Thorofare, we came to Stonington and tied up at a gas dock to get fuel and unwind a three-foot length of yellow polypropylene pot warp that had wrapped itself around our little propeller. The rope had been whipping itself out of water, and in, and out, going thwack, thwack in a highly disconcerting manner. We were lucky it hadn't jammed worse than it did. We weren't always courageous and buoyant, especially this day. It rained, the sun came out, and it rained again. Rows and rows of squarish, unlovely houses rose up from Stonington's apology for a harbor, every one of the houses white. The "harbor" was only an exposed passage inside Crotch Island, another unlovely place scarred by old quarries and derelict loading-boom cranes from a long-ago era when hundreds and hundreds of Italian stoneworkers breathed the dust of the area's pink granite. We wondered whether they sang of sunny Italy, or whether the islands of naked rock silenced them, after a year, two years, how many? Now the quarries were silent, cluttered with rusting machinery at the edge of pits full of water, scraps of broken, frayed cable among the rubble, and always the drunken wooden cranes seeming about to fall but not doing it. Great jetties of "grout," the broken blocks of granite that didn't split right, stuck out from the points, adding to the hazards of reefs among the maze of islands off Stonington.

The town's waterfront was rough and rolly. Taking a hint from the ever-helpful *Cruising Guide,* we decided to "retreat to perfect peace in the upper reaches of Webb Cove" not far away. An abandoned fish weir of solid stakes on the port hand near the entrance was to be avoided.

Inside, we were ringed by solid stone, with evidences of rock quarrying everywhere, and so much grout it looked as though more than half the stone worked had been left behind in enormous jagged fragments. Little *Sunrise* sat placidly in the middle of this gigantic Stone Age nightmare like a fly in a cathedral, and the rattle of her anchor chain running out sounded sacrilegious.

Ah, but next day was another kettle of fish, clear, sharp, and inviting. I had been troubled that fog among the crowd of rocky islets off Stonington might keep us from McGlathery Island that we had read about. Carefully we picked our way out toward McGlathery, dodging ugly reefs by means of eagle-eyed piloting, around a can, past another Green Island that wasn't green at all, through between Coombs and Bare. *Sunrise* slid quietly, sail tipping ever so slightly, drawing a V of ripples as we navigated among the rocks, carefully, carefully, while Kay held the main sheet in her hand and I held the chart and tiller, till we came to the tickle between Round Island and McGlathery that formed quite a well-protected anchorage.

McGlathery was fairly large; Round Island was small, with a brush and woods. Where the two came close together in a sort of hooked beak at the head of our snug refuge, waves were breaking. But boulders and stone occupied the narrow opening so that the seas produced little disturbance inside.

Nobody was there in this wild and charming place. On the near shore of Round Island, an abandoned summer fisherman's shack was falling in ruin. In front of it a long, sloping ledge of smooth granite gradually subsided into the water, making a natural ramp, with a few old iron ringbolts in the rock where he used to haul up his boat. Many stains marked places where he tarred his nets.

On the other side, McGlathery was grassy, with sheep. Clear wavelets lapped the pink granite ledges as we rowed around our paradise in the dinghy. This was Maine at its best. Kay in the stern, I at the oars, we drifted slowly around the point, looking to seaward at Gooseberry Island and other rocks outside us that broke the swell. We came to a small indentation in the barnacled rock where we looked down at bits of purple shell on the bottom. A small slope was there, too, cushioned with seaweed smelling of iodine. Watching out for some extra-big swell that might disturb the rise and fall of the sea's breathing, we hauled up our inflatable without scratching its bottom. This was a great place to loll and dream, to contemplate one's navel or one's sins.

Instead, I pulled off my shirt and jeans and slid into the ice-cold water. By this time I was moderately accustomed to its fiery touch.

Kay slipped in, too; she is better at standing the cold than I am. Then the joy of a sun-warmed rock! Such a dip makes a fellow feel like a new man if he isn't shivering too much.

Back at the harbor, we had to go exploring McGlathery. It was much bigger than Round, maybe seventy-five acres. By its harbor shore, a sheer wall of stone with plenty of water at its base had been used as a handy dock for loading and unloading fishing boats. An old log scaffold and boom still leaned over it, where they had hoisted casks and barrels, perhaps stoves for the houses.

In and out among the boulder outcrops and bushes, sheep trails wound, not going anywhere. A few shy sheep peeked at us sleepily, then went to cropping again. We found five old cellar holes where fishing families must have lived for generations. Whether they lived on the island in the winter or not we wondered. Perhaps they did—certainly in the summer for the fishing and lobstering. In those old days of oars and sail, the mainland was too far away for frequent trips. By contrast, the outer islands are now more deserted than they used to be; fishing families that used to summer there have grown too old or passed away. Their progeny, the young, won't put up with such isolation. And anyway, they can motor out here and back before the night almost anytime in their powerful lobster boats. The place had an atmosphere, like Damariscove, of old, unhurried times, and we fondly imagined that someday we would camp there for a whole, happy summer. It takes time to get the feel of a place and sense its rhythms.

Next day, this being Maine, in came the fog to McGlathery Island, thick and woolly from the far pastures of the eastward sea, where it hangs almost forever. The trees dripped, the boom dripped, and when we put a brick on the Primus stove for heat, our condensing inner walls dripped. If you stayed outside looking at it long enough, your eyelashes dripped.

I returned to my bunk, determined I wouldn't get up all day. I'd stay there tight as a cocoon to keep my bed from soaking up the all-pervading damp. I got to wishing we had a charcoal stove, or perhaps a big-boat diesel-oil heater, with a stovepipe to carry off the fumes. But the stovepipe would have to be fairly close to the boom, and wouldn't its heat burn holes in the mains'l? Yes, but at such times as this the mains'l was so soaking wet you could hardly burn it with a torch. I told Kay about this. She was also bundled up tight in a blanket in her bunk. She put down her book and said, "Well, we haven't got a stove like that, so no problem." We really enjoy such days; they give us a fine rest.

# CHAPTER XVI

*Interlude*

## COASTAL CRUISING

GOING IN AND OUT OF THE ISLANDS along a coast seems to me a much more enchanting experience than sailing across the broad oceans on some gung ho voyage of achievement. Here are all the charms of trees, rocks, flowers and endlessly opening vistas, whereas the ocean tends to be a great salty sameness. Some people feel they have to cross the oceans in little boats. I shall have to someday, I suppose.

So many transocean sailing books are a catalog of hardships bravely endured—a feat, an epic—we really shouldn't have any more of that kind. The charm of Slocum, Robinson, Pigeon, Guzzwell, the Peter Pyes, Hiscocks, and the other gay ones is that they enjoyed it; that's what they went for. Sir Francis Chichester, Alain Gerbault in his unsuitable *Firecrest,* and some others had the wrong idea; it's all heroics, tribulations, till one throws the book in

179

the corner and says, "Oh for heaven's sake, if you didn't like it, why didn't you stay home?"

Many of the truthful world cruisers say it's the islands and beaches, the people, and the places visited that they liked most. In their books you see the Hiscocks in some island paradise preparing reluctantly for another long ocean leg. You see William Robinson aboard his *Varua,* perhaps the most beautiful yacht in the world, returning after a long voyage, sailing in to his home in Tahiti with such surges of joy he can hardly speak of it.

As has been often said, cruising is going out in order to come in, and coming in so that you can joyfully go out again.

One of the best things about cruising is the dawnlight. When on a cruise, we tend to go to bed at dark and to get up at daybreak. Usually there is only a faint breeze when the sun struggles over the rim of the world, making mist on the water begin to stir and features of the harbor emerge and sharpen. Other boats at anchor are asleep on the quiet water, no sound at all. We tend to speak in whispers, trying to steal out silently, not from any sense of guilt as though we had robbed a bank but in an effort not to mar the pristine quality of the morning. In Maine, dark spruces stand around, not approving not disapproving, like Quaker elders waiting to see whether we will behave with proper decorum.

I take off the dew-wet sail ties, uncoil the main halyard from its cleat, and hoist the mains'l. Its climbing up the mast fills me with gladness and I can't help it. My mate, like as not clad only in her nightie (we haven't even had coffee yet), loosens the main sheet to let it flap. She is ready at the tiller as I bring in the anchor chain. Then the anchor comes aboard, snarled in seaweed as usual. Expecting that, I am barefoot to sluice it off later. Mate knows just what to do; she waggles the tiller vigorously one way, softly the other, to head the boat's bow off the wind's eye, and then hauls in the main sheet so that our lovely white triangle begins to draw. Ripples form at the stem, making a faint tinkle, and we are under way, moving out. As we ghost past an anchored thirty-footer, a tousle-headed man slides back the hatch and gives us an understanding wave of the hand. We're picking up speed, heading for the harbor mouth. When *Sunrise* has achieved some space and elbow room, I get up the jib, while we begin to feel the swells lifting and cradling us as we slip out from under the lee of the land and the breeze starts to heel us. Mate goes below to light the stove and put on the coffee as well as some clothes, while I take the tiller.

And now all day the magic surge and whisper, foam at the bow, wake streaming astern

> *Sun, wind, and beat of sea,*
> *Broad lands stretching endlessly;*
> *Where are bonds to bind the free!*
> *All the world was made for me.**

For us all day the shining water glinting in the sun, blue islands moving closer, and changing scenes changing our moods, but always above all the boat, the boat, our winged Pegasus. The ideal day is clear, with good visibility, so in studying the chart and plotting our course we know exactly where we are—blessedly no apprehension wondering where the hidden ledges lie.

*Richard Halliburton

And so we soar, fast or slow according to the strengthening or slackening of the breeze, till by afternoon we old folks grow weary as the sun sinks low (often right in the eye). We've been figuring on that, studying the chart so that another heavenly harbor will open its rocky arms to us. We sail in, readying the anchor, furling the jib, circling and picking the exact spot where *Sunrise* will have plenty of room to swing even at low tide when water level has sunk ten feet. What would we do without the lead line, the fourteen-foot pole, and the chart?

Down with the main. Our nice new anchor, beginning to get rusty already, sinks into clear, cold depths, so clear in this beautiful Maine water I can see its galvanized angles on the bottom as I pay out anchor rode. Mate has our little outboard in slow reverse to stretch the sagging chain while I test whether we are holding. From the foredeck I give her the hand signal, Yes, holding.

Twilight, supper, stars. In the night chill, we are overwhelmed with gladness at the prospect of all this tomorrow and tomorrow (if the weather will cooperate). Surf rumbles on the ledges outside the cove. Let it rumble. Good night, world.

# CHAPTER XVII

# FRENCHMAN AND BLUE HILL BAYS AND APPROACHES

BROOKLIN–CENTER HARBOR is a particularly beautiful anchorage. Its inner haven is full of handsome boats lying behind a wooded island. The outer harbor, where you enter from Eggemoggin Reach, is not very well protected. On its edge is a gray-shingled, folksy little yacht club. The inner end, where Joel White's boatyard stands, is fairly snug.

Joel White is a dark, slight, but rugged fellow with something intriguing about him. His yard must be growing, since it contains huge storage sheds for hauling out boats in the winter. But he had no room for us at any of his slips, so we anchored among the moored craft. I found that he and his crew of Maine craftsmen build a yacht each winter, in addition to doing many repair jobs. One of his creations is a small black sloop with bowsprit, built for his father.

Joel White's father is E. B. White, of *New Yorker* fame. E. B. White and James Thurber were great pals, so congenial that they once organized an absurdly comic safari "To Discover the Sources of the Bronx River," complete with guides, beaters, boats, headmen, porters, and sun helmets, all in Great White Hunter style. Mrs. E. B. White is Kathryn White, long a *New Yorker* editor, and these three in the heyday of the *New Yorker* were, in my estimation, what made the magazine great.

Joel can't seem to endure having you mention his illustrious father. It clams him up so that he will hardly speak to you. I guess he's sick of summer-visitor lion hunters who have nothing to do but roam around boring everybody. He is shy. But his quiet desire for privacy is as nothing to that of his famous father. Many of Maine's prominent residents, like White and the Wyeths, are that way. They didn't come to Maine to be devoured by strangers.

I met a nice old man when I went up along the road for water with my five-gallon jerrycan. Joel's dock didn't have drinking water. This contented chap, retired like me, lives in a tiny house beside the road that straggles up from the town dock, which is shared by Joel's yard. We got acquainted through the water business and his garden hose. Then, one afternoon when I was aboard doing a little varnishing and maintenance, he rowed alongside in his skiff. He showed me some mackerel he had just caught, trolling. The harbor mackerel were here now, he told me, and if you troll in the morning or evening you are sure to catch some. He advised me about the kind of hooks and leads and leaders to use, and said he had an old set he'd give me if I wished. He used to work for the Maine Telephone Company, and he knew all about this area, especially Center Harbor–Brooklin. The storekeeper at the crossroads grocery was a migrant from far away too, he said, one of those mavericks who had fled the city to find simplicity. Maine is full of people who have come there and made their own jobs in this land of little money. Lobsters and summer folks are the principal sources.

I pricked up my ears when he mentioned E. B. White. My new friend said, "He's very standoffish, you know. He won't talk about *One Man's Meat* or *The Second Tree from the Corner*, or any of his writings. Once in a while he goes fishing with me in my little boat. But he won't talk about his books. We were trolling for mackerel not long ago, and I told him I'd listened to a program the day before that gave an hour to reading the works of E. B. White. I could see he didn't like me to talk about that. All he said was, 'I must have missed it.'"

E. B. lives in a charming old white farmhouse on a hill over-looking the water, surrounded by flowers and grassy fields amid an apple orchard. This is the house he paid the mortgage on and wrote of, his beloved escape hatch. I walked miles to go by it—the purest hero worship. I felt a fierce desire to knock on the door and say, Mr. White, thank you for all the joy and wisdom you have given me. But what could he say? I have to remember I know him from his works, but he doesn't know me. I imagine him as a great man, simple, brave, independent, and alone. I have to go past that house slowly, not knocking on that door. It will be a long time before I forget that rambling white house among its flowers, its stone walls, amid the green fields above the blue water. I do not even know what Mr. White looks like.

I asked Joel if he had ever thought about building an L. Francis Herreshoff Nereia ketch. He said yes, he had the plans, but hadn't found anyone who would pay for the massive lead keel and all that hand labor. Then he turned back to the job he was on, fastening down a mooring cleat that had ripped off the foredeck of a yawl. I decided that when Joel and his Maine-ites got through with it that cleat will not rip off again. Not one of them will have a single word to say about it, not how flimsy the original was, not what they do to remedy the defect, nothing. It will be there like a rock from now on.

We were in Naskeg Harbor and from there sailed across Casco passage and York Narrows into an enchanted hole in the wall called Buckle Harbor. It is a little kingdom of sea-fronting cliffs and shelly coves, spruce woods, inner harbor—an island—and in the sheltered harbor is a big timber mooring, all said to belong to the Rockefellers. We tied onto it. Ashore is a fairyland cottage of flower gardens and porches, very simple. We never see anyone, though we have been there twice—once going up, once on the way back. Great for mussels.

In Burnt Coat Harbor, we walked to the lighthouse, and picked wild strawberries, talked to a fisherman working lobster pots of spruce slats and twine. Saw a yacht come in and anchor, suffering from a spinnaker wrap that flapped and popped for two hours, shaking their mast to its roots. They couldn't get it down, so finally from a bosun's chair cut it down in ribbons. Next morning went out so cautiously under short sail in light air, we could not help laughing—they looked so chastened, just the general air of their sailing.

Blue Hill Bay, Bass Harbor, Mount Desert, Northeast Harbor, the cruisers' delight. Somes Sound, the Cranberry Isles, Frenchman Bay, Bar Harbor, Sorrento. We were very sad that we did not get beyond that invisible dividing line, Schoodic Point, for beyond there is the wild coast, where summer resorts peter out and the fogs are thicker and the tides run harder and there are even more surf-encircled islands where nobody lives. Rocque Island, Cutter, Passamaquoddy, New Brunswick, and Nova Scotia will have to be for another time. Three times we got geared up and supplied to sail

186

beyond Schoodic, with gas tanks topped, plenty of stove kerosene, a new patch on the mainsail clew, food galore, all charts, water jerrycans full—and three times at Schoodic we met cold east winds, rough, fog, rain. We would punch into the frigid ocean soup for an hour and say, "My God! this is supposed to be fun!" Then we'd run back up Frenchman's Bay into the sunshine where we could lie on a rock in the sun and swim in some lovely cove, or Blue Hill Bay islands where we could pick blueberries and walk ashore for hours even on sandy beaches. We felt like horrible sissies, because we had vowed we would get to Rocque Island, the cruisers' mecca, where the boys get separated from the men.

It was September, time to start south—southwest, rather, for that is the way the coast trends—right square into the prevailing southwest wind. No wonder they talk about "Down East," for the downwind, the fair way. Getting back to Hilton Head Harbor, South Carolina, was not going to be easy.

# CHAPTER XVIII

# CAPE ELIZABETH TO CAPE COD BAY

# CAPE COD CANAL AND APPROACHES

SUCH A LOVELY SUNNY DAY, clear and cool, as we hoisted sail and leaned briskly out of Northeast Harbor. Bound south now, with more than a thousand miles to go, we passed close beside an anchored big black schooner on whose deck sat a gray-haired man in a folding canvas chair, legs crossed, reading *The New York Times.* I said to myself, He's a cruising millionaire. He doesn't have to go anywhere: He's been.

At first I did it all wrong, as usual. Each morning I'm crazy to hoist the sails and sail away. So that's what I'd do, the only trouble being that there wasn't any wind. Summer mornings are characteristically calm until about noon, when the southwest wind comes up almost as regularly as a trade wind. So we'd drift along all morning, hardly getting anywhere until noon when up comes the southwest wind, right on the nose. Then, in order to make a little distance toward home that day, we'd motorsail with flattened main, tacking, tacking all afternoon and not getting very far along our way. This was all wrong. We found that the thing to do if we must motor was to motor during the calm morning, motoring more or less south and more or less west, along the outer coast outside some of the islands. Then in the afternoon's strong breeze we were positioned slightly out to sea and could shut off the kicker and sail close-hauled all afternoon far up into some bay west or west-southwest for our night's shelter. In this way the wind served us and we accomplished a long dogleg each day and began making some progress.

Returning south—"to the westward"—we got quite brave. We felt we had won our spurs and began to take some considerable chances. We anchored two nights in a cove niche of Damariscove, the harbor open to the south, described by the *Cruising Guide* as precarious. A fascinating place made barren by sheep. We explored ruins and remains, roving the island for two days. The nights were quiet, fortunately. But it was September, and we had to make tracks south now. In fog we passed across ugly Muscongus and weathered Pemaquid via many seaward tacks, to stock up supplies again in Boothbay Harbor. Small Point. Past Portland and Cape Elizabeth in haze and rain to Biddeford Pool. We often saw people, but did not go ashore and did not speak to anybody for three or four days. Fog, fog, fog varied by rain with fog. Every stitch we owned was wet. To Annisquam. Big jumps, six hours in fog. Gloucester Harbor so thick we had to anchor close to shore. Could scarcely see the light of the boat, afraid we'd get run down. All went well from Portland to Gloucester, and from there to Scituate, Massachusetts—a name and pronunciation we thought odd. I considered sending cards to friends saying "We are situated in Scituate." In Scituate we heard that a hurricane was coming up the coast. Every day reports were more alarming. September is the time for them. "September remember," the hurricane-watchers say. It was off the Carolinas, it was off Cape May. Maximum winds were ninety miles an hour according to the radio. Two days later Rhode Island was feeling its fringes. If it held its present course straight north, it would strike Massachusetts full force.

As expected, the pretty harbor was crowded with moored craft. There would be no room for us to ride to an extended anchor chain such as we'd need in a big blow. Over in one corner, finger floats with perhaps five feet of water extended their arms. One of the slips between the floats being vacant, we rented it and prepared for the worst.

Down came the hurricane's outriders of deluging rain. Winds were said to be a hundred miles an hour, and it was headed right for us. The day was muggy with tropic air, heavy, sopping, oppressive.

Out on the broad harbor peppered with hundreds of boats, the scene was alive with yellow figures all in oilskins tending their craft. From Boston, from Newton Center, from all the suburbs they had come, dropping their appointments, leaving their offices and shops to add another anchor, to put chafing gear on the mooring pennant, or to reduce windage. Many were removing the furled mains'l from the boom and stowing it below. All in the pouring rain that flooded decks and gushed out of scuppers. Roller-furling genoas were being wrapped all around with line so they couldn't unroll, as happens sometimes in gales, especially when a corner has been left sticking out.

A man in a dinghy, carrying out a heavy anchor, capsized and had to be rescued in his boots and heavy rain gear, providing a welcome note of hilarity to break the tension. Weekenders were removing awnings and Biminis, lashing down spray-hood-dodgers, taking cockpit cushions below, closing ventilators, lashing every bit of gear tight. Everybody was drenched, cheery, and helpful, the way people are in emergencies. Dinghies scurried here and there like waterbugs.

Rain poured off the roads and down grassy banks into the harbor in waterfalls. Working at our dock lines, Kay and I were soaked to the skin despite our first-class foul-weather gear. We put on breast lines fore and aft, as well as bow and stern lines port and starboard. That made eight lines. Then for good measure we added forward spring lines and aft spring lines both sides, making twelve lines in a virtual spiderweb to hold our seagoing treasure. I was surveying this handiwork, when an elderly inhabitant of the town came by.

"That's all very well," he said, "but the last hurricane to hit here, those floats you're tied to landed up on the New York, New Haven, and Hartford railroad tracks. I had a nice little outboard. I sank her with rocks in the shallows thinking for sure she'd be safe there. Well, a big ketch broke her moorings and came ashore right on top of her—smashed my boat to kindling."

He told us of a taxi man we could phone. The radio bulletins were even more ominous. The full force of the storm might be upon us in a couple of hours, and we didn't need any reports to see that the wind was rising as gusts tore the harbor. We went below to stuff a little bag with express checks, dry clothes, and our few valuables. I hated to leave beloved *Sunrise,* and felt it was wrong.

192

Nevertheless, we had done all we could, and if the floats were to tear loose, we couldn't stop them.

I had been reading about a hurricane in Nantucket that wrecked almost every vessel in the harbor. It raised the water level six feet above high-tide marks and sent great breakers crashing against the harbor shores. The idea of doing anything for one's boat at that point was ludicrous. People had to flee to higher ground, to lie prone behind hillocks to keep from being lifted off their feet and pinned against walls. Houses were lifted off their foundations.

With sad backward glances, we went up to the taxi. Our boat was built stronger than most of them. It would be better to save our lives; perhaps then we could repair *Sunrise* after the storm. We had our mains'l off too, and not a thing on deck, hatches bolted shut, chafing gear on all four chocks.

The taxi man knew of a house where they rented rooms. Sheets of rain blew across the gleaming streets, under the tossing trees. It was a big old house belonging to a woman named Ellen Craig, who lived there alone. She was very kind to a couple of drowned rats who dripped on her floors. She gave us a nice, square, second-story room with a bay window, also blankets to wrap up in, as we were thoroughly chilled, and let us hang our wet things in the kitchen. Tight inside our blankets in the big bed, we listened to the weather on our little portable radio that was our most cherished possession on that stormy day. The afternoon wore on. The landlady said she would provide us with supper in the large oak dining room. The radio reports became sporadic; they had lost touch with the hurricane center. Then came the climax: "This is the hurricane that wasn't. Winds at the end of Cape Cod are two miles an hour. The

hurricane center has veered out to sea, and danger is past. No further bulletins are planned for the Massachusetts Bay area."

We were only too glad to spend that anticlimactic night in Ellen
Craig's big comfortable house. During the evening, we scribbled
postcards to the children telling them how Pa and Ma were situated
in Scituate.

Here we are at Cape Cod Canal again, all the way from Scituate.
The East Basin is crowded, as usual. After leaving Maine and its
beautiful solitudes, everything seems to get more crowded the farther south we go. As night falls and more and more boats come in,
the basin becomes so crowded it becomes a joke, a jolly joke. And
we enjoy it. Boats are even in the entrance. The Coast Guard patrol
boat going out on a call—will it order them away? Away to where?
No, it shaves past half a dozen boats and appears to share the joke,
shrills its siren, noses out, and is gone.

What a change in us, in me. It was all ominous and threatening
here on our way north. I was so unfamiliar, so expectant of disaster. The black tide boiling past the basin entrance, the way the menacing lights wavered on the water—would someone ram us, crowd
us, crunch a dent in us?

No, of course not. Should we live always fearing they might?
Would that keep the dents away? We are changed, relaxed, knowing we will cope with any squeezes as best we can and not worry.
Worry spoils everything. We will sleep calmly, and if we bump the
sloop to starboard or the yawl to port—well, we'll lash the rubber
dinghy alongside for a fender, and probably everything will be all
right. How different we are from our former selves on the way up!
Our private, solitary island of ourselves—it is not good if it is

invaded by worries. We must keep them resolutely at bay, smile, and be happy, sure that the world will roll on blissfully without us. So, why worry? It is wonderful for a worrier like me to be free of care. We are transformed. The cruise has done a lot for me. I say to the great globe of stars above my head in this black basin where the wind sighs, "If I love you, what is that to you?" Nothing, obviously. And that frees me, frees me for the little time I live—instead of being dead all the time.

# CHAPTER XIX

# MARTHA'S VINEYARD TO BLOCK ISLAND

# BLOCK ISLAND SOUND—POINT JUDITH TO MONTAUK POINT

# BLOCK ISLAND SOUND AND GARDINERS BAY, LONG ISLAND

THIS PAGE OUGHT TO SMELL OF KEROSENE, for I have just been hanging out the riding light lantern. We are near the ferry dock of the Great Salt Pond, Block Island, it is a black night and a huge fishing trawler has just come in. They don't seem to pay much attention to night or day; probably they were born here.

This has been a great and wonderful day for us, just as it would have been for any learning cruisers, sailing more than forty miles on a crossing from Martha's Vineyard to Block Island. It was Vineyard Sound in good mood, an area that has some of the steadiest summer winds on the East Coast.

*Sunrise* poked her stubby nose out of Menemsha's millrace channel at daybreak in a strong fair wind. Visibility was about three miles—pretty good as things go, and a blessing since there are some bad shoals just to the westward between Martha's Vineyard and the Elizabeth Islands. The Eldridge piloting book says that many coastal schooners used to pile up on those shoals because of currents that carried them off course, not only on the flood but also on the ebb.

We soon got into an impromptu racing brush with a twenty-four-foot sloop on the same heading as we were. The wind was quartering, almost astern but not quite, so his main blanketed his genoa, which fell limp no matter what he did. He should have put up his spinnaker, but maybe he didn't have one. He wasn't one of the salty ones, you could tell. Anyway, I stuck the end of our long whisker pole into the clew ring of our masthead genoa, boomed it out with the foreguy, lift, and sheet to hold it fast, and then we had two big sails drawing to his one. "The secret weapon wins again," my helmswoman remarked as I came aft and we began to pull away from him. He was trying to hold his jib out with a boathook for a pole, but it wasn't long enough. In a little while he became a tiny white speck, while we rolled over the swells toward Cuttyhunk, which was at first lost in haze, then appearing blue and mysterious. By and by we were passing it. I could have spent a week going in there again and exploring the fabulous Elizabeth Islands. How I would have liked to poke into the stony coves of Nashawena, Pasque, or Naushon, to run the swift tide of Robinsons Hole or anchor off a sandy beach in Quicks Hole, and walk along the bare green moors that look like pictures of Ireland. But it seemed as though we should be getting south. Next year, next year!

It was a joy to be receiving good RDF bearings from the powerful signal on Buzzards Bay Light Tower, for that would give us a good course check partway across to Block Island. Cautiously, we were going to head right for the tower, though it was considerably out of our way. We often make such doglegs on foggy days, to a bell, to a whistle, to a lighthouse, so that we will have a sure point of departure for long crossings and be keeping track of our position. Already Cuttyhunk was fading, and we would be a long time out of sight of land. When you are quite close to a powerful station, that's when the radio direction finder really works. We could home in on Buzzards regardless of the thickening mist that had lessened visibility to a mile; and in fact pretty soon we saw the tower's penetrating blink, yellow and bright ahead. We came quite close to the tower's iron legs, wondering what the men up there were thinking about as the swells swished under. They must have been glad to be stationary instead of rolling and pitching in the anchored lightship that was there only a few years ago. They're scared, I'm sure, of being run down by ships homing in on them days like this, but the shrill blast of their foghorn must be some protection. What they're thinking about, no doubt, is the same old thing—their girls, and when will the helicopter land on the rooftop pad to take them ashore? As usual, we saw nobody, and all our wonderings as to what they thought of a little sailboat appearing out of the mist and disappearing into it again were vanity, vanity.

When we changed course for the thirty-mile run to Block Island, the rising wind came dead astern. What a chance for our magnificent blue-and-white spinnaker! It must be rigged with all the lines carefully led outside the shrouds, halyard free and snapped to the head of the sail, the cloth carefully folded in the bag accordion-fashion so that it will emerge without a tangle. All this is a joy to me because of the long years when I didn't have a boat and the many more years when I had a boat but no such challenging sail as this. Even when you've got a boat and spinnaker it may be years before you experience a thirty-mile spinnaker run in a spanking breeze. I have at last learned that it is wise to jibe the main so that it masks my genoa, and then, with wind spilled out of the tugging sail and no thrust to fight against, it is an easy matter to unship the long whisker pole and get the genny down. All this takes careful steering but we have a good helmswoman, and soon we had the genny down and the great parachute arched aloft. The spinnaker is a heart-filling sail, the most uncontrollable but the most enchanting. Every now and then a puff would make its forward-reaching curve rise toward the sky and the boat soar in a surge that subsided in white foam. Hour after hour we flew along, eating up the miles, alone in our misty circle of ocean.

Who can say what the ocean is, what sailing feels like? When a cat's paw comes stealing on a calm day, dark and gleaming over the breathing sea, and my boat begins to move, to trail her V, to come to life—what is it but a caress, a magic touch, a stirring. When the wind heels her to the chainplates, when the wind screams so that she must bow her head and give with a blast in order to live, it is a passion exceeding sense or logic or understanding. The ocean is like love, immense, omnipotent, moody, nothing, everything.

I kept checking the course every half hour by radio bearings backward on Buzzards Tower, and also got a good cross-fix via the beacon at Brenton Reef. It has taken me a long time to learn that a progression of bearings—say, four at intervals of about half an hour—are infinitely more valuable than just one. In fact, one isn't worth much, as it may be in error. Oddly (and yet typically), I couldn't raise the Block Island Southeast Light radio direction station. Newport was only thirteen miles to the northwest of us, but we got no sight of land. A motor cruiser came up astern and passed us, on the same course bound the same place, obviously. She was going fifteen knots to our seven, heading a degree or two to starboard of our course. Maybe he knew something I didn't about tidal currents that would set us off course. There is a fierce tide around Block Island, part of the great volume that runs past the Race in and out of Long Island Sound. The north end of Block Island dies away in a point extended farther by a long shoal known as Block Island North Reef. Across this reef surges a fearsome current that has carried swimmers away never to be seen again. Its end is marked by a bellbuoy that we must round, being very careful not to get into the current sucking across that reef.

We had our lunch and took our turns at the tiller. For a spell when the breeze fell light, our spinnaker threatened to wrap, but then the wind picked up again. By and by in the thinning haze, Block Island appeared ahead, a long blue hump, and sure enough we were too far to port, heading for the center of the island instead of for the bellbuoy off the north end. What a joy to find it! We had formerly been surprised to find any mark after a long crossing, but now we were surprised if we didn't. Not that we still hadn't plenty of worries, but it added a lot to cruising joys to have tackled some of the problems before.

The wind was blowing so hard I had a job to drag the spinnaker down when we rounded the north point bell and changed course for a close reach south alongshore toward the Great Salt Pond entrance. I didn't do it right, didn't blanket the chute with the main, and could hardly pull the big bag down. If you let the halyard go on the run, the whole spinnaker falls into the water, where the boat

201

rides over it. My present system is to put one foot on the halyard line on the deck, gather in the folds, and pull the sail down against the friction. It helps a lot to have the forehatch off and then keep stuffing the cloth down the hatch before the wind can get into it. The racers have three or four people, or more, to handle spinnakers.

The entrance to the harbor is a narrow dredged channel, well buoyed, with a Coast Guard station on the starboard hand. Inside, it opens up into the Great Salt Pond, perhaps half a mile wide and a mile long. Except for a few shoal spots, the water tends to be deep, thirty feet or more. Consequently, it being a weekend, many cruising boats were clustered over the ten- to fifteen-foot depths so they wouldn't have too much anchor line to haul in at departure time. We anchored among a covey of them with hardly room to swing, near the head of the harbor not far from a dock where the steamboat ferries from Newport and Point Judith tie up. They blast their whistles as they come foaming in, and blast again as they leave, a wild, windy screech, forever exciting.

We went ashore in the dinghy to go for a walk, and found the island surprisingly quiet, as so many resorts are after Labor Day, the hotels and summer cottages mostly closed. I've never seen so many mansard roofs, as though every building had had its top story built to accommodate maximum summer boarders. Not having read up on it, we hadn't realized the island would be so large, miles and miles in extent, with roads and cars, fields, stone walls, marshes, and high bluffs overlooking the sea. The Old Harbor on the east side, with its stone jetty and the hotels looking down on it, seemed somehow English and ancient. The sun was sinking low, with long slanting light that made the green fields and the bayberry bushes and wild roses by the roadsides and the white houses very pretty, as though a pink searchlight were playing on them, as though this day were too lovely ever to fade. The breeze blew very hard as we walked along, feeling the strange exhilaration that comes of sailing into a fascinating new port. We arrived at a beach that stretched almost out of sight, where waves were pounding, and sat on the sand in the wind looking at the steely sea all dancing with whitecaps, a little awed that we had sailed from way out there below the horizon.

Two young couples were wandering barefoot along the edge of the waves. One boy and girl strayed off into the sand dunes and did not reappear.

Back aboard again, we began to drag, at one o'clock in the morning in heavy wind and thick fog—an unpleasant combination. What woke me was the chain grating on the bottom as the anchor skipped and tightened. I was out on deck in a second, feeling the chain, confirming the sad fact. Why do these things have to happen to us, I wondered. Looking to leeward, I thought I could make out a hunched figure on the boat astern. When I went aft to see better, sure enough, he was crouched at the bow rocking up and down, saying with a mixture of resignation and annoyance, "I was just about to call you." Who was he, and would we have been friends under more favorable circumstances, instead of potential enemies, as now?

He had reason to be angry, for I was guilty of that worst sin— anchoring too close and then dragging down in the night on a boat that was there first. When people do that to me, I tear my hair out in handfuls. Only a few yards were separating us now from his plunging stem. Kay was up. "We're leaving right away," I called to him as I dived for the motor and cranked it to life.

203

All around were the ghostly boats, beginning to roll and plunge. My blatting exhaust was waking their crews, no doubt. Where would we go, how would we find the way? I must get the anchor up first of all. Everything was wet and clammy. I could hardly see three boat lengths.

At the controls Kay eased us ahead while I stood on the fore-deck hauling in, feeling desolate, no security anywhere, and lost as to the next course of action. In daylight with the whole harbor to choose from I had made a mess of it; now how was I going to do any better in the foggy dark and wind? Directly ahead was the channel leading to the ferry dock and town wharf; I couldn't anchor in that fairway of ferries and fishing boats coming in and out all day and night.

Kay circled slowly within sight of a channel marker, clinging to the one certainty of its dim shape while I ducked below to chart a course for a cove nearly a mile across the harbor where I'd seen three boats anchored when we came in. By golly, we'd have plenty of room to swing this time. Fortunately, we had a large-scale harbor chart, and we could expect to pick up a black can partway; also, there were no obstructions nearby if we wandered from our course. Protection from the wind was poor over there, but maybe the seas wouldn't get too big. Our anchor gear was of the best. Automatically I looked at my watch.

We crept away on our compass course at three miles an hour, slow that we might not hit anything if it loomed ahead, fast enough to minimize leeway en route. Lost in the nothingness of fog, the old fears assailed me. Did we know what we were doing? Hell, I thought, we wanted adventure, and this is adventure! Hadn't we coped with Maine coast fogs just as thick as this, with rocks all around instead of sand? Meanwhile I was measuring off distance on the chart. It was three-quarters of a mile to the cove; well, at three miles an hour that would be one mile in a third of an hour, or a mile in twenty minutes; then three-quarters of twenty equals fifteen. So fifteen minutes from departure was our ETA.

Already seven minutes were gone. Nothing, nothing, just wetness and fatigue, then we passed the fat round can, almost close enough to touch. At fourteen minutes on the tick we saw the first boat swinging to her anchor, a shadowy blob without substance. It was the cove. I blessed our compass! We circled back perhaps eighty yards and dropped the hook, a good distance from any boat, with plenty of room to swing in all directions. It was thirty-five feet deep, but I didn't mind that. Kay reversed the kicker while I paid out two hundred feet of line, and finally felt the rope stiffen as our twenty-five-pound CQR anchor dug in and stopped all sternway. That ought to hold us. Had I done the right thing for once? Time would tell.

I shut off the motor and went below, thinking how easy it sounds in the cruise books quoting a terse log: "Changed to storm jib as gale was blowing fifty knots," or "Anchor dragged, so moved to east-side harbor where more room to swing."

Sleep engulfed us, even more welcome than usual.

Waiting at Block Island for the fog to lift became monotonous. We were reminded of a tale told by a returnee: "I've been cruising on the Maine coast—I think."

On the third day, in murk as thick as the proverbial pea soup, we set off across for the Rhode Island mainland, heading toward an unobstructed stretch of shore at Quonochontaug, where the chart showed no off-lying dangers. It was an expanse east of Watch Hill Light, where we would have room for several miles of error as we came in from our obscure gropings. Watch Hill has a powerful horn that we ought to hear at least two miles off. Bells, whistles, and any other audible aids are blessings at such times. The RDF beacons from Little Gull or Montauk were no help, probably being too weak and far away. We would sound our way toward the beach with the lead line, and the fog could stay as thick as it liked.

And so, after a time, with Kay sailing in a moderate breeze and me swinging the lead, we crept on. No bottom, no bottom—and then I felt it, at fifty feet. Next it was forty, thirty, eighteen—we must be getting close—and then we could hear and even see the dim white ruffle of surf. We feel a thrill and sense of achievement when we are traveling in thick fog. But the concentration required is tiring, and I find myself worn out when we come to anchor.

Following the beach westward toward the Watch Hill horn, we passed the lighthouse fairly close abeam to starboard in slightly improved visibility, knowing exactly where we were as we threaded the ugly reefs at the entrance to Fishers Island Sound. These were the crucial rocks we had thought about all morning. I had studied them on the chart, and the gaps between them, wondering which opening we should choose. Now here they were, close beside us, grinning sociably as a small surf broke among them.

Visibility continued to improve; the reefs thinned out; but the day stayed gloomy, and the tides ran strong.

Deciding to call it a day, we anchored in the West Harbor of Fishers Island, not far from the Fishers Island Yacht Club. After a cup of tea, we pumped up the dinghy and went for a row into the shallow inner basin at the southern end of the harbor. It was all commercial and for fishing boats, but had much better protection from the northeast than the spot where we were lying. I suppose that in a blow a little boat like ours could poke and push and shove in there to tie up alongside a lobsterman or trawler whether they liked it or not. Legally speaking, no one owns the water; it all belongs to the public—a pleasant theory and fallacy. The reality is that the people who live here all their lives take, quite naturally, everything available; and the cruiser, who is there one night in his life, takes what's left, if anything. Fishers Island is full of lovely homes and gracious estates. Blessedly isolated from the vulgar mainland, it has no bridge, just a ferry from New London. It might be nice to live there, as many wealthy folks have apparently discovered. Anyway, it was a pleasant place to have our anchor down as darkness came and the fog shut in close around our yellow riding light. It had a halo, as though it were saintly.

# CHAPTER XX

# FISHERS ISLAND SOUND

# NORTH SHORE OF LONG ISLAND SOUND— NIANTIC BAY AND VICINITY

# CONNECTICUT RIVER—LONG ISLAND SOUND TO DEEP RIVER

# LONG ISLAND SOUND— EASTERN PART

# LONG ISLAND SOUND— WESTERN PART

SPRAY WAS FLYING, water sliding to and fro across the deck, slapping into the sail, especially into the belly of the jib. Most of it stayed outside the cockpit coaming, at least the solid part. Although considerable scud flew over the coaming onto the cockpit seats. It poured off the edge in cold little waterfalls into the foot well, and gurgled down through the cockpit drains. The sky was smudgy gray and black, cheerless with chill and wet, not much prospect of clearing, as squalls beat the boat down. Because steering required judgment and bearing up in puffs, the work at the tiller became arduous after some hours.

My time for respite and a relaxed hour in the cabin came. Kay took over.

Down below, what a change, so quiet and dry. Especially, it was a joy to be relieved of the pressure of the wind, dehydrating, pushing, flapping, chapping, making your skin burn and your eyes hurt. What a blessing to get the streaming oilskins off and to stretch out on the bunk. I put my head down and watched water splattering onto the closed Plexiglas hatch, the elliptical puddles and globules crawling back and forth on the transparent cover like drops of mercury that don't want to lodge anywhere.

The bow rose and fell as we rolled and pitched, clawing violently to windward. Under the floorboards the bilge was dry, as usual. The twisting, wringing strains of a thirty-foot mast in a twenty-foot boat are tremendous, but she never leaks, she never squeaks, and she hasn't opened up. We had a pretty good idea where we were on the chart, many miles from the nearest obstruction. I couldn't see Kay's hand on the tiller because of the washboards closing the companionway opening. But I knew it was there, steady and firm.

From Fishers Island we had hoped to make Clinton, Connecticut, again for the night, it being a familiar harbor to enter in the dimness. But against the headwind and head tide Clinton was plainly too much that day. We'd be lucky to get to Saybrook at the mouth of the Connecticut River. Always to windward, tacking and motoring in combination, we couldn't do much motoring on the port tack because the outboard propeller lifted and raced as the boat heeled. We had been punching to and fro off Niantic Bay for hours when we picked up the black-and-white whistle "P1." The wind was piping up, cold and wet. We could not see the Connecticut mainland, though it was close. Then suddenly in a burst of color half a dozen yachts with spinnakers straining leaped out of the haze ahead and roared down on either side of us. They were thirty-five- and forty-footers looking very handsome as they ran before the fair wind—such a fair wind for them—that we'd been punching into all day. It must be a race to Newport, we decided. They were yachty yachts, their spinnakers pale blue and yellow, some purple, pastel pink, blue-and-white, red-and-white. One had a smiling face on its great balloon. Another had a girl's closed eye leering from its bulge, with long lashes. Three of the boats were yawls carrying the ultimate "rag," a smart little creampuff mizzen chute, tailored with broad shoulders to hold maximum wind, impeccable, matching the big spinnaker in color and design, like those mother-and-daughter outfits favored in the suburbs. As if to emphasize our slow, wet slogging, this covey of stylish birds disappeared in the fog with smug rapidity while we seemed to be standing still or just going up and down.

On compass course we punched along for the Connecticut River sea buoy, I on my knees in the cabin, charting, drawing lines on the chart on the bunk, Kay at the tiller, feet braced, her oilskins shining in the spray. We had to see that outer buoy because it marked an immense shoal at the river's mouth. It was only about twenty miles from Fishers Island to the Connecticut River, but we couldn't seem to get there. The seas were so rough and the wind so strong we shut off the motor to keep it from racing on the lifted-up tack. Oddly enough, we always feel better in tough going when the motor has been silenced. The motor is too weak to do much in blowy times, anyway. At last we reached red bell "8" and could go about and beat for the harbor breakwaters. This course was very close-hauled for us, but at least we seemed to be making progress through the steep chop. The edge of the shoal close on our starboard hand was clearly defined by a long line of breakers uncomfortably close. Pinching along like that, close-hauled on the edge of a shoal, our maneuverability was severely restricted. Consequently, a tugboat materialized almost immediately dead ahead and coming for us on collision course—a tugboat specialty. He also was skirting the shoal, on a line a little farther off than we, since he drew more water. Surely he would turn aside a little and give us room to pass port to port in the usual manner. Or would he? We couldn't turn to the right because of the breaking shoal beside us. We couldn't turn to the left and cross in front of him because it was too late and he was coming too fast. Besides, that was to windward for us. It was a perfect trap. So now what? Surely he could see the situation for the little sailboat and would give over to allow us a little room, even a few feet.

But no, he kept straight on and wouldn't twist his wheel one spoke, the Great Stone Face in his dry, steam-heated pilothouse. He had the whole sound on his right; we had the breakers on our right and were standing on end, almost unable to steer, strapped down tight, pinching to windward as close as we could go in this fierce tide rip. I took the main sheet in my hand as his cruel bow loomed close, and I bore off within inches of the sand. He squeezed us almost into the breakers, and so we passed, tossing madly about twenty feet from the black side of that black-hearted tugboat. He sat up there in his pilothouse, not waving, not acknowledging our existence.

In our cruising we have acquired, rightly or wrongly, a distinct hostility toward tugboats or tugboats-and-barges, because of their conduct toward us. Later we read of two yachtsmen run over and drowned by a tug-and-barge off Point Judith. Perhaps they resent the fact that we are doing for fun what they are doing for pay.

As we beat into the river's mouth past its two huge lighthouses, I was charitably recalling a yachting story about a good tugboat captain. Years ago during a yacht race in the South, the skipper of a tall racer was so intent on trimming sail neither he nor his crew peered under the genoa to see a tug with barge on a long towline. As the racing sloop bore straight for the cable, disaster seemed inevitable, with great danger that the yacht, brought up short by the cable, would then be run over and sunk by the oncoming barge. It is a widely held belief that nobody ever comes out alive from under a barge. But this exceptional tugboat man, seeing the impending catastrophe, stopped his engine, went full astern to make the cable sag, and while everybody held his breath (for the yacht crew now saw their peril), the racer's keel scraped across the sunken towline and she was safely over. So somewhere there exists at least one kindhearted tugboat skipper.

The Connecticut River shores opened to us as a light rain began to patter on the sails and twilight softened outlines of the low, sandy land. Here in Saybrook, marinas were everywhere, packed with thousands of boats at finger floats. Obviously there'd be no peace for us if we anchored in the tide-rip river's mouth, where motorboats and commercial traffic were churning up and down. A marina that had a protecting bulkhead shutting off the swell looked good, even though its name was Terra Mar. We rounded up in the river to lower and furl the main, then drifted through a sort of gateway in the bulkhead, under jib alone, and came alongside the gas-dock float. To confirm our faith in the Affluent Society and the American Way, we were greeted by a friendly, barefoot dock boy ("Take your lines, Captain?") who took us along to show us his yacht, which was a twenty-six-foot varnished mahogany sloop far grander than our own, and we were soon exchanging sailing yarns and hearing about his cruises up and down the sound.

The marina was glamorous and extensive, with snack bar, restaurant, swimming pool, cabanas, all closed for the season. Still open was a two-story sumptuous motel and a glassed-in yacht club lounge. The swimming pool was all lit up with strings of colored lights, while sprightly tunes of canned music tripped out of loudspeakers set on gaily painted posts. Nobody was there, of course, this cold, rainy, fall evening with dry leaves whirling out of the sky into the pool. But the music played on, forlorn and mindless.

In the night I pulled back the hatch and looked out. Stars were glowing bright as lamps, in crisp air close to the freezing point, all the mist blown away—a splendid norther to whisk us south. In reality, Long Island runs almost east and west, so I should say "to the westward."

As we were finishing our scrambled eggs and bacon, a pleasant man and woman off a nearby bargelike houseboat appeared and hung about, wanting to ask questions. They had plainly wanted to ask questions the evening before but had seen we were tired and considerately wandered away. They had seen us come in out of the misty fog, which now caused the woman to say, "I'm scared out there in the fog. Aren't you scared?"

Before I could make a clean breast of it and admit this is a condition not unknown to me, the husband chimed in, "How do you find your way in fog? We go out of this harbor and as soon as we begin to lose sight of the outer buoy we get panicky. Yesterday the waves smashed right over the front windows and across the sundeck. My wife was terrified. It's clear today, but it's too rough." I didn't like to say that his luxurious tub looked like a floating greenhouse. Instead, I asked him if he didn't have a compass and hadn't studied up on piloting and charting compass courses from one marker to another. It developed that they had chartered this houseboat for their vacation, it was the first time they had ever been "to sea," the compass was acting strangely, and he knew very little about piloting. "I took a piece of paper, two pieces," he said, "and tried to draw a course. I don't have a ruler."

"No parallel rules or such?"

"No."

I felt I must help him if I could. Maybe I could get him started on the rudiments of compass courses—simple enough in principle, though not always so simple in practice. "Let's take a look at your setup," I said, and grabbed up my own little hand-bearing compass, which is a gem and very accurate. The bridge of his modern monstrosity was a mass of dials, a countertop nearly four feet long with dozens of indicators, mostly electric, and embedded in the middle of these error-making circuits sat a small, poor-quality compass. It didn't have a chance: When he turned on his electric bilge pump the compass went one way, and when he connected up his second air conditioner it did something else. I stood amidships holding up

215

my hand-bearing compass some six feet away from all those magnetic attractions and, squinting at the bow, asked him for his bearing straight ahead.

The twenty-five-degree error in his ship's compass would foil anybody trying to find his way in fog. It was all quite hopeless. This houseboat was a perfect example of cart-before-the-horse, with "comforts" and superficialities taking precedence over the true, the essential, and the safe. Their so-called boat must have cost seventy-five thousand dollars, and it wasn't even seagoing. Those windows, that vast expanse of glass—and not very thick either! The back porch, with its screen door—how long would it take a big following sea to crash that in?

"What shall I do?" he asked.

I told him the owner shouldn't send him out so ill-equipped. "Perhaps you could wait for a clear day when it's calm and return where you came from." He conferred with his wife, and by the time we were ready to leave they had decided to phone the owner to tell him to come and get his houseboat. They themselves would go home by bus and taxi. They cast off our lines, waving bravely but quite sadly. They were so kind, so deluded. I felt like a sham, too, for they plainly looked upon us as Viking navigators of giant stature. "Don't be discouraged," I called to him. "Take the Power Squadron or Coast Guard piloting courses. Get some books on piloting and charting. Get Chapman, get Mixter. It's quite simple, honest it is."

"I will, I will," he promised. And so we sailed away, thinking how tragic that many little cruises come to a bad end through lack of even the simplest preparation. And a lot of these people are apprehensive forever after. Even if he'd had a good compass he wouldn't have known how to use it.

I didn't know, either, a few years ago. I hope he won't sit on the edge of the blue, beckoning water all his life, dreaming and pining just because the builder and the owner gypped him and he also short-circuited himself.

I said to Kay, "They remind me of the motor cruisers who say, 'Oh, how we'd love to sail, but we tried it one summer and we got in such a mess. It's not for us.'"

As we soared off down the river's mouth we were thinking how many messes we've been in and how lucky we are. Our sole wreck took place in the Sand Hole and didn't cost us our boat.

That was a day as different from yesterday as light from dark. *Sunrise* outdid herself—as though she hadn't done well enough before—running down Long Island Sound in one of those powerful, cold northwest blows that come raging out of the Arctic in October. They tear the clouds to pieces, leaving only little white, fleecy puffs. They are full of squalls that turn the water blue-black, ripping the tops off and throwing them in your face if you're going to windward, which fortunately we weren't.

So we came out of Saybrook with a rush, and set a course to pass beside the Long Sand Shoal, which extends five miles in a westerly direction from the Connecticut River's mouth. It is outlined by spread-out buoys at each end and along the middle. Soaring like a gull, we passed Falkner Island Lighthouse as though it was standing still (which indeed happened to be the case). The yachty-est thing we saw all day was a big Coast Guard cutter doing maneuvers or time trials or something, throwing spray right over her masthead. We ran forty-five miles under genoa alone in seven hours. A hard little red-topped bulge the sail was, yanking us through the water like a giant's hand. I stood in the cockpit looking back at those breaking crests and

217

could have sworn she was going to get pooped. But she never did. This was a day when we had to explore the crawl-in spaces at the foot of our bunks for our long johns, sweaters, flannel shirts, mittens, and extra socks. The wind had the breath of winter in it, reminding us we weren't getting south any too soon.

Right on the button, after a run of twenty-two miles from Falkner, we picked up Stratford Shoal Light to starboard and turned in for the big, Long Island–side harbor of Port Jefferson. In that northwest wind we had a tossed-up, rough time of it between the stone breakwaters, but on a broad reach were quickly through. I hadn't done my homework in the *Cruising Guide,* so didn't know about Mount Misery Cove to the left as we entered (anyway, it was full of barges), or the large cove to our right inside Old Field Beach. We sailed on into the end of the harbor close to the town and anchored in the shadow of three enormous power-station stacks. There were rocks to avoid near our anchor spot, and we avoided them. The harbor, being large, is rolly in a northwest wind. But we were accustomed to rolling. Our plow anchor, chain, and line held firm; that was the important thing.

Remnants of the northwester next day wafted us another goodly jump across the chart. At evening, far down the Long Island shore, within view of the tips of Manhattan skyscrapers, we ducked into a bay and farther around behind a point to the silent cove known as Prices Bend, where moonlight silvered the water. On shore was a man puttering around a vacation cottage back from the beach, a gray-head, like me. Happy from the day's run, I felt like calling out, "Hail, brother!" Wouldn't he have been surprised!

# CHAPTER XXI

# HUDSON RIVER—NEW YORK TO WAPPINGER CREEK

SUNRISE CAME THAT EVENING to City Island, where the Long Island Sound narrows into New York's East River bottleneck. We rather dreaded threading all down the length of Manhattan Island through New York City again. The metropolis is so overwhelmingly enormous, so complex, so unknowable that it shrinks our smallness even smaller. Though we usually feel big enough on the open ocean, New York casts a mysteriously threatening spell over us, its people so unfriendly, its ferryboats ferocious, its tugboats-and-barges menacing as they swing fast around the East River's tideswept bends.

An hour before dawn, to catch the swift-flowing ebb, we tightened our belts and set out. Soon sweeping through Hell Gate and past the Con Ed plant, we made wonderful time riding the back of the current, which gurgled and foamed and showed sullen whirlpools. Sailing, motoring, charting, avoiding collisions, and narrowly missing a garbage scow near the Harlem River kept us busy past Welfare Island and down past the United Nations building and the East River apartments that hang over the river. Their window boxes and gardens weep expensive plants tier on tier, way up there above the water, with a supercivilized air so different from the windswept beaches of Massachusetts or the rocky coves of Maine. We felt ourselves in a different world. Imagine taking that garden soil up in elevators! I'll bet it cost a dollar a pound.

Close beside us, women in high heels pecked the pavement, and mothers complete with perambulators and toddlers strolled the riverside stone walks. A jogger went past. Taxis streaked down FDR Drive, flashing under overpasses and reappearing again. But they encountered so many jams we were going almost as fast as the taxis. We were studying the shore with intense curiosity, but hardly any of the people looked at us. Maybe life in the city, with its millions of stimuli, teaches you to quit looking at things. To our right stood Manhattan's tenements and spires, to our left Brooklyn's ten thousand labyrinths, and we were plunging into the city's maw.

A little crosstown breeze wafted down through Forty-Second Street to fill our sails. Should I put a quarter in a slot, or hand somebody two dollars, or in some way pay the endless cost the city demands? But we were separated and protected by a water moat and sliding fast on the dark stream oceanward to escape the turnstiles and the landlords.

A few yachts passed, hurrying up and down, mostly motor cruisers. A lordly ketch some ninety or a hundred feet long steamed by with a cheery wave from its captain. All gleaming bronze and spotless teak, the tender on her midships deck was bigger than *Sunrise*. She was graceful with that grace that only length can give, like a long-stemmed rose, or a long silken leg.

Looking at a detailed map, you see how extensive New York Harbor is, one of the finest harbors in the world, surpassed only by Sydney, Australia. Its maze of waterways is impressive. And how beautiful Manhattan Island must have been when it was thickly wooded, with smoke from a few campfires rising. It is strange and sad how the loveliest and most desirable places on earth, the harbors and valleys and river junctions, are often so very desirable that we humans turn them into congested antheaps, where they become the worst. Then we go to Glacier National Park for vacations— which nobody had any use for on account of its solid-rock peaks and twenty-foot snowdrifts.

Here is the East River, leading to Long Island Sound, Shelter Island, Montauk, Fishers Island, and the sea. Across the top of Manhattan runs the short Harlem River, connecting with the magnificent Hudson, the colonial "Warpath of Nations" leading to Lake Champlain and even Quebec on the St. Lawrence. Into New Jersey run the Passaic and Hackensack Rivers, which, though small, were big enough for flatboats in the days before roads. Down the bay is the Shrewsbury, flowing inside the Jersey coast beaches to Redbank. A navigable channel runs inside Staten Island, and the vast Lower Bay includes Hoboken, Perth Amboy, Newark Bay, and a canal over there that used to connect with the Delaware River. Most useful of all is deep water to the shore for berthing ships. Florida has mazes of waterways, too, but they are deceptively thin water, often with two feet or less. The old Queen Mary and Queen Elizabeth used to pull right in to the Cunard piers at the end of Fifty-Ninth Street. And many other liners docked handily at Manhattan piers in the heyday of the harbor. Docks in Brooklyn's Red Hook, docks all up and down the East River, docks on the

Jersey and Manhattan sides of the Hudson, docks in Hoboken and Perth Amboy, docks everywhere.

The great salt marshes of the Meadows over in New Jersey, a true savannah, were a teeming paradise of birds when the Dutch settled here, and didn't smell, as now.

Then we were past the Battery, dodging Staten Island ferries, which run very fast on a beeline and seem not to vary an inch for tugboats, freighters, or twenty-foot peanut shells. They rush upon the latter with terrifying speed.

The course could have been off through Red Hook's crowded waters bordered by miles of warehouses and docked freighters. We had come through there on the way north and been enchanted by its heady aromas of coffee, jute, cocoa, bananas, cinnamon, Carnauba wax, spice, onions, and the smells of a dozen other products from South America and the Far East. Red Hook had made us savor again John Masefield's unforgettable "Cargoes":

*Quinquireme of Nineveh from distant Ophir*
*Rowing home to haven in sunny Palestine,*
*With a cargo of ivory,*
*And apes and peacocks,*
*Sandalwood, cedarwood, and sweet white wine.*

*Stately Spanish galleon coming from the Isthmus,*
*Dipping through the Tropics by the palm-green shores,*
*With a cargo of diamonds,*
*Emeralds, amethysts,*
*Topazes, and cinnamon, and gold moidores.*

*Dirty British coaster with a salt-caked smoke stack*
*Butting through the channel in the mad March days,*
*With a cargo of Tyne coal.*
*Road-rail, pig-lead,*
*Firewood, iron-ware, and cheap tin trays.*

This time, instead of going through Red Hook, we turned down the harbor's rough expanse torn by wakes and whitecaps as both the Hudson and the East River poured their waters toward the ocean. Now the Lower Bay was opening, where ships from Hong Kong, Israel, Sweden, Britain, Russia, Germany, Indonesia, and the usual tankers from Monrovia lay at anchor, all pointing upriver into the tide.

As *Sunrise* sailed close by a stone wall at the entrance to Gravesend Bay, some old men in a park were leaning on a railing at the water's edge watching the boats with a faraway look in their eyes. I used to be like that. But now at last I was aboard one, sailing one, very grateful to whatever fates may be.

We tacked close to the Statue of Liberty, after which with close-hauled main and small jib we could just lay a roadway of buoys like the aisle of a church, leading to the long stone breakwater forming Atlantic Highlands Harbor. It lies just inside Sandy Hook. The ebb was gone, and the flood was beginning to run against us.

Now, astern of us, the city was a fairyland of blue, storied castles. *Sunrise* had slipped under all the bridges successfully. The ominous Gotham Gods had let us through without exacting tribute. Good-bye Camelot.

We hadn't gone far when purple-black clouds loomed over New Jersey. Lightning-torn rain and wind struck us a couple of miles from our harbor-for-the-night. Thank goodness we had the sails furled and the outboard cranked when the screaming white squall hit us. The rain felt freezing cold. The driving deluge almost filled the cockpit, and we couldn't see ten yards. When it cleared away, we were able to locate ourselves as being about a mile off the Atlantic Highlands breakwater and see we had been driven backward toward the beaches inside Sandy Hook. Then down came a second screamer worse than the first, completely shutting us in. The wind was so strong we couldn't punch it, and the bow began to blow off. Those beaches behind us! I got the bow into the wind between squalls, only to have it blow off again. Kay took the tiller while I crawled forward to overhaul the anchor as quickly as possible. Before I could get the anchor over, this second storm cleared away.

Thunder squalls are often short like that. If you can only manage to stay alive for fifteen or twenty minutes, lo and behold, the sun comes out and you wonder how it could all have seemed so perilous. The perilous aspects are real enough, too, for many a craft caught with her sails up has been dismasted or capsized.

Chilled to the bone, we motored up the long harbor inside the barnacle-encrusted rocks, past all the moored yachts. In the harbor master's second-floor office, I asked him about a slip. No slips. Soaked and dripping, my teeth chattering, I made the mistake of remarking, "Those were two hellacious thunderstorms!"

He gave me a seedy look and replied, "You sailboaters have an awful time, don't you?"

I should have known this was motorboat country. I managed not to say, Ah, but we have more fun than you do.

So it was find a hole among the moored craft and anchor in the harbor's soft ooze—poor holding ground. While we were warming up with a hot cup of tea, Kay glanced over and saw a boy in a little plastic-foam sailboat slipping along down the breakwater not far away. The breakwater's big stone blocks were covered with barnacles and slime. His sail was ripped, and he had no oars. He was clawing at the rocks but being carried out toward Sandy Hook by the strong ebb tide. As we watched, he pulled his little rudder off the transom and tried to paddle with it, but made no progress and continued to drift.

We couldn't let that go on, so I quickly buoyed the anchor, cranked the outboard, and went over to him in handy little *Sunrise*. "You want some help?" I asked.

"Yes please."

I tied a line to his bow and he came aboard. He didn't have a line of his own. His sail was torn clean in half from leach to luff. After taking it down, we motored back to our anchor.

His name was Harold. But that's all we could learn. We couldn't get him to say anything except his name. He wouldn't take a cup of tea or a cookie. He just sat on the stern deck clasping his knees, shivering occasionally, and looking a picture of misery.

It being a long way to the head of the harbor, I didn't want to up anchor, so I hailed an inbound motor cruiser and asked them to take Harold and his plastic bathtub to the town dock at the edge of town.

"Why, sure," said the skipper, and put his own line on the little boat.

Just before stepping across, Harold surprised us by putting out his hand, giving us a big smile, and saying, "Thanks a lot." Then he was gone.

As the harbor chop rocked me in my bunk that night, I was thinking that odd things occur when you're cruising, living a sort of catch-as-catch-can life, never knowing what will happen next. It was a blessed relief for us, of course, to have made a safe passage through menacing New York City, but the event of the day was Harold. How odd that in all our travels we should have come upon him at the exact time of his brief troubles, and then be able to remember the transformation in him that brought on his firm hand-shake and smile. In the jumble of existence you are at a certain place at a certain time and meet by chance a certain person— which changes the whole course of your life. Maybe that was the way today for Harold. I decided New York City is big, but the return of Harold's confidence was big, too. I wondered if he'd grow up to be a sailor, often scared, sometimes brave, always try-ing to be more of the latter.

CHAPTER XXII

# SANDY HOOK TO LITTLE EGG HARBOR

# LITTLE EGG INLET TO CAPE MAY

IN ATLANTIC HIGHLANDS almost everything had been holed up for days because of a huge swell that had been rolling in from the northeast for a long time. Enormous it was, like mountains.

We left there at dawn rounding Sandy Hook for a forty-mile stretch down the long, straight sandy beaches of the Jersey coast, bound for Manasquan-Brielle Inlet.

We hung off Manasquan breakwater, almost afraid to run the inlet. The harbor mouth is just a narrow cut through the beach, lined on each side by stone-block jetties, enormous cubes about ten feet square, with small light towers on their seaward ends. The place becomes a maelstrom when a big tide is running out against wind and swell. This particular afternoon the enormous swell was hitting the breakwaters on a diagonal from the northeast, and sometimes as we watched, a big one would slop right over the northern arm, further roiling the entrance channel as its crest swept sidewise across the soapsuds between the rocks. As best I could see, none of the big swells was actually breaking, though they rose up in a menacing dark curl as they felt the ground. The main danger was that we might get carried broadside into the rocks on the back of a huge swell as we entered. I decided that, like the swells, I would enter on the bias—not in the middle, but close to the windward, upswell side.

All this time we were jogging to and fro, sinking so deep into the troughs of the seas that we couldn't see the breakwater at all when we were in the valley. Then the boat would be flung high so that half the inner harbor became visible. I had a mind to go on all night to Atlantic City, which is a broader, safer inlet. I was recalling the story of a 150-foot Gloucester schooner trying to make harbor between similar breakwaters in a storm at Ocean City, Maryland. A huge wave broached her to, lifted her up, and set her square on top of the jetty. The impact broke her back, and she became a total loss.

We were faced with no such storm as that. But the Jersey coast inlets are frequently tricky and dangerous for a low-powered sailboat. By rights we should have stayed out, but we were tired, as usual at the day's end, and wished very much that we could make harbor and rest. We watched a sportfisherman run in, twin screws turning quite fast to give him maximum steering control. A big wave boosted up his stern, and he surfed down its back but did all right. We would have a reaching wind to help our little motor, and we had the last of the flood running in, too. If we were going, we must go now.

So we let draw and put her for it. I shut up the companionway and closed all the hatches and ventilators in case a wave broke over us. We cut the windward point within about twenty-five feet, were lifted high and slammed almost over to the opposite wall, but there the backwash knocked us into the middle again. Then we were through, purling up a peaceful little river between green salt marshes and a sandbar with its usual complement of gulls. The afternoon sunshine had a tranquil quality, making me wonder how, amid this peacefulness, I could have been so worried. Then we heard a boom and roar, looked back, and saw a comber climbing over the rocks.

Such a strange place, Manasquan! I don't know what it is to people who live there. But to crews coming in from the sea, the railroad drawbridge shows up mighty fast. There is only a short distance between the ocean entrance and this bridge—a bad one with a millrace tide running through its narrow gut. It has so little clearance when down that even a rowboat can't get under. It is a fearsome black thing that hinges open from one side, upward against the sky, like a crocodile's jaw, and it can get you coming down, just as it can get you by going up too late as you rush toward it with wind and tide behind you. Unlike some rather inactive railroad draws, this one was opening and closing every eight or ten minutes as late-afternoon commuter trains of the Jersey Central came through from New York City, while shoals of boats above and below the span jockeyed in the current waiting for the bridge to open. The bridge tender blew the same horn for opening as for closing—an antique sort of klaxon, AA-000-AH!—and you'd better be somewhere else when the contraption comes down. I noticed the boats were punctilious about letting downcurrent craft have first turn through the wasp-waist bridge—probably an aspect of survival.

We aimed to stay below this monster, to seaward. But of course, the few outside marinas were extremely crowded. I inquired at two of them, and there seemed to be no room for us. Almost all the berths were taken by permanent craft as usual. At the third, a combined bar-restaurant-dock, a black-haired woman bartender accepted ten dollars in the surly New York City manner and told me with her thumb, "Ovah daah." We barely had room to squeeze between two fat motor cruisers in the berth indicated, but by putting out fenders and springs we managed. The tide sucked past our mooring at four or five knots—in all, a horrible place, but we were happy to be tied up to four strong pilings, alive and in one piece.

The drawbridge blew its goofy horn, whereupon ponderous machinery began to clank and thunder as the towering ironware came down out of the sky. Soon a long red commuter train rumbled over, only a few tired businessmen showing in the windows of the cars, for this was near the end of the line. Poor devils! I used to be doing that some years ago.

Late in the afternoon, I was strolling the waterfront stretching my legs and went to the dock end to look at a big motor cruiser. She was a fifty-six-foot Chris Craft, on whose deck stood a vigorous-looking gray-head leaning over the rail. "Big swell outside," I said, by way of inane remarks.

"Big enough for this one," he replied. "She's got a built-in roll. Where'd you come from today?"

"Atlantic Highlands."

"Thought so. We came from there. Was going on to Atlantic City, but we were laying the cabin windows in the water. A mile or so past here, we turned back. I was afraid my wife would get hurt. I made her sit right on the pilot stool beside me, and I strapped her in."

Thus it was that we became acquainted with Captain George Luther Burns, of Carvers Harbor, Vinalhaven, Maine. Born in Maine, he first went out to the Grand Banks on a Gloucester schooner when he was sixteen. Captain Burns had a quiet way, jolly, but with the authority of experience. His zest for life and knowledge of the sea were boundless. I later decided that of all the seagoing people we had met up and down the coast Captain Burns had put the most water under his keel.

"You like to sail," he said. "Well, Gloucester schooners had no power in those days you know. Ten men hauled in the main sheet, tailed on a line. Chain sheets for the tops'ls. You had to climb halfway up the mast and throw them over your shoulder when she came about. Seven-part tackle. Took three men to get the jib down. We had bridles on the main boom, seventy feet long it was; to reef, men had to climb out on the boom, got shook off, that's how we lost 'em. Not so much fun, sailing those days. Come aboard. We'll have a drink."

I could see this was going to last more than a minute. I said I'd get my wife, for she loves a good story as much as I do. We climbed aboard and met his wife, bustling about in a miraculously well-appointed galley, complete with bar, cocktail glasses, electric fridge, all the trimmings. This twin diesel yacht, he told us, belonged to a lady doctor, for whom he ran the ship, summers in New England, winters in Florida. The Burnses were taking the boat to Florida now, to meet the owner there in early December. In her home port in the summertime the lady doctor liked to come aboard for lunch, which Captain Burns cooked for her. She was fond of broiled fish. She never entertained any visitors aboard. I had an idea, pure guess-work, that Captain Burns bossed the lady doctor in a tactful way for the first time in her life, and that she liked it. I was at least quite sure that he—like many old-time yacht skippers we had met—took few orders from "his" owner.

In the luxurious and spacious main cabin, with drink in hand and his wife beside him, Captain Burns delighted us for nearly an hour.

"I was telling you about the Gloucester schoonermen. I almost got mine on the bowsprit a couple of hundred miles off Block Island one November. I was eighteen then. The jib was in the water. I could almost heave it up with one hand, but not quite. One hand for the ship, you know. I watched my chance between plunges, and gambled on hauling in the canvas with both hands. I almost had it, when the wind gave the sail a flap and knocked me off. Right under her bow I was, and she charging along at eight knots. I grabbed the bobstay and held on under there, but she'd rise and pound me with the stem. Three times she came down on me, and the last time she hit me on the head and hurt me bad. I was getting groggy and had to let go. Went right under the vessel, she cutting me with barnacles on her way over. It was the cook who saved me. He saw me go, and ran up the mast. From there he spotted my cap in the wake. It was on my head, I reckon. I was semiconscious by this time, could just keep afloat. They brought 'er round and threw me a line. I remembered dropping the bight of it around me. I was pretty banged up, my shoulder stiff and a big cut on my head. Couldn't work for ten days."

In later years Burns had spent much time as yacht captain for a man named Lloyd, also a doctor. First they made long voyages in a forty-six-foot ketch. "We were almost wrecked coming in to Atlantic City one rough night in December. You know how the sea breaks on the bar to starboard of the entrance channel. Well, it was a northeast gale, and we should never have gone in. A big one broke across the bar, and, instead of slowing down, it swept right on across. It picked us up in midchannel and surfed us sidewise. I thought sure it was going to heave us onto the beach portside of the channel. But at the last minute it went on under us and we got in."

Burns owned a freighter during one period of his career, running between Caribbean and Gulf ports. He said he made seventy-five thousand dollars his best year. But there were many bad years, and we gathered it was an up-and-down gamble.

"I was in the old Miami Harbor years ago when a hurricane sank a vessel in the main channel. Every ship there was penned in. I said to another captain I knew, 'We can get a big motorboat for fifty dollars a day, with gear and all. Will you pay half?' He got the idea, and said he would, so we took off along another way, the old channel, sounding, sounding, and putting out our own markers. Then we came back and quietly took our four vessels out the back way early one morning. The insurance companies heard about it and wouldn't let anybody else try it. The ships were bottled up two weeks, while I was making my run among the islands."

His wife said she was trying to get him to retire. "Seems to me he's been enough places."

"Yes," he said, "we've got a twelve-room house in Carvers Harbor, Maine, lookin' right over the water. I'm going to go there pretty soon and have a little thirty-foot motorboat and spend my time lobster fishin'. I'm seventy-five years old, and I suppose she's right, I better settle down."

We all had another drink while he told us of his Navy days in World War II. "I was in charge of a flotilla of minesweepers out of Boston. We set off for Newfoundland in the middle of the winter and of course their engines pretty soon began making trouble. We tried to stay in groups of four, but it was so stormy we couldn't keep

233

contact. Halfway, a minesweeper broke down astern of me, one of our group. I sent the others on and shot a line across him, come daylight. We had monstrous seas. I got a little too close one pass, and a big sea lifted me and I thought it was going to throw me right on top of him. But it passed under. We broke the towline. I knew we would. So at last we rigged anchor chain, thirty fathoms of his and thirty fathoms of mine, and I got him to Argentia at three knots. It took days and days. Another minesweeper was lost somewhere, so we stocked up and steamed out again. 'Where are you going?' the commander signaled me. I said I was going to look for the lost vessel, of course. We steamed all over hell and gone and finally we heard a faint radio signal. We kept trying and trying to home in on it, and after about a week we brought him into Argentia, too, on the end of a towline."

At this point a question popped out of me that I couldn't repress. "Captain Burns," I asked, "how do you find your way? On all those voyages, off a strange coast, at night, in snowstorms—?"

He looked at me with a kindly sort of wisdom and said, "I'm a bottom man myself. Many's the time I've sounded my way around Cape Sable in thick fog. All the fishermen have. And found my way on the Banks and along Nantucket Shoal. Your echo sounder or your lead line tells you when you're coming in. We had our other aids, our Consolan, our loran, and our radar. But the bottom contours as you come in—it starts rising under you—and the contours are all on the chart. You get so many fathoms, and you know you're so many miles off."

Navy talk and the war set more memories stirring.

"Did you know I was a naval reserve captain? There were lots of navy reserve captains, but not many were allowed to captain ships. I had a ship. I've got a full license in sail and a full license in steam. Very few men have both full licenses, because there's no way to get 'em anymore, no sailing vessels.

"They sent me out to Seattle to command a big new hospital ship just being launched."

The new ship was destined for island invasions of the Pacific War, among them Saipan, but he didn't know that at the time. Right away he got into hot water with a certain admiral who was to be a passenger for the voyage to Pearl Harbor. The admiral quite tactlessly called in both Reserve Captain Burns and a regular navy commander. While the two of them stood before him, he told the commander he was sorry to have a reserve officer in charge of the new ship, but nobody else was available. The Annapolis graduate said, "Admiral, I'm sure you couldn't find a better-qualified man than Captain Burns."

The admiral told him they were to sail on a certain morning. Captain Burns made his preparations. He was lying at a long dock, with a ship astern and a ship ahead, a difficult slot to get out of. "I had a man with a telephone to be on the bow, another on the stern, and an officer out on the bridge wing. They were to tell me how many feet of clearance I had as we moved up or back. If they said thirty feet, I figured fifteen. I always cut it in half. I was going to keep a bow spring line on the dock and give her half ahead to swing her stern out before letting go the line. The admiral called for me the night before we were to sail and he said, 'Is the pilot aboard?'

"I said, 'I don't need a pilot. I've studied this harbor.'

"He wanted to know, 'Have you ordered a tug?'

"I said I didn't need a tug.

"He said, 'Captain, do you think you can take this ship to Pearl Harbor?' I said, 'Admiral, I can back this ship to Pearl Harbor if you want me to.'

"Morning came, and everything went fine. I put the power to her and swung her just as I'd figured. Those big ships, you can't be fainthearted with 'em. They get away from you. We went off down the harbor first rate. We had a good voyage.

"We were at Saipan. A wicked assault that was. We took aboard six hundred casualties. We had some medical teams, mister! We never lost a single thorax case, not one, and we had hundreds of 'em."

"Don't you think it's about time he gave up the sea and took it easy?" said his wife.

"I think he ought to write a book," said my wife.

It was getting late and we had to go. He handed us down the ladder to the dock in courtly style, the grand old man. We were hoping to spend a week in Vinalhaven some summer listening to his yarns. He didn't seem old to us.

We went away to our supper, walking on clouds, wondering what makes some people so miraculous. Here was a man who'd inherited nothing but hard work. The ordinary fisherman who goes to sea on trawlers doesn't have much of a flair for doing it with a swish that makes life gorgeous. But this man had all the rich joy associated with sportsmen who pilot planes around the globe. Such a man loves to tell a story, of adventure, of tough odds cheerfully encountered, and half the time—the way he tells it—the joke is on him. Everybody loves people like that.

We were up early, but not early enough to beat Captain Burns. He was gone, no sign of his big cruiser, though it was scarcely daylight. No doubt he intended to bypass Atlantic City and make Cape May, about eighty-five miles in one day. Meeting Captain Burns cheered me. Maine people are often that way; they are so strong some of their strength flows into others. I didn't feel so scared of facing the Manasquan breakwater or of plugging down the coast in the giant swell. What child's play compared to the Newfoundland coast in blizzards!

I made a serious mistake going out through the jetties, or perhaps two. First of all, I found when we arrived at the narrow pass that the tide was late in ebbing and hadn't started to run out in our favor. I should have waited for it to ebb. Second, I did not carry any sail, because the wind seemed, I repeat *seemed* to be dead ahead through the gullet and I thought the flapping main would only retard us in that rough alley too narrow for tacking. Such bottle-necks are motorboat country; they are not for little sailboats with five-horse motors.

As a result, we just about stood still in the worst of the soap-suds between the seething walls. The little mill was puttering faithfully away, but we were only moving out inch by inch against wind and tide. A little slant of wind developed, and if I had had the main up, it might have given us a much-needed bit of help. I was afraid to turn around and run back. So we sat there, making a foot or so to seaward between waves, while the white breakers smashed against the jetty rocks close alongside. At last we reached the open ocean, hoisted sail, and soared away, laughing to think how glad we had been to get into Manasquan, and how glad we were to get out of it. The dawn was still red, the clouds edged with gold. The great dark blue waves enclosed us in their gulfs, shutting us off from the land. We were aboard our windship, with a powerful northeast breeze rolling us south along the coast. Out here we were better off than the motor cruisers, our keel and sails steadying us, so that we only rolled about half as much.

The sun came out and set the sea to winking, which cheered us, and we needed it, for the great seas astern rose up into the sky, rushed upon us, and seemed to leer right down the companionway into the cabin. It was fearsome looking astern, because every big one threatened to inundate us, overwhelm us, but they weren't breaking. Thus the procedure was to look ahead. A day or two previously I had put paraffin on the companion slide to make it run easier, but now the thing was sliding back and forth with the pitching seas. It nipped Kay's finger when it slid back against its stop and could have injured her severely. Fortunately, it was a flesh pinch, missing the bone, but bad enough. As always, she was Spartan, pretending it didn't hurt much.

I put in the companionway boards and jammed the slide tight, closed all the ventilators again, and fastened myself aboard by means of the safety harness in case a big wave should break onto us; they were right on the verge. We were making good time down along the heavily populated beaches past the miles and miles of hotels, towns, cottages, despite the fact that we lost our wind in the deep troughs, where the sails slatted with destructive force against their fastenings. Most of the motor cruisers stay in port when conditions are like this, with an east wind that has continued for weeks, building the waves higher and higher across a fetch of thousands of miles. However, a few party boats passed us, bound out from Manasquan for offshore fishing banks. Most of them seemed exclusively devoted to males, who sat or stood around the decks like rows of crows, but no matter how big the boats were—some with as many as fifty people aboard—they sank out of sight in the cavernous valleys only a few hundred feet away. Now and then a smaller one carried a few women, and sometimes one of the women tried to snap a picture of us as we rose on a crest. We wished we could see ourselves, the fluttering sails soaring up and sinking down, looking proud to us, though perhaps pitiful to them.

Rushing down the coast, the boat was being thrown about so violently we couldn't steer. While Kay did her usual good job at the tiller, I pulled down the main, which left us roaring on with the genny hung out on a pole, pinned down fore and aft. This was one of the days when the foredeck went out from under me. But it is really nothing; you expect to get tossed and to hang on, or you wouldn't go to sea. I was glad of my strong, four-inch-high hand-holds all around the foredeck.

Our compass courses were working out well. After about twenty miles, we picked up the whistle buoy off Barnegat Inlet. We got a good radio direction finding bearing on Barnegat as we passed at right angles. We were yawing a good fifteen degrees either side of the compass course, which made steering arduous. Since the wide compass swings couldn't be prevented, the only way to sail an accurate course was to try to swing equally either side. It was a guess any way you went about it.

At Barnegat we were five miles off the coast. From there we laid a course of twenty-one miles to the black-and-white bell off Little Egg Inlet, edging closer to the shore. When we got there, the surf in Little Egg was fierce, and I wouldn't have run it for anything. Shoals shift, and the Coast Guard changes the buoys with the shifts, local knowledge being required, for you have the breakers on all sides as you enter—so we had been told. Inside, we could see more mazes of shallows, which were good places to stay away from.

Visibility being good, we could make out the distant shore, but you never know when the haze will close in. Such a shore is not as much help as you'd think, bending away in deep bights such as Little Egg Inlet, or sinking to nothing in very low land, so that you cannot be sure how far off you are unless you find the buoys. We were picking them up first rate, only half a mile or so in error despite our yawing. Apparently there was no tidal set.

The charts of the Jersey coast are forever showing HOTEL, TANK, STACK. We kept peering through the glasses trying to identify one or the other or groups of them. But the beaches are practically solid with hotels, tanks, and stacks, making position finding almost impossible by that means.

Everything domestic seemed impossible, even getting a cup of water to one's mouth. We took turns steering, the off-watch lying on the floor between the bunks to get some rest. I felt wonderfully happy to see my little boat kicking up her stern, not a drop coming aboard. We had a total of fifty miles to go this day.

After Little Egg, the next thing we had to watch for was Brigantine Shoal, which sticks out a long way. We set a course that should take us outside the red nun that marks the seaward edge of the shoal, and we hoped also to see the red whistle buoy that lies three miles farther out to sea. A large sloop was our constant companion all day, first miles behind us, then passing ahead, and then when I put up our reefed main she dropped astern again for some strange reason. Maybe they were having a nap and making her steer herself. We had to carry plenty of sail if we were going to make it through Absecon Inlet (the sea name for Atlantic City) before dark and before the tide turned against us. We were a cat's cradle of lines, with the main boom tied down via a foreguy so it couldn't jibe, and sheet leading aft. The poled-out genoa was made fast three ways, with sheet aft, foreguy forward, and spinnaker boom-lift holding it up—lines all over the place and nothing could go anywhere except the boat surfing and twisting and corkscrewing and tossing her tail, with the crew tumbling end over end every time they didn't hang on. You have to be extremely careful not to get injured. You simply expect to get thrown and thrown violently unless you go from handhold to handhold. We were becoming accustomed to it. The only relaxation was wedged on the floor between the bunks, and very important it seemed to get rested for a capable performance running Absecon Inlet.

Through the binoculars in the late afternoon we picked up the red nun tossing off Brigantine Shoal, a little closer inshore than I had intended, though I was very glad to locate it. The shoal can be extremely dangerous on a rough day, though our companion sloop apparently neither knew that nor saw the nun. He went far in across the shoal, where a big wave could have broken on him, but the Lord must have been watching out for him while he slanted across the sands. We never did see the offshore whistle, lost in the swells, but we could set a course for the Atlantic City sea buoy from Brigantine nun, and did so. The sun's path was a blazing mirror dead ahead as the afternoon waned (one of the disadvantages of sailing to the westward instead of Down East). We donned black glasses, pulled our hats low over our eyes, and looked at the compass instead of that blinding glare. One cannot use the binoculars to westward at such times, a considerable handicap when looking for harbor.

241

All went well, with the Atlantic City sea buoy showing up right where it was supposed to be. We watched our all-day companion, the big sloop, flutter in toward the channel, then bear away past the resort piers down the coast. They were using the fair wind to sail on all night to Cape May, as we would have done if we'd had more crew to take tricks at the tiller. It's bad luck, they say, to waste a fair wind, and we've often found it so.

The inlet was rough, but it is broader and deeper than Manasquan. A beam wind and the last of the flood were boosting us in. It was just getting dusk, so that in another half hour we'd have had darkness and a head tide to contend with, in addition to the combers thundering on the bar beside the channel. At one point as we came in, it looked as though they were breaking all across, but that proved to be illusion. In the most crucial spot the usual three-hundred-horsepower twin-screw sportfisherman threw a wake-wave eight feet high at us, full throttle, the fish killer in from the sea and his day's sport, proudly from the lofty flying bridge steering his racy status symbol. Passing some twenty feet away, he pretended to be unaware of our existence. We slid into the center of his wake where motion was less violent, and with pleasure watched him disappear in the direction of the vast municipal marina. Our anchor spot was in the basin not far from the Coast Guard station. There we sat for a moment and sighed before I began gratefully coiling all those lines. Kay went below to light the Primus and start supper. Laughing to herself, she was no doubt thinking of my favorite salutation from the marina dock boys, when she called up, "What a thrilling day. We did all right today, Captain, sir."

* * * *

Next day we were bound south from Atlantic City to Cape May, about thirty-four miles. The Jersey coast is 120 miles of open ocean, with few harbors, a stretch not to be sneezed at. We had the same powerful north wind with the breath of autumn in it, and we made good progress though the sea was rough and we got a dollop of spray.

Cape May, at the tip of New Jersey, is a great place for bird migrations, especially in the fall. This rushing wind had blown many land birds out to sea, and they were struggling toward the beaches against the wind in exhausted condition. We were about two miles offshore and many flickers and warblers landed on us to catch their breath. The first flicker came down on the gunwale about four inches from Kay's hand on the tiller. She was entranced by the bright colorings in the morning sunlight, the brilliant red patch on the back of the head, gold-striped wing feathers, dark spots on the chest, a beautiful black bib. And over all, an iridescent sheen of gray-green-purplish fawn.

The birds would perch on top of the mast, on the end of the boom, on the cabintop, at the stem, at the stern, and one alit on Kay's hat. They were in a sorry plight, for when a land bird comes down on the ocean he cannot as a rule take off again. The seagulls were unbelievably cruel (territorial rights, I suppose), diving on the poor tired ones as they streaked lower and lower toward the safety of the beach. A flicker sat on our aluminum mast woodpecker-fashion, or tried to. He kept slipping down its impossible surface and hunching himself up again. He was so tired his eyes were shut. At last in a hitch-up he got his claw into a brass grommet hole in the leading edge (luff) of the mainsail, and that secured him first class. There he rested and ignored all the noise, the enormous blue-and-white spinnaker, our voices, and even seemed fast asleep while I was just below him, fixing a line. He went to sleep there for nearly an hour, while I tried to keep the sail from fluttering or flapping in the strong wind. It was one of those dark blue days, with scudding little puffball clouds, very clear, quite cold, with squalls every six or seven minutes.

It was cold in the late afternoon when the warblers arrived. One sat resting and sleeping on Kay's gloved hand. It was grayish with a yellow wash on the sides of its breast. A yellow patch at the base of the tail showed when it flew away.

A little flycatcher made himself more at home than any of them. He caught and ate five flies off the mainsail (I guess the flies were being blown off, too) and hopped around looking for a snug spot, finally flitting into the cabin with an inquisitive air that gave way suddenly to drowsiness and dreamland.

Many of them, of many species, stayed only five minutes or so. We strained our eyes watching them grow small, and felt a pang in our hearts as well as a kinship for those brave little creatures at the mercy of the wind. With a fierce intensity we yearned to have them gain the land, arrowing for their lives against the vast current of air that had come down from the Arctic. But this was for real, and I fear many of them died that day.

# CHAPTER XXIII

# Cape May to Cape Hatteras

# Cape Hatteras to Charleston

# Port Royal Sound and Inland Passages

So what is it, this cruising racket? Just self-indulgence, just the luxury yachting has always implied? No sir! It is storms and calms, lonely beaches, rivers, harbors, clouds, the wind. It is the natural world we all need, the world that children know and men most generally lose. It has to be won, for fear, and competence, and fighting with one-self are a part of it as well as contentment and sunset at anchor in some peaceful, hard-won cove in Maine. Work, sweat, pain, exhaustion, strength, peace, and exhilaration go into it! Like love, it is dangerous, for you can get hurt in your innermost being—as when you fail your-self and flunk out. But—also like love—it's ultimate ecstasy and joy in the world, the natural, unashamed, primitive, naked, lovely world.

The Chesapeake in autumn was something to savor, almost everybody gone except us and the wild ducks and geese. As evening settled over those endless creeks and bays we heard the tired geese kronking, calling, looking for a resting place, and very often other geese that had already pitched and were feeding answered as though to reassure the ones coming in. Thousands of empty cottages stood by the beaches. Boats as lonely as clouds swung at their moorings, and we could half shut our eyes and imagine they hadn't any owners. The green trees on the bluffs were luxuriant and huge, like tree ferns or old-fashioned landscape paintings. We noticed them particularly, after weeks along the rocky Maine coast, miles of Jersey coast sand, and the endless Delaware marshes.

The Chesapeake autumn days were blue and dreamy. I enjoyed lying on the foredeck as we sailed, watching the peak of our mast tipping to and fro against the sky, hearing the bow wave rush and whisper, thinking, *Life is good, brother.* We always wanted to cruise in our own boat, and now we were doing it, and thank God it was as good as we thought it would be.

On down the waterway we cruised, familiar now, stopping at marinas often, anchoring out whenever we could find a deep spot removed from the channel, put-putting the long, straight cuts, sailing Currituck, Albemarle, and Pamlico Sounds, as well as all the broader rivers. No more heat this time; instead, lots of cold, fair north winds that made woolen underwear and parka hoods a necessity. It was November, with frost on the deck at daybreak as we set off for each day's run. When at last *Sunrise* came creaming down Calibogue Sound to Hilton Head again, we had sailed more than three thousand miles and been aboard four and a half months. "Next year," said Kay, "we'll get to Rogue Island, won't we, to Cutler and even beyond the Canadian line maybe to Grand Manan Island."

Stowing sails for the last time, we ran over in our minds the times we'd had, the mistakes, the lessons, the joy, the confidence and competence we'd gained. Proud of our jewel-like little boat, we were thinking of the surprising people we had met, and the marvelous East Coast. We'd see dozens more of those enchanting harbors next year.

# ELLIOTT T. MERRICK III

ELLIOTT T. MERRICK, ninety-one, died on April 22, 1997, after a short illness. He had a varied career as editor, teacher, farmer, writer, and sailor. A graduate of Yale in 1927, he took up newspaper and publicity work in and around New York City, and then went to Labrador for two and a half years, where he taught in the Grenfell Mission's most northerly school. In Labrador, he met and married Kay Austen, a trained nurse from Australia, and they traveled all one winter in the wilderness with trappers. The couple returned to Craftsbury, Vermont, and there ran a small subsistence farm for ten years.

Scribner's editor Maxwell Perkins was attracted to Merrick's Labrador stories, as a result of which Scribner's published his books *True North, Frost and Fire, Northern Nurse,* and *Ever the Winds Blow. Northern Nurse* was on the *New York Times* best-seller list for seventeen weeks. The Macmillan Company later published Merrick's *Green Mountain Farm* and a novel titled *Passing By* about the United Nations Merchant Marines in the World War II U-boat conflict and Battle of the Atlantic. He shipped as an ordinary seaman aboard a tanker in convoy to gather material for the story, having been previously a writer for the Office of War Information.

His teaching included three years at Craftsbury Academy, three years in the English Department at the University of Vermont, and one year as associate professor of English at Black Mountain College in North Carolina. For twenty-two years he was science editor and publications officer at the Southeastern Forest Experiment Station of the USDA Forest Service, with headquarters in Asheville, North Carolina. The station had experimental forests in five states and a staff of 120 researchers. He used to say, "I'm trying to teach them to write readable reports, and they're trying to teach me forestry."

His literary career included stories in *Reader's Digest, The New Yorker, Scribner's Magazine, Yankee, Collier's, Saturday Evening Post, American Mercury, Story,* and *Encore.* One of his short stories that has been reprinted more than fifty times appears in five different U.S. high school reading books and two Canadian.

In 1984 he was awarded an honorary doctor of letters degree by Memorial University, St. John's, Newfoundland, for his Labrador books and stories.

When he retired from the Forest Service, he built a twenty-foot oceangoing sloop that he and his first wife, Kay, sailed from Georgia to Maine and back three times. Another summer, in a larger boat, he sailed to Bermuda and the Virgin Islands.

Kay Merrick died at the age of ninety-four. Several years later, Mr. Merrick married Patricia Herring Stratton, a widow and an accomplished equestrian artist and portrait painter from Southern Pines, North Carolina. He and his second wife cruised to Cape Cod, to Maine, and for many seasons on the Chesapeake Bay. His stories of these voyages appeared in *Rudder Magazine, Yachting,* and *Cruising World.* The Merricks made their home on a small farm in the Riceville area, nine miles from Asheville, North Carolina.

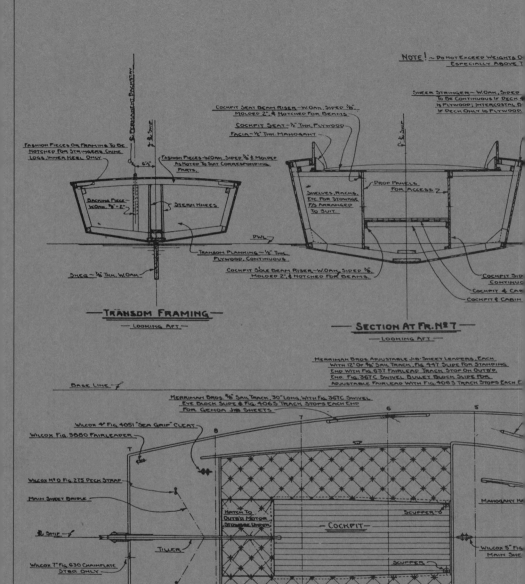

NOTE! ~ DO NOT EXCEED WEIGHTS O—
ESPECIALLY ABOVE T—

FASHION PIECES OR FRAMING TO BE
NOTCHED FOR STRINGERS, CHINE
LOGS, INNER KEEL ONLY

CENTERLINE OF FASTENING

BACKING PIECE~
W.OAK. ⅞"× 2"—

STERN KNEES

FASHION PIECES~W.OAK. SIDED ⅜" & MOLDED
AS NOTED TO SUIT CORRESPONDING
PARTS.

SHEG ~ ⅜" THK. W.OAK

## — TRANSOM FRAMING —
— LOOKING AFT —

COCKPIT SEAT BEAM RISER~W.OAK. SIDED ⅜",
MOLDED 2", & NOTCHED FOR BEAMS
COCKPIT SEAT~½" THK. FLYWOOD
FACIA~½" THK. MAHOGANY

DWL

TRANSOM PLANKING ~ ½" THK.
PLYWOOD, CONTINUOUS

COCKPIT SOLE BEAM RISER~W.OAK. SIDED ⅜",
MOLDED 2", & NOTCHED FOR BEAMS.

SHEER STRINGER~W.OAK. SIDED
TO BE CONTINUOUS IF DECK &
IS PLYWOOD; INTERCOSTAL &
IF DECK ONLY IS PLYWOOD

PROP PANELS
FOR ACCESS 2

SHELVES, RACKS,
ETC. FOR STOWAGE
F/S ARRANGED
TO SUIT

COCKPIT SID—
CONTINUO—
COCKPIT & CAB—
COCKPIT & CABIN

## SECTION AT FR. Nº 7
— LOOKING AFT —

MERRIMAN BROS. ADJUSTABLE JIB-SHEET LEADERS, EACH
WITH 12" OR ⅝" SAIL TRACK, FIG. 447 SLIDE FOR STANDING
END WITH FIG. 637 FAIRLEAD TRACK STOP ON OUTB'D.
END. FIG. 36TC SWIVEL BULLET BLOCK SLIDE FOR
ADJUSTABLE FAIRLEAD WITH FIG. 400S TRACK STOPS EACH E—

BASE LINE

MERRIMAN BROS. ⅝" SAIL TRACK, 30" LONG, WITH FIG. 36TC SWIVEL
EYE BLOCK SLIDE & FIG. 406S TRACK STOPS EACH END
FOR GENOA JIB SHEETS

WILCOX 4" FIG. 4051 "SEA GRIP" CLEAT

WILCOX FIG. 5080 FAIRLEADER

WILCOX Nº0 FIG. 275 DECK STRAP

MAIN SHEET BRIDLE

& SHIP

WILCOX T" FIG. 630 CHAINPLATE
STBD ONLY

TILLER

HATCH TO
OUTB'D. MOTOR
STOWAGE, UNDER

— COCKPIT —

SCUFFER

SCUFFER

MAHOGANY H—

WILCOX 5" FIG—
MAIN SHE—

WILCOX 4" FIG. 4055 "SEA GRIP" JIB SHEET JAM CLEAT

WILCOX FIG. 8—